Scrumptious Side Dishes to Complement
Every Meal in Dinner is Ready!

By Deanna Buxton

Cover art by Ryan Lindahl

———————————

Library of Congress Control Number: 2006939238

ISBN: 978-0-9787765-2-7

———————————

Enjoy all 30 Meals in One Day™ titles by Deanna Buxton:
Dinner is Ready
Lunch is Ready
On the Side

For additional books, software, and other products, visit us online at
www.dinnerisready.com
www.30MealsinOneDay.com

For David,
always by my side

Contents

Introduction

Once you've chosen a main dish for dinner, do you ever wonder, "What shall I serve with this?" There are always the old standbys to fall back on but some recipes scream for something more than boring rice or plain pasta. *On the Side* is a collection of recipes that are simple, fun and fabulous that will add delicious variety to your meals.

If you are preparing meals from the book *Dinner is Ready*, turn to page 3 of *On the Side* and you'll find a **Menu Guide** that identifies delicious matches of entrees and side dishes. It will make deciding, "What shall I serve with this?" not just easy, but a simple pleasure. If you love variety, you'll appreciate that each meal in *Dinner is Ready* has its own unique side dish recommendations that are not paired with any other recipe. However, with more than 350 side dish recipes in *On the Side*, you'll want to mix and match them according to your own preferences. There are endless fabulous combinations.

The recipes here are so versatile and delicious. There is a recipe collection for every side dish category - Vegetables, Rice, Pasta, Bread and Salad, right down to the Dressings and Sauces that put the finishing touch on your meals. There is even a recipe section called "Everything Else" for delicious tidbits that don't quite fit in the other categories. There are so many to choose from, you are sure to find many to add to your list of family favorites that you'll serve again and again.

Some of these side dishes can be prepared in advance, many can even be frozen. This is a wonderful solution for some recipes that make more servings than you need at once. Just divide the recipe into the desired portion sizes and serve or freeze. Since it doesn't take much more effort to prepare a double batch of a favorite recipe, you can intentionally pre-pare more than is needed, and freeze some for later.

Freeze a few side dishes along side your frozen main dishes for time saving convenience. This is especially helpful in preparation for a special occasion in which you desire to spend time with your guests rather than in the kitchen cook-ing for the masses! Recipes that are freezer worthy are iden-tified and are complete with freezing instructions.

Whether you make them now or freeze them for later, whether you use the **Menu Guide** for side dish suggestions for recipes from *Dinner is Ready*, or you just want more choic-es of side dishes, you'll find these recipes a welcome change from boring pasta, plain rice or humdrum green salad.

You'll find endless combinations and delicious variety, and best of all, no more wondering, "What shall I serve with this?"

There is now a *30 Meals in One Day* computer program available. The *On the Side* version contains every recipe in this book and will allow you to enter any other recipes you desire. This program will adjust recipe sizes and print recipe cards. It will generate printable grocery shop-ping lists. It will print your chosen Menu complete with the date and the number of each meal you have frozen. It will print labels, ready to put on meals for the freezer, complete with recipe title and cooking/serving instructions. This pro-gram will streamline your efforts and is available in stores and at **www.dinnerisready.com**.

Menu Guide

Use this Menu Guide to easily identify side dishes to serve with main dishes from **Dinner is Ready**. The bold, underlined titles are **Dinner is Ready** recipes. Subsequent recipes are suggestions from **On the Side** to complete the menu.

Almost Ravioli
- Italian Salad, 167
- Simple Italian Dressing, 285
- French Loaves, 338

Bacon Chicken
- Mashed Red Potatoes, 82
- Company Peas, 28
- Layered Salad, 208
- Catalina Dressing, 266

Bacon Meat Loaf
- Cheesy Bacon Potatoes, 72
- BLT Salad, 156
- Ranch Dressing, 264

Baked Chicken in Gravy
- Mushroom Pie, 61
- Tortellini Spinach Salad, 253
- Creamy Cheese Dressing, 274

BBQ Beef and Biscuits
- California Vegetables, 22
- Fruit Salad, 223

Beef and Broccoli
- Cucumber Stuffed Tomatoes, 103

Beef and Cheese Rolls
- Tortellini Primavera, 133
- Broiled Garlic Rolls, 366

Beef and Pork Chop Suey
- Baked Mushroom Rice, 122
- Green Beans and Bean Sprouts, 58

Beef Noodle Onion Bake
- Celery Bacon Green Beans, 56
- Onion Cake, 350

Beef Stroganoff
- Orange Carrots, 41
- Baked Mashed Potatoes, 86
- Buttermilk Salad, 246

Beef Stuffing Bake
- Sweet Potato Salad, 219
- Cranberry Cabbage Slaw, 206

Beefy Chinese Rice
- Chow Mein, 143

Beefy Macaroni
- Green and Gold Salad, 162
- Onion Poppy Seed Rolls, 374

Beefy Spanish Rice
- Chicken and Rice Burritos, 390
- Refried Beans, 59

Bird's Nest Pie
- Italian Broccoli, 30
- Ranch Garlic Bread, 340

Biscuit Beef Bake
- Tomatoes and Cucumbers, 102
- Club Salad, 153
- Roquefort Dressing, 273

Broccoli Chicken and Rice
- Spinach Cran-Apple Salad, 198

Brown Sugar Pork Ribs
- Oriental Noodle Salad, 257
- Baked Hash Browns, 63
- Frozen Strawberry Salad, 233

Cabbage Patch Stew
- Corn Muffins, 330
- Honey Butter, 304

Calico Beans
- Bacon and Egg Potato Salad, 217
- Vegetable Kabobs, 26

California Dip Meat Loaf
- Monterey Potatoes, 75
- Garlic Green Beans, 53
- Orange Tossed Salad, 180
- Sweet Honey Mustard Dressing, 271

Candied Chicken
- Cheese Potatoes, 71
- Baked Corn, 46
- Frozen Fruit Salad, 231

Cantonese Meatballs
- Carrot Rice, 119
- Sweet and Sour Vegetables, 17
- Lettuce Wraps, 386

Cheese Manicotti
- Spinach Salad, 190
- Layered Pineapple Carrot Salad, 240

Cheesy Chicken and Rice
- Baked Broccoli, 36
- Raspberry Avocado Salad, 214
- Raspberry Dressing, 301

Cheesy Ham and Noodles
- Green Beans and Carrots, 57
- Lime Sour Cream Salad, 245

Cheesy Ham and Potatoes
- Cheesy Green Beans, 51
- Frozen Raspberry Salad, 235

Cheesy Lasagna
- Elegant Salad, 154
- Simple Caesar Salad Dressing, 297
- Vegetable Cheese Texas Toast, 342

Cheesy Meat Loaf
- Saucy Vegetables, 21
- Bacon Cauliflower Salad, 176
- Sweet Dijon Salad Dressing, 287

Chicken a'la King
- Puff Bowls, 367
- Dried Cherry Salad, 185
- Poppy Seed Dressing, 289

Chicken and Biscuits
- Asparagus Bacon Salad, 212
- Creamy Frozen Apricots, 238

Chicken and Broccoli
- Potato Bake, 70
- California Salad, 160

Chicken and Dressing
- Baked Sweet Potatoes, 93
- Broccoli with Mustard Sauce, 32
- Sweet Potato Biscuits, 320

Chicken and Ham Dinner
- Curly Red Salad, 159
- Creamy French Dressing, 268

Chicken and Mushrooms
- Potato Puff, 87
- Sweet and Sour Salad, 166
- Sweet and Sour Dressing, 275

Chicken and Rice
- Broccoli and Mushrooms, 33
- Banana Salad, 179

Chicken Cacciatore
- Pasta Primavera, 134
- Spinach Slaw, 203

Chicken Cordon Bleu
- Mustard Red Potatoes, 66
- Cheddar Vegetables, 19
- Swiss Salad, 158

Chicken Enchiladas
- Mexican Salad, 168
- Garlic Tomato Dressing, 278

Chicken Fried Steak
- Mashed Potatoes, 79
- Confetti Corn, 49
- Raspberry Ribbon Salad, 251

Chicken Ham Roll-Ups
- Bacon Fettuccine Alfredo, 131
- Strawberry Romaine Salad, 188

Chicken Stroganoff
- Homemade Egg Noodles, 130
- 24 Hour Fruit Salad, 227

Chicken Stuffed Manicotti
- Red, White and Green Salad, 152
- Creamy Italian Dressing, 286
- Mushroom Puffs, 370

Chicken Tortellini Soup
- Cheese Squares, 352

Chicken with Mushroom Gravy
- Italian Fettuccine, 139
- Crunchy Spinach Mushroom Salad, 192
- Honey Dressing, 270
- Cheddar Biscuits, 316

Chili
- Calico Corn Muffins, 332

Chili Beef and Rice
- Piñata Salad, 171
- Chile Dressing, 283
- Nachos, 389

Chili Soup
- Cheddar and Chile Pinwheels, 372

Cola Chicken
- Lemon Garlic Angel Hair Pasta, 141
- Broccoli Raisin Salad, 207

Continental Chicken
- Asparagus Linguine, 140
- Strawberry, Kiwi, Spinach Salad, 202
- Strawberry Dressing, 301

Corkscrew Chicken
- Broccoli Tomato Salad, 210
- Green Goddess Dressing, 277
- Hawaiian Sweet Bread, 353

Corn Chowder
- Bread Bowls, 355

Corned Beef and Cabbage
- German Potato Salad, 218
- Sour Cream and Chive Biscuits, 318

Cornflake Chicken
- Zucchini and Tomatoes, 100
- Wild Rice Salad, 258
- Onion Rings, 62

Corny Meat Loaf
- Peppered Broccoli, 34
- Creamed Corn, 45

Country Barbequed Ribs
- Potato Skins, 89
- Apple Salad, 226
- Apple Cider Biscuits, 322

Country Chicken and Vegetables
- Five Fruit Salad, 221
- Honey Lime Dressing, 272
- Easy Yeast Rolls, 359

Country Style BBQ Ribs
- Baked Beans, 60
- Pasta Fruit Salad, 255
- Corn Bread Salad, 215

Cowboy Barbeque
- Fried Green Tomatoes, 104

Crab, Shrimp, or Lobster Newberg
- Shrimp Salad, 213
- Scones, 358

Cranberry Chicken
- Dried Cranberry Salad, 189
- Celery Seed Dressing, 290
- Honey Cranberry Muffins, 328

Cream Cheese Chicken
- Candied Carrots, 38
- Whipped Potatoes, 80
- Broccoli and Cheddar Salad, 209

Creamed Corn and Beef
- Lemon Glazed Asparagus and Carrots, 23
- Pretzel Salad, 241

Creamy Chicken and Pasta
- Lemon Pepper Vegetables, 25
- Almond Spinach Salad, 195

French Onion Soup
- Strawberry Spinach Salad, 199
- Onion Dressing, 293
- Stuffed Crescent Rolls, 373

Glazed Meat Loaf
- Scalloped Potatoes, 67
- Cheddar Green Beans, 55

Grandma's Beef Stew
- Corn Bread, 333

Green Chile Chicken Soup
- Onion Poppy Seed Bread, 351

Ground Beef Stroganoff
- Mashed Cauliflower, 44
- Honey Mustard Vegetables, 24
- Lime Pear Salad, 244

Ham and Chicken Roll-Ups
- Swiss Green Beans, 54
- Frozen Fruit Cocktail, 236

Ham and Noodles
- Asparagus Salad, 178
- Buttermilk Ranch Dressing, 263

Ham and Potato Scallop
- Maple Carrots, 39
- Maple Corn Bread, 334

Ham Loaf with Pineapple Sauce
- Hawaiian Baked Potatoes, 92
- Glazed Carrots, 40
- Pineapple Cole Slaw, 205

Ham Primavera
- Layered Red and White Salad, 177
- Strawberry Bavarian Salad, 252

Hawaiian Chicken
- Confetti Fried Rice, 112
- Mandarin Salad, 174
- Mandarin Dressing, 300

Hawaiian Meatballs
- Rice Ring, 110
- Crispy Wonton, 382
- Red Sauce, 303

Honey Barbequed Ribs
- Potato Pancakes, 76
- Fresh Fruit Salad, 225
- Southern Corn Muffins, 331

Honey Lime Chicken
- Lemon Rice, 115
- Lime Vegetables, 16

Italian Chili
- Pepperoni Puffs, 368

Italian Meat Sauce
- Garlic Pasta, 135
- Lime Avocado Salad, 187
- Cheesy Texas Toast, 343

Italian Roast
- Corkscrew Broccoli, 137
- Caesar Salad, 155
- Caesar Salad Dressing, 296

Italian Shells
- Bacon Spinach Salad, 193
- Brown Sugar Dressing, 295
- Three Cheese Bread, 356

Jack Soup
- Bacon Biscuit Balls, 319

Lasagna
- Bleu Cheese Salad, 157
- Bleu Cheese Dressing, 298
- Bread Sticks, 348

Manhattan Clam Chowder
- Apple Pasta Salad, 256
- Dinner Rolls, 360

Maple Almond Beef
- Fried Noodles, 145
- Cream Cheese Wonton, 383

Mayonnaise Chicken
- Spinach Bean Sprout Salad, 196
- Russian Dressing, 288
- Sour Cream Croissants, 371

Meatball Soup
- Vegetable Bread, 345

Meatball Spaghetti
- Fresh Pear Salad, 186
- Ginger Dressing, 294
- Cheese-Onion Bread Sticks, 349

Meatballs in Gravy
- Garlic Mashed Potatoes, 81
- Simple Spinach Salad, 191
- Buttermilk Dressing, 265
- Potato Bread, 357

Meatballs in Sour Cream Sauce
- Baked Rice, 123
- Snow Pea Stir-Fry, 27
- Potato Rolls, 363

Meat Loaf and Potatoes
- Bacon Green Beans, 50
- Lemonade Salad, 249

Mexican Beef Stew
- Jalapeño Quesadillas, 379

Mexican Lasagna
- Mexican Avocado Salad, 170
- Avocado Dressing, 280

Minestrone
- Corn Fritters, 369

Mock Filet Mignon
- Garden Stuffed Baked Potatoes, 91
- Tomato Wedges, 101
- Batter Fried Shrimp, 388
- Cocktail Sauce, 306

Nacho Meat Loaf
- Monterey Rice, 114
- Honey Glazed Stir-Fry, 18
- Chili Cheddar Biscuits, 317

Navajo Tacos
- Gazpacho Salad, 172
- Gazpacho Dressing, 282

New England Baked Beans
- Paradise Pasta Salad, 254
- Sweet Braided Bread, 354

New England Clam Chowder
- One Hour Rolls, 361

Old Fashioned Bean Soup
- Ham and Cheese Muffins, 326

Onion Soup Meat Loaf
- Onion Roasted Potatoes, 78
- Red and Orange Salad, 163
- Honey French Dressing, 269

Oven Stew
- Onion Cheese Muffins, 329

Peachy Chicken
- Coconut Rice, 120
- Walnut Broccoli, 37
- Layered Peach Salad, 239

Pineapple Meatballs
- Pepper Rice, 116
- Pineapple Salad, 182

Pizza in a Dish
- Frozen Sour Cream Fruit Salad, 237
- Garlic Cheese Bread, 344

Pizza Meat Loaf
- Italian Scalloped Potatoes, 65
- Honey Lime Fruit Salad, 222

Polynesian Pork Roast
- Shrimp Rice, 121
- Carrot Pineapple Salad, 248
- Sweet Potato Rolls, 364

Porcupine Meatballs
- Au Gratin Potatoes, 68
- Broccoli with Cheese Sauce, 31
- Frozen Peach Salad, 232

Pork Chops and Potatoes
- Bacon Carrots, 42
- Creamy Apple Salad, 228

Pork Chops, Carrots and Gravy
- Cream Cheese Mashed Potatoes, 85
- Frog Eye Salad, 230
- Buttermilk Oatmeal Muffins, 327

Pork Loaf with Applesauce Glaze
- Parmesan Potatoes, 73
- Glazed Carrots and Apples, 43

Ravioli Soup
- Cheese Wraps, 385

Salisbury Steak and Gravy
- Duchess Potatoes, 84
- Honey Mustard Peas, 29
- Cheese Biscuits, 315

Scalloped Pork Chops
- Cheesy Broccoli Rice, 124
- Melon Cucumber Salad, 220

Simply Lasagna
- Green Salad, 151
- Thousand Island Dressing, 291
- Buttery French Bread, 339

Skillet BBQ Chicken
- Crisp New Potatoes, 69
- Speedy Fruit Salad, 224
- Western Zucchini, 346

Skillet BBQ Pork Chops
- Golden Fried Potatoes, 88
- Bacon Corn, 48
- German Cole Slaw, 204

Slow Cooked Chili
- Zucchini Rounds, 99
- Corn Meal Bread, 335

Slow Cooked Goulash
- Noodles Romanoff, 132
- Wilted Salad, 165
- Cloverleaf Rolls, 362

Slow Cooked Short Ribs
- Bacon Potato Salad, 216
- Apricot Salad, 243

Slow Cooked Stew
- Sour Cream Corn Bread, 336

Slow Cooked Stroganoff
- Roasted Onion & Garlic Potatoes, 83
- Tomato Green Beans, 52

Smoky Maple Chicken
- Bacon Pilaf, 118
- Parmesan Zucchini, 98
- Triple Orange Salad, 242

Smothered Steak
- Herbed Corn, 47
- Twice Baked Potatoes, 90
- Deep Fried Zucchini, 97

Southwest Stew
- Corn Pudding, 337

Spaghetti and Meatballs
- Parmesan Pimento Salad, 164
- Parmesan Dressing, 276
- Toasted Garlic French Bread, 341

Spaghetti Sauce
- Tangy Linguini, 138
- Italian Broccoli Salad, 211
- Italian Dressing, 284
- Italian Twists, 347

Steak and Vegetable Pie
- Sweet and Sour Lettuce, 161

Stuffing Meat Loaves
- Pecan Stuffed Acorn Squash, 96
- Fresh Cranberry Salad, 247

Swedish Meatballs
- Pasta Ring, 129
- Fruit and Lettuce Salad, 181
- Apple Carrot Muffins, 324

Sweet and Sour Chicken
- Oven Steamed Rice, 109
- Egg Rolls, 384

Sweet and Sour Meatballs
- New Year Fried Rice, 113
- Coconut Shrimp, 387
- Marmalade Dipping Sauce, 305

Swiss Ham and Noodles
- Swiss Spinach Salad, 194
- Simple Thousand Island Dressing, 292
- Cherry Freeze, 234

Swiss Steak and Gravy
- Home-Style Potatoes, 64
- Blueberry Salad, 183
- Blueberry Muffins, 323

Taco Pie
- Chicken Fajitas Salad, 169
- Salsa Dressing, 279

Taco Soup
- Steak Taco Quesadillas, 378

Teriyaki Beef
- Oriental Rice Pilaf, 117
- Chinese Dumplings, 381

Teriyaki Chicken
- Oriental Noodles, 144
- Pot Stickers, 380

Tomato Beef Stew
- Cheese Rolls, 365

Tomato Stroganoff
- Zucchini Garlic Bow Ties, 136
- Apple Lettuce Salad, 184

Tomato Swiss Steak
- Baked Sliced Potatoes, 74
- Swiss Broccoli, 35

Tortilla Chicken
- Guacamole Salad, 173
- Guacamole Dressing, 281

Tuna Bow Ties
- Spinach Raspberry Salad, 197

Tuna Broccoli Au Gratin
- Orange Cauliflower Salad, 201
- French Dressing, 267

Tuna Chow Mein
- Oriental Salad, 175
- Chinese Salad Dressing, 299

Tuna Fettuccine
- Blackberry Spinach Salad, 200

Tuna Stroganoff
- Broccoli Fettuccine, 142
- Taffy Apple Salad, 229

Turkey and Stuffing Roll-Ups
- Maple Glazed Sweet Potatoes, 94
- Cranberry Pineapple Salad, 250
- Orange Cream Cheese Muffins, 325

Turkey Dressing Pie
- Orange Candied Sweet Potatoes, 95
- Cranberry Sauce, 302

Vegetable Beef Soup
- Pimento Cheese Biscuits, 321

Very Best Meat Loaf
- Spicy Red Potatoes, 77
- Simple Cheesy Vegetables, 20

Waikiki Turkey
- Fried Rice, 111
- Chinese Green Peppers, 105

Vegetables

Is there a meal that is complete without vegetables? Not only are vegetables an important part of a balanced diet, they are also delicious and beautiful. The long list of vegetables and their combinations provide a wide variety of recipes to enjoy.

Fresh vegetables are the clear winner of any taste test, with garden fresh topping the chart. Next best is fresh produce from the market. Frozen vegetables add the advantage of immediate convenience plus the satisfaction of enjoying them out of season. Vegetables that you have frozen from your garden (if frozen very soon after harvesting) are hardly different from fresh. Next in line are frozen vegetables from the supermarket.

Freezing Vegetables

Most vegetable dishes are fairly simple to prepare. Even though many are not time consuming, you may still benefit from preparing some ahead for situations when there is not even time for simple preparation. A few bags of already assembled vegetable dishes in the freezer ensures the ability to serve them with only a few seconds of effort. Freezing also provides the ability to store an abundance of produce, perhaps from the garden, and have it available for later.

Most vegetables freeze well. It should be understood, however, that freezing does change vegetables. Vegetables have rigid cell walls and a high moisture content. Freezing causes the water in the vegetable cells to expand and burst the cell walls. This softens vegetables somewhat. This is usually not noticed when serving cooked vegetables except when you desire to serve crisp crunchy vegetables, such as in a stir-fry recipe. If you desire crisp, crunchy vegetables, whatever the recipe, you should not freeze them. However, if you prefer your vegetables cooked slightly soft or completely soft, even in a stir-fry recipe, you can probably successfully freeze the recipe.

When using fresh vegetables in a recipe being prepared for the freezer, most should be at least partially cooked to halt or at least lessen enzyme activity that can cause vegetables to become starchy, tough and undesirable. If a recipe does not call for complete cooking before freezing, be sure to blanch the vegetables, (cook in boiling water for 2 or 3 minutes), to stop the enzyme activity which causes vegetables to become starchy and undesirable.

When using previously frozen vegetables in a recipe being prepared for the freezer, it is usually best to not thaw the vegetables unless the recipe calls for complete cooking prior to freezing.

Most of the recipes in this section have freezing instructions. An absence of freezing instructions does not necessarily mean the recipe absolutely cannot be frozen, just that perhaps it is not practical or preferable.

Fresh or frozen, vegetable recipes provide variety and allow for beautiful presentation, for any meal from simple to spectacular.

Vegetable Recipes

continued...

Lime Vegetables

2 tablespoons peanut oil
1 teaspoon minced garlic
1 (16-ounce) package frozen stir-fry vegetables
    (pea pods, carrots, onions, mushrooms)
2 tablespoons lime juice
2 tablespoons soy sauce
3 tablespoons packed brown sugar
2 tablespoons peanut oil

Heat oil in a skillet with garlic.
Add thawed vegetables to hot oil.
Stir-fry until hot and crisp/tender.
Remove vegetables to serving plate.
In a small saucepan, combine lime
juice, soy sauce, brown sugar and
peanut oil. Heat and stir just until bubbly. Immediately
drizzle over hot vegetables. 6 servings.

Complete Menu

Honey Lime Chicken
- Lemon Rice, 115
- Lime Vegetables, 16

To juice a lime quickly, easily and thoroughly, place
lime in a glass bowl in the microwave. Heat until
lime bursts. This will take approximately 1 minute,
depending on the size of the lime. Turn off microwave
as soon as lime bursts. Allow to cool for a few minutes.
Juice can then be squeezed easily from the hole made
by the escaping steam.

Sweet and Sour Vegetables

3 tablespoons canola oil
1 cup sliced carrots
1 cup chunked green bell pepper
1 cup snow peas
1 (8-ounce) can sliced water chestnuts, drained
1/2 cup sliced, quartered cucumber
1 cup chunked tomato
3/4 cup **French Dressing**, (page 267)
2 tablespoons packed brown sugar
2 teaspoons soy sauce

Heat oil in a skillet. Add carrots, green pepper and snow peas. Cook for about 5 minutes over medium heat, stirring frequently. Add water chestnuts, cucumber and tomato. Combine dressing, brown sugar and soy sauce. Pour over vegetables. Stir gently and simmer covered for about 5 minutes until vegetables are tender. 6 servings.

Complete Menu

Cantonese Meatballs
• Carrot Rice, 119
• Sweet and Sour Vegetables, 17
• Lettuce Wraps, 386

 This recipe is also great with commercial French, Sweet & Spicy French or Russian dressing.

Honey Glazed Stir-Fry

1/3 cup honey
1/3 cup prepared stir-fry sauce
1/4 teaspoon crushed red pepper flakes
2 tablespoons peanut oil
2 cups broccoli florets
1 cup pea pods
2 cups sliced mushrooms
1/2 cup onion chunks
1 cup sliced carrots

In a small bowl, combine honey, stir-fry sauce and red pepper flakes. In a large skillet, heat peanut oil over medium-high heat. Add broccoli, pea pods, mushrooms, onion and carrots. Stir-fry about 3 minutes. Add the honey sauce. Stir until all vegetables are glazed and the sauce is bubbling. 6 servings.

Complete Menu

Nacho Meat Loaf
- Monterey Rice, 114
- Honey Glazed Stir-fry, 18
- Chili Cheddar Biscuits, 317

Cheddar Vegetables

4 cups vegetables in any combination
      (carrots, cauliflower, broccoli, zucchini,
         yellow summer squash, pea pods, asparagus)
2/3 cup evaporated milk
1 teaspoon mustard
1/4 cup water
2 tablespoons flour
2/3 cup shredded Cheddar cheese
1/4 teaspoon pepper

Cook vegetables in salted, boiling water for about 12 minutes or until tender. Drain. In small saucepan, combine milk and mustard. Whisk flour into water until well combined. Add to saucepan. Stirring constantly, cook over medium heat until thickened and bubbly. Remove from heat. Add cheese and stir until cheese is melted. Add pepper and pour over vegetables. 6 servings.

Complete Menu

Chicken Cordon Bleu
- Mustard Red Potatoes, 66
- Cheddar Vegetables, 19
- Swiss Salad, 158

Simple Cheesy Vegetables

1 (20-ounce) package frozen vegetables
      (carrots, broccoli and cauliflower)
1 (8-ounce) loaf or jar of processed American cheese
1 cup crushed butter cracker crumbs
1/2 cup melted butter

Cook vegetables in salted, boiling water for 8 minutes. Drain. Arrange vegetables in baking dish. Cube cheese (if from a loaf) or spoon cheese (if from a jar) over vegetables.
In a small bowl, combine cracker crumbs and melted butter. Sprinkle crumbs on top of vegetables and cheese. Bake at 350° for 20 to 25 minutes. 6 servings.

Complete Menu

Very Best Meat Loaf
- Spicy Red Potatoes, 77
- Simple Cheesy Vegetables, 20

Saucy Vegetables

2 (16-ounce) packages frozen vegetables
        (carrots, broccoli, cauliflower)
1 (10.75-ounce) can Cheddar cheese soup
1/2 cup sour cream
1/4 cup milk
1/2 teaspoon seasoned salt
1 cup shredded Cheddar cheese, divided
1 1/2 cups French fried onions, divided

Place thawed vegetables in greased baking dish. In a small bowl, combine soup, sour cream, milk, seasoned salt, 1/2 cup of cheese and 1/2 cup French fried onions. Mix and pour over vegetables. Bake covered at 375° for 45 minutes. Uncover and top with the remaining cheese and French fried onions. Return to oven for 5 minutes. 10 servings.

Complete Menu

Cheesy Meat Loaf
• Saucy Vegetables, 21
• Bacon Cauliflower Salad, 176
• Sweet Dijon Salad Dressing, 287

To Freeze: Do not thaw vegetables. Do not bake. Combine soup, sour cream, milk, seasoned salt, 1/2 cup cheese, and 1/2 cup French fried onions. Mix with frozen vegetables and place in freezer bag. Label and freeze.

To Serve: Thaw. Place in greased baking dish. Bake covered at 375° for 45 minutes. Uncover and top with 1/2 cup cheese and 1 cup French fried onions. Return to oven for 5 minutes.

California Vegetables

1 1/2 cups fresh broccoli florets
1 1/2 cups fresh cauliflower florets
1 cup sliced carrots
1 (10.75-ounce) can cream of mushroom soup
1 (8-ounce) loaf or jar processed American cheese
1 (6-ounce) box stuffing mix
1/2 cup melted butter

Cook broccoli, cauliflower and carrots in salted, boiling water for 8 minutes. Drain. Add soup and cheese to pan with vegetables. Stir to combine and partially melt cheese. Arrange vegetables in greased baking dish. Sprinkle stuffing cubes over top. Pour melted butter over all. Bake at 350° for 30 minutes. 6 servings.

Complete Menu

BBQ Beef and Biscuits
• California Vegetables, 22
• Fruit Salad, 223

To Freeze: Cook vegetables 4 minutes. Drain. Add soup and cheese to pan. Stir to partially melt cheese. Allow to cool. Place in freezer bag. Label and freeze.

To Serve: Thaw. Place in a greased baking dish. Sprinkle stuffing over top. Pour melted butter over all. Bake at 350° for 45 minutes.

Lemon Glazed Asparagus and Carrots

2 cups sliced carrots
4 cups asparagus, cut into 1-inch lengths
1/4 cup butter
1 teaspoon cornstarch
3 tablespoons water
1 tablespoon lemon juice
1 teaspoon grated lemon peel
2 tablespoons chopped toasted pecans

Cook carrots and asparagus in salted, boiling water for 10 minutes. Drain. Melt butter in a large skillet. In a small bowl, combine cornstarch, water and lemon juice. Stir into butter in skillet. Cook and stir over medium heat until sauce is thickened. Stir in lemon peel. Stir in carrots and asparagus. Stir to coat. Pour into serving dish. Top with toasted pecans. 6 servings.

Complete Menu

Creamed Corn and Beef
- Lemon Glazed Asparagus and Carrots, 23
- Pretzel Salad, 241

Honey Mustard Vegetables

1 (16-ounce) package frozen mixed vegetables
2 tablespoons packed brown sugar
3 tablespoons butter
2 tablespoons honey
1 tablespoon mustard
1/8 teaspoon salt

Cook vegetables in salted, boiling water until tender. Drain. In a small saucepan, combine brown sugar, butter, honey, mustard and salt. Heat until bubbly. Pour over vegetables. Stir to coat. 6 servings.

Complete Menu

Ground Beef Stroganoff
• Mashed Cauliflower, 44
• Honey Mustard Vegetables, 24
• Lime Pear Salad, 244

Lemon Pepper Vegetables

2 cups fresh cauliflower florets
2 cups fresh broccoli florets
1 cup sliced carrots
2 tablespoons melted butter
1 teaspoon lemon pepper
1 teaspoon minced garlic

Cook cauliflower, broccoli and carrots in salted, boiling water for about 15 minutes or until tender. Drain. Combine melted butter, lemon pepper and garlic. Drizzle over vegetables.
6 servings.

Complete Menu

Creamy Chicken and Pasta
• Lemon Pepper Vegetables, 25
• Almond Spinach Salad, 195

Vegetable Kabobs

2 ears fresh corn
2 small zucchini
8 pearl onions
1/2 cup melted butter
2 tablespoons minced chives
2 tablespoons snipped fresh parsley
1/2 teaspoon garlic salt

Cut corn into 2-inch pieces. Cut zucchini into 1-inch pieces. Thread corn, zucchini, and onions alternately onto 4 large skewers. In a small bowl, mix together butter, chives, parsley and garlic salt. Brush kabobs with butter mixture. Broil kabobs for 8 to 10 minutes, until tender, turning and brushing with butter every 2 minutes. 4 servings.

Complete Menu

Calico Beans
- Bacon and Egg Potato Salad, 217
- Vegetable Kabobs, 26

Snow Pea Stir-Fry

3 tablespoons butter
2 cups fresh or frozen snow peas
1 1/2 cups sliced mushrooms
2 teaspoons cornstarch
1/2 teaspoon chicken bouillon
2/3 cup water
1 tablespoon soy sauce

Heat butter in a large skillet. Stir-fry peas and mushrooms for about 5 minutes. In a small bowl, combine cornstarch, bouillon, water and soy sauce. Whisk until smooth. Add to skillet and bring to a boil. Cook and stir for about 5 minutes until thickened and vegetables are coated. 6 servings.

Complete Menu

Meatballs in Sour Cream Sauce
- Baked Rice, 123
- Snow Pea Stir-Fry, 27
- Potato Rolls, 363

Company Peas

1 tablespoon butter
1 teaspoon chicken bouillon
2 tablespoons water
1 1/2 cups sliced mushrooms
1 cup sliced celery
2 tablespoons chopped red bell pepper
1 (16-ounce) package frozen petite peas
1 (8-ounce) can sliced water chestnuts

Melt butter in a large skillet. Add bouillon and water and mix well. Add mushrooms, celery and red bell pepper. Cook and stir over medium heat for about 5 minutes or until vegetables are tender. Stir in peas. Cover and cook for about 2 minutes or until peas are hot. Add drained water chestnuts and cook for another minute or until heated through. 6 servings.

Complete Menu

Bacon Chicken
• Mashed Red Potatoes, 82
• Company Peas, 28
• Layered Salad, 208
• Catalina Dressing, 266

You could substitute regular peas for the petite peas. However, petite peas are so much better, you won't want to.

Honey Mustard Peas

1 (16-ounce) package frozen petite peas
1 teaspoon salt
1 teaspoon sugar
2 tablespoons melted butter
2 tablespoons honey
1 1/2 teaspoons mustard

Fill a saucepan with water and add salt and sugar. Bring to a boil. Add peas and cook for about 2 minutes. Drain. In a small bowl, combine melted butter, honey and mustard. Pour over peas. Stir to coat. 6 servings.

Complete Menu

Salisbury Steak and Gravy
• Duchess Potatoes, 84
• Honey Mustard Peas, 29
• Cheese Biscuits, 315

Petite peas are younger, smaller and more tender than regular peas. Find them in the frozen section, right next to regular peas.

Italian Broccoli

1 1/2 pounds fresh broccoli
2 tablespoons olive oil
1 tablespoon butter
2 tablespoons shredded fresh Parmesan cheese

Cut broccoli into bite-sized pieces. Cook broccoli in salted, boiling water for about 15 minutes or until tender. Drain. In same pan, heat olive oil and butter. Add broccoli. Cook and stir until broccoli is a delicate brown. Sprinkle with cheese. 6 servings.

Complete Menu

Bird's Nest Pie
• Italian Broccoli, 30
• Ranch Garlic Bread, 340

 1 (16-ounce) package frozen broccoli may be substituted for the fresh broccoli.

Broccoli with Cheese Sauce

1 1/2 pounds fresh broccoli
1 (8-ounce) jar or loaf processed American cheese
1/3 cup milk
1/4 teaspoon onion salt

Cut broccoli into bite-sized pieces. Cook broccoli in salted, boiling water for about 15 minutes or until tender. Drain. In small saucepan, over medium heat, stir cheese,

Complete Menu

Porcupine Meatballs
• Au Gratin Potatoes, 68
• Broccoli with Cheese Sauce, 31
• Frozen Peach Salad, 232

milk and onion salt until cheese is melted and smooth. Pour over broccoli. 6 servings.

 1 (16-ounce) package frozen broccoli may be substituted for the fresh broccoli.

Broccoli with Mustard Sauce

1 1/2 pounds fresh broccoli
1 tablespoon butter
1 tablespoon half-and-half
1/2 teaspoon ground mustard
1 teaspoon sugar
1/8 teaspoon pepper

Cut broccoli into bite-sized pieces. Cook broccoli in salted, boiling water for about 15 minutes or until tender. Drain. Melt butter in a small saucepan. Stir in half-and-half, ground mustard, sugar and pepper. Mix well. Pour over broccoli. 6 servings.

Complete Menu

Chicken and Dressing
• Baked Sweet Potatoes, 93
• Broccoli with Mustard Sauce, 32
• Sweet Potato Biscuits, 320

 1 (16-ounce) package frozen broccoli may be substituted for the fresh broccoli.

Broccoli and Mushrooms

2 cups fresh broccoli florets
1 cup sliced mushrooms
1 (10.75-ounce) can cream of mushroom soup
1/2 cup processed American cheese
1/4 cup salad dressing
1/4 cup milk
1 egg, beaten
1/4 cup dry bread crumbs
1 tablespoon melted butter

Cook broccoli in salted, boiling water for 5 minutes. Drain. Arrange broccoli and sliced mushrooms in a baking dish. In a small saucepan, heat soup

Complete Menu

Chicken and Rice
• Broccoli and Mushrooms, 33
• Banana Salad, 179

and cheese. Stir until cheese melts. Remove from heat. Add salad dressing, milk and egg. Mix well. Pour over broccoli and mushrooms. In a small bowl, combine crumbs and melted butter. Sprinkle evenly over broccoli and sauce. Bake at 350° for 45 minutes, until crumbs are lightly browned. 4 servings.

To Freeze: Do not cover with crumbs or butter. Do not bake. Place in freezer bag. Label and freeze.

To Serve: Thaw. Place in greased baking dish. Top with buttered crumbs. Bake at 350° for 50 minutes.

Peppered Broccoli

6 cups broccoli florets
2 tablespoons olive oil
2 teaspoons minced garlic
1/8 teaspoon crushed red pepper flakes
1/2 cup red bell pepper strips
1/2 cup onion slices
1/2 teaspoon salt
1/8 teaspoon pepper

Cook broccoli in salted, boiling water for 5 minutes. Drain. Heat oil in a large skillet. Add garlic and red pepper flakes to hot oil. Stir in red bell pepper strips and onion slices. Stir to break onion into rings. Cook and stir until onion begins to soften. Stir in broccoli. Cook, stirring occasionally, for about 5 minutes. Season with salt and pepper. 8 servings.

Complete Menu

Corny Meat Loaf
• Peppered Broccoli, 34
• Creamed Corn, 45

Swiss Broccoli

3 cups fresh broccoli florets
1 1/2 cups sliced summer squash
1/2 cup butter
1 egg, beaten
1 cup shredded Swiss cheese
1/4 cup milk
1/4 teaspoon ground mustard
1 teaspoon salt
1/8 teaspoon pepper
dash cayenne pepper
1/2 cup shredded fresh Parmesan cheese

Cook broccoli in salted, boiling water for 5 minutes. Add summer squash and boil 2 additional minutes. Drain. Arrange in greased baking dish. Melt butter and mix with egg, Swiss cheese, milk, ground mustard, salt and peppers. Pour over vegetables. Top with Parmesan cheese. Bake at 350° for 20 minutes. 6 servings.

Complete Menu

Tomato Swiss Steak
• Baked Sliced Potatoes, 74
• Swiss Broccoli, 35

To Freeze: Cook vegetables for 2 minutes. Combine with sauce. Do not add Parmesan cheese. Place in freezer bag. Label and freeze.

To Serve: Thaw. Place in greased baking dish. Top with Parmesan cheese. Bake at 350° for 35 minutes.

Baked Broccoli

6 cups fresh broccoli florets
1 (10.75-ounce) can cream of mushroom soup
1 cup mayonnaise
4 eggs, lightly beaten
1/4 cup chopped onion
1/2 teaspoon salt
1 cup shredded Cheddar cheese

Cook broccoli in salted, boiling water for 5 minutes. Drain. Arrange broccoli in a greased baking dish. In a mixing bowl, combine soup and mayonnaise. Add lightly beaten eggs. Mix well. Stir in onion and salt. Mix in cheese. Pour over broccoli. Bake at 350° for 20 to 30 minutes. 8 servings.

Complete Menu

Cheesy Chicken and Rice
- Baked Broccoli, 36
- Raspberry Avocado Salad, 214
- Raspberry Dressing, 301

To Freeze: Cook broccoli 2 minutes. Add sauce. Place in freezer bag. Label and freeze.

To Serve: Thaw. Place in greased baking dish. Bake at 350° for 35 minutes.

Walnut Broccoli

1 (14-ounce) package frozen broccoli florets
2 tablespoons butter
1 teaspoon minced garlic
1/4 cup walnut pieces

Cook broccoli in salted, boiling water for about 10 minutes, or until tender. Drain. Melt butter in a small saucepan. Add garlic and cook until butter is lightly browned, stirring constantly. Stir in walnuts. Pour over broccoli. Toss gently to coat. 6 servings.

Complete Menu

Peachy Chicken
• Coconut Rice, 120
• Walnut Broccoli, 37
• Layered Peach Salad, 239

Candied Carrots

1 (2-pound) package carrots
1 teaspoon salt
1 teaspoon sugar
1/2 cup butter
1/2 cup packed brown sugar

Peel and slice carrots. Place in pan and cover with water. Add salt and sugar. Bring to boil, reduce heat to medium and boil gently for about 20 minutes or until carrots are very soft. Drain. In the same pan, heat butter and brown sugar until melted and bubbly. Immediately pour carrots back into pan. Stir to coat. 6 servings.

Complete Menu

Cream Cheese Chicken
- Candied Carrots, 38
- Whipped Potatoes, 80
- Broccoli and Cheddar Salad, 209

To Freeze: Allow to cool. Place in freezer bag or freezer container. Label and freeze.

To Serve: Heat and serve.

Maple Carrots

1 (2-pound) package carrots
1 teaspoon salt
1 teaspoon sugar
1/4 cup butter
1/2 cup maple syrup
1/2 teaspoon salt

Peel and slice carrots. Place in pan and cover with water. Add salt and sugar. Bring to a boil, reduce heat to medium and boil gently for about 20 minutes or until carrots are very soft. Drain. In the same pan, heat butter, maple syrup and salt until melted and bubbly. Return carrots to pan. Stir to coat well. 6 servings.

Complete Menu

Ham and Potato Scallop
• Maple Carrots, 39
• Maple Corn Bread, 334

To Freeze: Allow to cool. Place in freezer bag or freezer container. Label and freeze.

To Serve: Heat and serve.

Glazed Carrots

2 cups sliced carrots
1/4 cup butter
1/4 cup pineapple juice
1 teaspoon sugar
1/2 teaspoon salt

Cook carrots in salted, boiling water for 10 minutes. Drain. Place in ungreased baking dish. Melt butter. Add pineapple juice, sugar and salt to melted butter. Pour over carrots. Cover and bake at 375° for 40 minutes. 4 servings.

Complete Menu

Ham Loaf with Pineapple Sauce
- Hawaiian Baked Potatoes, 92
- Glazed Carrots, 40
- Pineapple Cole Slaw, 205

To Freeze: Place cooled carrots in freezer bag or container before or after baking. Label and freeze.

To Serve: Unbaked: Thaw and place in ungreased baking dish. Cover and bake at 375° for 45 minutes.
Baked: Heat and serve.

Orange Carrots

2 cups julienned carrots
2 tablespoons sugar
1 1/2 teaspoons cornstarch
3/4 teaspoon salt
6 tablespoons orange juice
3 tablespoons butter or margarine

Cook carrots in salted, boiling water for about 20 minutes or until tender. Drain. Remove carrots. In same saucepan, combine sugar, cornstarch and salt. Gradually stir in orange juice. Bring to a boil. Cook and stir until thickened and bubbly. Add butter. Return carrots to pan and stir to coat. 4 servings.

Complete Menu

Beef Stroganoff
• Orange Carrots, 41
• Baked Mashed Potatoes, 86
• Buttermilk Salad, 246

Bacon Carrots

4 cups julienned carrots
4 slices bacon
1/2 teaspoon salt
dash pepper

Cook carrots in salted, boiling water for about 10 minutes or until tender. Drain. Meanwhile, fry bacon in a skillet until crisp. Drain on paper towels. Drain all but 2 tablespoons bacon drippings from skillet. Add drained carrots, salt and pepper to reserved drippings in skillet. Crumble bacon into carrots. Stir. 6 servings.

Complete Menu

Pork Chops and Potatoes
- Bacon Carrots, 42
- Creamy Apple Salad, 228

Glazed Carrots and Apples

1 1/2 cups sliced carrots
2 tablespoons butter
1/4 cup packed brown sugar
1 tablespoon lemon juice
dash cinnamon
1 cup peeled diced firm apple
1 tablespoon cornstarch
2 tablespoons cold water

Cook carrots in salted, boiling water for 20 minutes or until very tender. Drain. Return carrots to pan. Add butter, brown sugar, lemon juice and cinnamon. Mix well. Add apple. Cover and simmer for 10 minutes. Dissolve cornstarch in water and stir into carrots. Bring to a boil. Cook and stir for about 1 minute until thickened. Continue to cook and stir for about 2 minutes longer to glaze carrots and apples. 4 servings.

Complete Menu

Pork Loaf with Applesauce Glaze
- Parmesan Potatoes, 73
- Glazed Carrots and Apples, 43

Mashed Cauliflower

4 cups fresh cauliflower florets
1/2 cup cream
1 tablespoon cornstarch
1 teaspoon sugar
1/2 teaspoon salt
1/2 teaspoon garlic salt
1/4 teaspoon pepper

Cook cauliflower in salted, boiling water for about 20 minutes or until tender. Drain and allow to cool. Place in a food processor or blender and process until smooth. Add up to 1/2 cup water if necessary to blend smoothly. In a medium saucepan, combine cream and cornstarch. Whisk until cornstarch is dissolved. Stir in sugar, salt, garlic salt and pepper. Bring to a simmer over medium heat. Cook and stir until thickened. Stir in pureed cauliflower. Continue to cook and stir until thick and bubbly. 6 servings.

Complete Menu

Ground Beef Stroganoff
- Mashed Cauliflower, 44
- Honey Mustard Vegetables, 24
- Lime Pear Salad, 244

Serve Mashed Cauliflower in place of mashed potatoes. You might not even be able to tell the difference! Delicious!

Creamed Corn

1 tablespoon butter
2 teaspoons flour
1 cup cream
1 (16-ounce) package frozen corn
1 teaspoon sugar
1/2 teaspoon salt
dash pepper

Melt butter in a heavy saucepan. Stir in flour. Cook and stir until golden and bubbly. Stir in cream and bring to a boil. Add corn and sugar and return to boil. Allow to simmer for about 2 minutes, until hot and slightly thickened. Stir in salt and pepper. 6 servings.

Complete Menu

Corny Meat Loaf
• Peppered Broccoli, 34
• Creamed Corn, 45

To Freeze: Cool and place in freezer bag or container. Label and freeze.

To Serve: Thaw. Heat and stir until smooth and bubbly. Add a little milk or cream, if necessary.

Baked Corn

2 (16-ounce) cans creamed corn
1 (16-ounce) package frozen corn
3 eggs, lightly beaten
1 cup cream
1 tablespoon sugar
1 teaspoon salt
1/4 teaspoon pepper
1 cup butter cracker crumbs
3 tablespoons melted butter

In a mixing bowl, combine creamed corn, corn, eggs, cream, sugar, salt and pepper. Pour into greased baking dish. Bake at 350° for 45 minutes. Mix crumbs and butter. Spoon crumbs on top of corn. Return to oven and bake an additional 15 minutes. 10 servings.

Complete Menu

Candied Chicken
- Cheese Potatoes, 71
- Baked Corn, 46
- Frozen Fruit Salad, 231

To Freeze: Combine corn, eggs, cream, sugar, salt and pepper. Pour into freezer bag. Label and freeze.

To Serve: Thaw. Pour into greased baking dish, stir. Bake at 350° for 45 minutes. Top with buttered cracker crumbs. Bake 15 minutes.

Herbed Corn

10 ears fresh corn
1/2 cup softened butter
1 tablespoon snipped chives
1 teaspoon snipped fresh dill
1 teaspoon snipped fresh parsley
1/2 teaspoon thyme
1/2 teaspoon garlic salt
dash pepper

Cook corn in rapidly boiling water for 3 minutes. Meanwhile combine butter, chives, dill, parsley, thyme, salt and pepper in a small bowl. Drain corn and quickly dry. Spread herbed butter on each ear of hot corn. 10 servings.

Complete Menu

Smothered Steak
- Herbed Corn, 47
- Twice Baked Potatoes, 90
- Deep Fried Zucchini, 97

To freeze: Wrap each ear in plastic wrap. Allow to cool. Place wrapped ears in gallon freezer bag. Freeze.

To Serve: Thaw. Unwrap. Microwave each ear until hot, about 60 seconds.

Bacon Corn

1/2 pound bacon
2 tablespoons butter
2 tablespoons minced onion
1/4 cup flour
2 (15-ounce) cans corn
1 cup sour cream

In a large skillet, cook bacon until crisp. Drain bacon on paper towels. Cut into strips. Remove all but 2 tablespoons bacon drippings. Add butter and onion to drippings in skillet. Cook onion until tender but not brown. Stir in flour and mix well. Drain one can of corn. Pour corn and undrained corn into pan. Cook and stir over low heat until mixture begins to thicken. Stir in sour cream and bacon. 8 servings.

Complete Menu

Skillet BBQ Pork Chops
- Golden Fried Potatoes, 88
- Bacon Corn, 48
- German Cole Slaw, 204

Confetti Corn

1/4 cup butter
1/2 cup sliced mushrooms
1/3 cup diced red bell pepper
1/3 cup sliced green onion
2 cups diced tomato
1 (16-ounce) package frozen corn
1 tablespoon sugar
1 teaspoon garlic salt
1/2 teaspoon dried parsley flakes

Melt butter in a skillet. Cook mushrooms, bell pepper and onion in butter until tender but not brown. Add tomato, corn, sugar, garlic salt and parsley flakes. Mix well. Heat about 5 minutes or until heated through. 6 servings.

Complete Menu

Chicken Fried Steak
- Mashed Potatoes, 79
- Confetti Corn, 49
- Raspberry Ribbon Salad, 251

Bacon Green Beans

8 slices bacon
1 (16-ounce) package frozen green beans
1 tablespoon sugar
1 teaspoon salt
1/4 teaspoon pepper

Slice or dice bacon. In a large, heavy skillet, cook bacon until almost crisp. Add green beans and cover with water to the top of the pan. Add sugar, salt and pepper. Cover with lid slightly ajar. Cook slowly for about an hour, until liquid is gone and beans are very tender. Continue to cook and stir just until beans start to brown. Do not allow to burn. 6 servings.

Complete Menu

Meat Loaf and Potatoes
• Bacon Green Beans, 50
• Lemonade Salad, 249

To Freeze: Allow to cool and place in freezer bag or container. Label and freeze.

To Serve: Heat and serve.

For delicious **Bacon Green Beans and Carrots**, add 1 to 2 cups of sliced carrots and cook with green beans and bacon.

Cheesy Green Beans

1 (16-ounce) package frozen French green beans
2 cups diced ham
1/2 cup salad dressing
2 teaspoons mustard
2 (10.75-ounce) cans cream of celery soup
2 cups shredded Cheddar cheese
1 cup shredded Mozzarella cheese
1/2 cup dry bread crumbs
2 tablespoons melted butter

Place frozen green beans under hot running water to thaw. Drain. Combine green beans with ham. Place in an ungreased baking dish. In a small bowl, combine salad dressing, mustard and soup. Pour over beans and ham. Sprinkle Cheddar cheese and Mozzarella cheese over top. Combine bread crumbs and melted butter. Sprinkle over top of cheese. Bake uncovered at 350° for 35 minutes. 10 servings.

Complete Menu

Cheesy Ham and Potatoes
• Cheesy Green Beans, 51
• Frozen Raspberry Salad, 235

To Freeze: Do not thaw beans. Combine frozen beans and sauce. Do not add cheese or buttered crumbs. Place in freezer bag. Label and freeze.

To Serve: Thaw. Place in ungreased baking dish. Top with cheeses and buttered bread crumbs. Bake uncovered at 350° for 35 minutes.

Tomato Green Beans

3 slices bacon
1/2 cup chopped onion
2 tablespoons packed brown sugar
1 (10.75-ounce) can tomato soup
2 (15-ounce) cans green beans, drained

Cook bacon until almost crisp. Drain on paper towels. Cut into 1-inch pieces. Add chopped onion to bacon drippings in pan. Cook until onion is soft but not browned. Remove from heat. Stir in brown sugar and tomato soup. Mix well. Stir in green beans and bacon. Place in greased baking dish. Bake at 350° for 25 minutes. 6 servings.

Complete Menu

Slow Cooked Stroganoff
- Roasted Onion & Garlic Potatoes, 83
- Tomato Green Beans, 52

Garlic Green Beans

1 (16-ounce) package frozen green beans
2 tablespoons olive oil
1 tablespoon melted butter
3 cloves garlic
1 tablespoon onion
2 teaspoons Italian seasoning
1/2 teaspoon salt
1/8 teaspoon pepper

Place frozen beans under hot running water to thaw. When completely thawed, drain thoroughly. Place into a baking dish. In a small bowl, combine olive oil and butter. Press garlic and onion through garlic press. Add to oil. Stir in Italian seasoning, salt and pepper. Mix well. Pour over beans and stir until well coated. Bake at 450° for 20 minutes, until crisp tender and lightly browned. 6 servings.

Complete Menu

California Dip Meat Loaf
- Monterey Potatoes, 75
- Garlic Green Beans, 53
- Orange Tossed Salad, 180
- Sweet Honey Mustard Dressing, 271

 For tender beans, boil in salted water for 20 minutes before placing in baking dish.

Swiss Green Beans

1 teaspoon salt
1 teaspoon sugar
1 (16-ounce) package frozen French green beans
1 tablespoon minced onion
2 tablespoons butter
2 tablespoons flour
1 cup sour cream
1 cup shredded Swiss cheese

Fill a large saucepan with water and add salt and sugar. Bring to a boil. Add green beans. Boil for 10 minutes. Drain. In saucepan over medium heat, cook onion in butter for about 2 minutes. Stir in flour. Stir constantly until smooth. Slowly add sour cream and cook until thick, stirring constantly. Remove from heat. Add cheese and beans. Pour mixture into a greased baking dish. Bake at 350° for 20 minutes. 6 servings.

Complete Menu

Ham and Chicken Roll-Ups
- Swiss Green Beans, 54
- Frozen Fruit Cocktail, 236

Cheddar Green Beans

1 pound fresh green beans
3 tablespoons butter
1/4 cup finely chopped onion
1 tablespoon flour
2 teaspoons sugar
1/2 teaspoon salt
1/4 teaspoon pepper
1 cup sour cream
1/2 cup crushed butter crackers
1 tablespoon melted butter
1 cup shredded Cheddar cheese

Cut beans into 1-inch pieces. Cook green beans in salted, boiling water for 10 minutes. Meanwhile, melt 3 tablespoons butter in saucepan. Stir in onions and cook until onion is tender but not brown. Stir in flour, sugar, salt and pepper to form a smooth paste. Cook and stir for about a minute. Remove from heat. Stir in sour cream. Drain green beans and stir into sour cream mixture. Pour into greased baking dish. Mix melted butter and cracker crumbs. Sprinkle buttered crumbs and shredded cheese over top. Bake uncovered at 400° for 20 minutes. 6 servings.

Complete Menu

Glazed Meat Loaf
• Scalloped Potatoes, 67
• Cheddar Green Beans, 55

To Freeze: Cook beans 5 minutes. Place beans and sauce in freezer bag. Do not add crumbs or cheese. Label and freeze.

To Serve: Thaw. Place in greased baking dish. Top with cracker crumbs and cheese. Bake uncovered at 400° for 30 minutes.

Celery Bacon Green Beans

2 (16-ounce) packages frozen green beans
6 slices bacon
1 cup chopped onion
1 (10.75-ounce) can cream of celery soup
1/2 cup cream

Cook beans in salted, boiling water for 20 minutes. Drain. Dice bacon. In a skillet, cook bacon over medium heat until almost crisp. Drain on paper towels. Remove all but 2 tablespoons bacon drippings. Cook onion in drippings until tender but not brown. Stir in soup and cream. Cook and stir until hot and bubbly. Pour over beans. Sprinkle bacon over top. 10 servings.

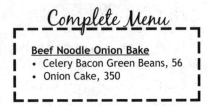

Complete Menu

Beef Noodle Onion Bake
- Celery Bacon Green Beans, 56
- Onion Cake, 350

Green Beans and Carrots

1 (16-ounce) package frozen green beans
1 cup sliced carrots
1 cup sliced onion
1/2 cup sliced celery
2 cups water
1 teaspoon salt
1/8 teaspoon pepper

In a large saucepan, combine beans, carrots, onion, celery, water, salt and pepper. Bring to a boil. Reduce heat and cover. Simmer for 30 minutes until vegetables are tender, stirring occasionally. Drain and serve. 6 servings.

Complete Menu

Cheesy Ham and Noodles
• Green Beans and Carrots, 57
• Lime Sour Cream Salad, 245

To Freeze: Allow to cool. Place in freezer bag. Label and freeze.

To Serve: Heat and serve.

Green Beans and Bean Sprouts

1 (16-ounce) package frozen French green beans
1/4 cup peanut oil
2 green onions, minced
2 cups fresh bean sprouts
1 teaspoon salt
1 tablespoon sugar

Place green beans under running hot water until completely thawed. In a large skillet, heat oil until very hot. Add green onion to flavor the oil. Add the beans and stir a few times, stir-fry for about 5 minutes. Add bean sprouts and stir-fry for about 30 seconds. Add the salt and sugar and stir-fry for about 1 minute longer. 6 servings.

Complete Menu

Beef and Pork Chop Suey
- Baked Mushroom Rice, 122
- Green Beans and Bean Sprouts, 58

Refried Beans

1 pound dry pinto beans
5 cups water
1 cup chopped onion
1/2 cup butter
salt

In a large pan, cover beans with water and bring to a boil. Cover and remove from heat. Allow to sit for 2 hours. Drain. Add 5 cups water and onion. Bring to a boil, reduce heat

Complete Menu

Beefy Spanish Rice
• Chicken and Rice Burritos, 390
• Refried Beans, 59

and simmer slowly until beans are very tender, about 3 hours. Remove from heat. Add butter and mash with a potato masher. Mix well. Return to heat and cook and stir until butter is absorbed and beans are thickened. Add salt to taste. Great as a side dish or in any recipe calling for refried beans. 8 servings.

To Freeze: Allow to cool. Place in freezer bag or container. Label and freeze.

To Serve: Thaw. Heat and serve.

Baked Beans

1 pound bacon
1 cup chopped onion
3 (15-ounce) cans pork and beans
1/2 cup ketchup
1/2 cup packed brown sugar
1 tablespoon mustard

Dice bacon. In a large skillet, cook bacon with chopped onion until bacon is almost crisp and onion is tender. Drain bacon drippings. Add beans, ketchup, brown sugar and mustard. Stir together. Pour into baking dish. Bake at 350° for 45 minutes. 10 servings.

Complete Menu

Country Style BBQ Ribs
- Baked Beans, 60
- Pasta Fruit Salad, 255
- Corn Bread Salad, 215

To Freeze: Cool and place in freezer bag. Label and freeze.

To Serve: Thaw. Heat and serve.

Mushroom Pie

1 (9-inch) unbaked pie crust
1 pound mushrooms
2 tablespoons minced onion
1/4 cup butter
4 eggs
1 cup cream
1 1/2 teaspoons salt
1/8 teaspoon pepper
3/4 cup shredded Swiss cheese
2 tablespoons butter

Crimp edges of unbaked pie crust. Bake at 450° for 8 to 10 minutes. Thinly slice mushrooms. Cook sliced mushroom and onion in butter until mushrooms are soft and the liquid is gone. Beat eggs with cream, salt and pepper. Add mushrooms. Pour into partially baked pie shell. Sprinkle cheese over top. Dot with butter and bake at 350° for 35 minutes or until puffed and slightly firm. 6 servings.

Complete Menu

Baked Chicken in Gravy
- Mushroom Pie, 61
- Tortellini Spinach Salad, 253
- Creamy Cheese Dressing, 274

To prevent the pie shell from shrinking while baking place waxed paper in pie shell and fill with dry beans or rice. Bake as directed. Allow to cool a bit and remove beans or rice and waxed paper.

Onion Rings

2 large sweet onions
2 1/2 cups buttermilk
3 tablespoons milk
2 eggs
1 3/4 cups flour
1 teaspoon salt
1 teaspoon garlic salt
1 teaspoon sugar
2 teaspoons chili powder
1/2 teaspoon pepper
oil for deep-frying

Slice onions and separate into rings. Soak rings in buttermilk for 30 minutes. In a separate bowl, whisk together milk and eggs. In a shallow dish, (such as a pie plate) combine flour, salt, garlic salt, sugar, chili powder and pepper. Drain onion rings. Dip first in egg mixture, then coat with flour mixture. Heat oil to 375° in electric skillet or deep-fryer. Fry onion rings for 1 to 1 1/2 minutes on each side or until golden brown. Drain on paper towels. 6 servings.

Complete Menu

Cornflake Chicken
- Zucchini and Tomatoes, 100
- Wild Rice Salad, 258
- Onion Rings, 62

To Freeze: Spread cooked onion rings in a single layer on a cookie sheet. Place in freezer. When rings are frozen transfer to a freezer bag. Label and freeze.

To Serve: Heat in toaster oven and serve.

 Onion Rings may be frozen prior to deep-frying. Freeze prepared rings in a single layer. Transfer to freezer bag. To serve, deep-fry desired quantity and serve.

 Onion Rings may be made with any onions, but sweet onions such as Walla Walla or Vidalia make the most delicious onion rings.

Baked Hash Browns

8 frozen hash brown patties
1 teaspoon salt
1/2 teaspoon garlic powder
1 cup cream
1 cup shredded Cheddar cheese

Place hash brown patties in a single layer in a greased baking dish. Sprinkle with salt and garlic powder. Pour cream over potato patties. Bake uncovered, at 350° for 50 minutes. Sprinkle with cheese and bake an additional 5 to 10 minutes or until cheese is melted. 8 servings.

Complete Menu

Brown Sugar Pork Ribs
- Oriental Noodle Salad, 257
- Baked Hash Browns, 63
- Frozen Strawberry Salad, 233

Home-Style Potatoes

6 potatoes
3/4 cup water
1/2 cup butter
1 (1.25-ounce) envelope onion soup mix
1/2 teaspoon dried parsley flakes

Wash and slice unpeeled potatoes into 1/4-inch slices. Arrange
potatoes in a greased baking
dish. In a saucepan, combine
water, butter, soup mix and parsley. Heat until butter is melted.
Pour over potatoes. Cover and bake at 350° for 40 minutes. Uncover and bake 20 minutes longer. 6 servings.

Complete Menu

Swiss Steak and Gravy
• Home-Style Potatoes, 64
• Blueberry Salad, 183
• Blueberry Muffins, 323

Italian Scalloped Potatoes

6 potatoes
1/2 cup chopped onion
1 cup shredded Mozzarella cheese
1/4 cup shredded fresh Parmesan cheese
1 (10.75-ounce) can cream of mushroom soup
1/4 cup milk
1/2 teaspoon Italian seasoning
1/2 teaspoon garlic salt

Peel and slice potatoes. Combine potatoes, onion, Mozzarella cheese and Parmesan cheese. Arrange potatoes in a greased baking dish. In a bowl, combine soup, milk, Italian seasoning and garlic salt. Pour soup mixture over all. Cover. Bake at 400° for 1 hour. Uncover and bake 10 minutes longer. 6 servings.

Complete Menu

Pizza Meat Loaf
• Italian Scalloped Potatoes, 65
• Honey Lime Fruit Salad, 222

Mustard Red Potatoes

18 small red potatoes
2 tablespoons canola oil
1/4 cup mustard
2 teaspoons minced garlic
1 teaspoon chili powder
1/2 teaspoon salt
1/8 teaspoon pepper

Scrub potatoes but do not peel. Prick each potato several times with a fork. Coat potatoes with oil. In a bowl, combine mustard, garlic, chili powder, salt and pepper. Mix well. Add potatoes, stirring to coat each potato. Arrange potatoes in a greased baking dish. Bake at 400° for 45 minutes or until potatoes are tender. 6 servings.

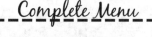

Complete Menu

Chicken Cordon Bleu
• Mustard Red Potatoes, 66
• Cheddar Vegetables, 19
• Swiss Salad, 158

Substitute other mustards, such as Dijon, spicy brown or honey mustard for the regular mustard.

Scalloped Potatoes

6 potatoes
1 1/4 cups milk
1 (8-ounce) package cream cheese
2 tablespoons minced onion
1 teaspoon salt
1/4 teaspoon pepper

Peel and slice potatoes. In a large saucepan, combine milk, cream cheese, onion, salt and pepper. Cook and stir until smooth. Remove from heat. Stir in potatoes. Spoon into a greased baking dish. Cover and bake at 350° for 1 hour and 10 minutes until potatoes are tender. 6 servings.

Complete Menu

Glazed Meat Loaf
- Scalloped Potatoes, 67
- Cheddar Green Beans, 55

Au Gratin Potatoes

1/2 cup chopped onion
2 tablespoons butter
1 tablespoon flour
1 teaspoon salt
1/4 teaspoon pepper
2 cups half-and-half
1 1/2 cups shredded Cheddar cheese
6 potatoes
1/4 cup dry bread crumbs
1/2 cup shredded Cheddar cheese

Cook and stir onion in butter in saucepan until onion is tender. Stir in flour, salt and pepper. Cook over low heat, stirring constantly, until mixture is smooth and bubbly. Remove from heat. Stir in half-and-half and cheese. Heat to boiling, stirring constantly. Cook and stir about 1 minute, until thickened. Peel and slice potatoes and place in an ungreased baking dish. Pour cheese sauce over potatoes. Bake uncovered at 350° for 75 to 90 minutes, until potatoes are tender and top is brown and bubbly. Mix remaining cheese and bread crumbs. Sprinkle over top of potatoes. Broil 3 to 4 inches from heat for about 4 minutes, until top is crusty and light brown. 6 servings.

Complete Menu

Porcupine Meatballs
• Au Gratin Potatoes, 68
• Broccoli with Cheese Sauce, 31
• Frozen Peach Salad, 232

Crisp New Potatoes

18 small new potatoes
1/2 cup oat bran hot cereal
3 tablespoons shredded fresh Parmesan cheese
1 teaspoon dried parsley flakes
1/3 cup milk
1 egg, slightly beaten
2 tablespoons melted butter
1/4 teaspoon garlic salt

Cook potatoes in salted, boiling water until tender. Drain, cool and peel potatoes. In a small bowl, combine oat bran cereal, cheese and parsley. In another small bowl, combine milk and egg. Dip each potato first in egg mixture then in oat bran mixture. Place in greased baking dish. Drizzle with melted butter. Sprinkle garlic salt over all. Cover and bake at 400° for 10 minutes. Uncover and bake an additional 10 minutes. 6 servings.

Complete Menu

Skillet BBQ Chicken
• Crisp New Potatoes, 69
• Speedy Fruit Salad, 224
• Western Zucchini, 346

Potato Bake

12 small new potatoes
1 egg
1 tablespoon milk
1 (2.5-ounce) envelope seasoned coating for chicken or pork
1 tablespoon shredded fresh Parmesan cheese

Boil potatoes in salted, boiling water until tender. Drain, cool and peel potatoes. In a small bowl, beat egg and milk. In a separate bowl, blend coating mix and cheese. Roll potatoes in egg mixture, then in coating mixture. Place potatoes in greased baking dish. Bake at 350° for 30 minutes. 4 servings.

Complete Menu

Chicken and Broccoli
• Potato Bake, 70
• California Salad, 160

Cheese Potatoes

6 potatoes
1/4 cup butter
1 teaspoon salt
1/4 teaspoon pepper
1 cup milk
2 cups shredded Cheddar cheese

Peel and slice potatoes. Melt butter in a large skillet. Add sliced potatoes, salt and pepper. Cook over medium heat until potatoes are almost tender and lightly browned. Add milk. Simmer, uncovered until milk is gone. Turn off heat, top with cheese, cover. When cheese has melted, stir and serve. 6 servings.

Complete Menu

Candied Chicken
• Cheese Potatoes, 71
• Baked Corn, 46
• Frozen Fruit Salad, 231

Cheesy Bacon Potatoes

2 cups water
3 teaspoons chicken bouillon
6 potatoes
1 cup chopped onion
6 slices bacon
3 tablespoons flour
1/2 teaspoon salt
1/4 teaspoon pepper
1 cup shredded Cheddar cheese

In a medium saucepan, heat water and bouillon to a boil. Peel and slice potatoes. Reduce heat and add sliced potatoes and chopped onion. Cover and simmer for about 5 minutes. Drain, reserving 1 1/2 cups broth. Cook bacon until crisp. Remove bacon and break into bite-sized pieces. Pour off all but 3 tablespoons drippings. Stir flour into reserved drippings. Stir in reserved broth, salt and pepper. Stirring constantly, cook until thickened and bubbly. Remove from heat. Add cheese and stir until cheese is melted. Add potatoes and bacon. Pour all into a greased baking dish. Bake at 400° for 35 minutes. 6 servings.

Complete Menu

Bacon Meat Loaf
- Cheesy Bacon Potatoes, 72
- BLT Salad, 156
- Ranch Dressing, 264

Parmesan Potatoes

6 potatoes
1/4 cup flour
1/4 cup canned Parmesan cheese
3/4 teaspoon salt
1/8 teaspoon pepper
1 tablespoon snipped fresh parsley
1/3 cup butter

Peel and cut potatoes into 1-inch cubes. In a paper bag, combine flour, Parmesan cheese, salt, pepper and parsley. Shake to mix. Add a

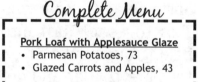

Complete Menu

Pork Loaf with Applesauce Glaze
- Parmesan Potatoes, 73
- Glazed Carrots and Apples, 43

few potato cubes to bag at a time. Shake to coat. Melt butter in bottom of a baking dish. Arrange coated potatoes in a single layer in butter in dish. Bake at 375° for 30 minutes. Stir potatoes to turn. Return to oven and bake additional 30 minutes. Potatoes should be golden brown. 6 servings.

Baked Sliced Potatoes

6 potatoes
1/2 cup melted butter
1 teaspoon salt
1/2 teaspoon pepper

Peel and slice potatoes. Place potatoes in a large bowl. Pour melted butter over potatoes. Sprinkle with salt and pepper. Toss to coat. Turn into greased baking dish. Bake at 425° for 40 minutes or until potatoes are tender and golden brown. 6 servings.

Complete Menu

Tomato Swiss Steak
- Baked Sliced Potatoes, 74
- Swiss Broccoli, 35

For a beautiful presentation of **Baked Sliced Potatoes**, arrange prepared potato slices in shallow round dish. Overlap potato slices in rings to cover bottom of dish.

Monterey Potatoes

6 potatoes
1/2 cup sliced red bell pepper
1/4 cup butter
1/2 cup chopped onion
2 tablespoons flour
1 teaspoon garlic salt
1/2 teaspoon ground mustard
1 cup milk
2 cups shredded Monterey Jack cheese

Peel and slice potatoes. Place potato slices and red bell pepper in a large saucepan. Cover with water. Bring to a boil and cook 5 minutes. Drain. Place potatoes and peppers in a greased baking dish. Melt butter in a medium saucepan. Stir in chopped onion. Cook and stir 5 minutes. Stir in flour. Add garlic salt, ground mustard and milk. Cook and stir until bubbly. Remove from heat. Stir in cheese until melted. Pour over potatoes. Bake at 375° for 40 minutes. 6 servings.

Complete Menu

California Dip Meat Loaf
- Monterey Potatoes, 75
- Garlic Green Beans, 53
- Orange Tossed Salad, 180
- Sweet Honey Mustard Dressing, 271

Potato Pancakes

4 cups shredded potatoes
1/2 cup minced onion
1 egg, lightly beaten
1/3 cup flour
1 1/2 teaspoons salt
1/4 teaspoon pepper
1/4 cup canola oil

In a mixing bowl, combine potatoes, onion, egg, flour, salt and pepper. Heat oil in a large skillet. Spoon 1/4 cup portions into hot oil and flatten. Cook over medium heat for about 5 minutes each side or until tender and golden brown. Drain on paper towels before serving. 6 servings.

Complete Menu

Honey Barbequed Ribs
• Potato Pancakes, 76
• Fresh Fruit Salad, 225
• Southern Corn Muffins, 331

 Frozen, shredded hash brown potatoes may be used for the shredded potatoes.

Spicy Red Potatoes

6 red potatoes
1 tablespoon onion
1/2 cup melted butter
1 tablespoon dried oregano
1/2 teaspoon salt
1/4 teaspoon pepper
1 teaspoon minced garlic
1/2 teaspoon crushed red pepper flakes

Do not peel potatoes. Slice potatoes and place in bottom of ungreased baking dish. Press onion through garlic press. In a small bowl, com-bine onion, melted butter, oregano, salt, pepper, garlic and red pepper flakes. Pour over potatoes. Bake uncovered at 450° for 30 minutes until potatoes are tender, stirring every 10 minutes. 6 servings.

Complete Menu

Very Best Meat Loaf
• Spicy Red Potatoes, 77
• Simple Cheesy Vegetables, 20

Onion Roasted Potatoes

16 small potatoes
1 (1.25-ounce) envelope onion or onion-mushroom soup mix
1/2 cup canola oil
1/4 cup melted butter
1 teaspoon sugar
1/4 teaspoon pepper

Wash and quarter potatoes. Dry thoroughly. In a large bowl, combine dry soup mix, oil, melted butter, sugar and pepper. Mix well. Stir in quartered potatoes. Pour all into a shallow baking dish. Bake at 450° for one hour or until potatoes are tender. Stir often during baking. 8 servings.

Complete Menu

Onion Soup Meat Loaf
- Onion Roasted Potatoes, 78
- Red and Orange Salad, 163
- Honey French Dressing, 269

Mashed Potatoes

6 potatoes
1/2 cup scalded milk
1/4 cup butter
1/2 teaspoon salt
dash of pepper

Peel and cube potatoes. Cook in salted, boiling water until tender. Drain. Pour scalded milk over potatoes. Add butter, salt and pepper. Mash, then beat until potatoes are light and fluffy. 6 servings.

Complete Menu

Chicken Fried Steak
- Mashed Potatoes, 79
- Confetti Corn, 49
- Raspberry Ribbon Salad, 251

Scalded milk is the secret to delicious mashed potatoes. To scald, place milk in a small saucepan. Heat milk just to boiling. Immediately pour over drained potatoes.

Whipped Potatoes

6 potatoes
1/4 cup butter
2 tablespoons cream cheese
1/2 cup cream
salt
pepper

Peel and chunk potatoes. Cook in salted, boiling water until tender. Drain. Mash. Add butter, cream cheese and cream. Whip with electric mixer until fluffy. Add salt and pepper to taste. 6 servings.

Complete Menu

Cream Cheese Chicken
- Candied Carrots, 38
- Whipped Potatoes, 80
- Broccoli and Cheddar Salad, 209

Garlic Mashed Potatoes

6 potatoes
4 cloves garlic, peeled
2 tablespoons olive oil
1/2 teaspoon salt
dash pepper

Peel and chunk potatoes. Boil potatoes and garlic in salted water until potatoes are tender. Drain, reserving 2/3 cup cooking water. Mash potatoes and garlic. Add oil, salt, pepper and the reserved cooking water. Stir until smooth. 6 servings.

Complete Menu

Meatballs in Gravy
- Garlic Mashed Potatoes, 81
- Simple Spinach Salad, 191
- Buttermilk Dressing, 265
- Potato Bread, 357

To peel fresh garlic, roll each clove briskly back and forth in the palms of your hands. The peel will come off easily.

Mashed Red Potatoes

12 small red potatoes
6 slices bacon
1/4 cup butter
2/3 cup cream
1 teaspoon salt
1/8 teaspoon pepper

Scrub and quarter potatoes. Do not peel. Cook in salted, boiling water until tender. Cut bacon in 1-inch pieces and cook until almost crisp. Drain potatoes and leave in pan. Add butter and allow to melt. Mash potatoes with peels. Add cream, salt and pepper. Stir to combine. Potatoes should be lumpy. Stir in bacon. 6 servings.

Complete Menu

Bacon Chicken
- Mashed Red Potatoes, 82
- Company Peas, 28
- Layered Salad, 208
- Catalina Dressing, 266

Roasted Onion and Garlic Potatoes

1 cup diced white onion
2 tablespoons coarsely chopped garlic
1 tablespoon olive oil
6 potatoes
4 cups water
3 tablespoons butter
1/2 cup sour cream
1 teaspoon salt
1/4 teaspoon pepper

In baking dish, combine onion, garlic and olive oil. Cover tightly and bake at 350° for 45 minutes. Remove from oven and set aside.

Complete Menu

Slow Cooked Stroganoff
• Roasted Onion & Garlic Potatoes, 83
• Tomato Green Beans, 52

Peel and cube potatoes. Boil potatoes in salted water until tender. Drain. Add roasted onion and garlic to potatoes. Add butter, sour cream, salt and pepper. Whip with electric mixer until well combined and fluffy. 6 servings.

Duchess Potatoes

6 potatoes
1/2 cup milk
1/4 cup butter
1/2 teaspoon salt
dash of pepper
2 eggs, beaten
2 tablespoons melted butter

Peel and cube potatoes. Cook in salted, boiling water until tender. Drain. In small saucepan, heat milk just to boiling to scald. Immediately pour over drained potatoes. Add butter, salt and pepper. Mash until potatoes are light and fluffy. Add eggs and beat until well blended. Drop potato mixture by spoonfuls in mounds onto greased baking sheet. Brush mounds with melted butter. Bake uncovered at 425° for 15 minutes or until potatoes are light brown. 6 servings.

Complete Menu

Salisbury Steak and Gravy
• Duchess Potatoes, 84
• Honey Mustard Peas, 29
• Cheese Biscuits, 315

Cream Cheese Mashed Potatoes

6 potatoes
1/2 cup sour cream
1 tablespoon butter
1 (3-ounce) package cream cheese, softened
1/2 teaspoon salt
dash pepper

Peel and cube potatoes. Cook in salted, boiling water until tender. Drain potatoes and return to pan. Mash with electric mixer. Add sour cream, butter, softened cream cheese, salt and pepper. Whip until fluffy. 6 servings.

Complete Menu

Pork Chops, Carrots and Gravy
• Cream Cheese Mashed Potatoes, 85
• Frog Eye Salad, 230
• Buttermilk Oatmeal Muffins, 327

To soften cream cheese, let sit at room temperature for about 30 minutes. If using cold cream cheese, allow cream cheese to warm and soften in the hot potatoes before whipping.

For extra zip, substitute other varieties of flavored cream cheese, such as chive and onion, for the plain cream cheese.

Baked Mashed Potatoes

6 potatoes
2 tablespoons butter
1/2 cup milk
1 (1.25-ounce) envelope dry vegetable soup mix
1 bunch green onions, sliced
3/4 cup shredded Cheddar cheese
1 egg, lightly beaten
1/4 teaspoon pepper
1/4 cup shredded Cheddar cheese

Peel and cube potatoes. Cook in salted, boiling water until tender. Drain potatoes. Add butter and allow to melt. Pour in milk. Mash potatoes. Stir in dry soup mix, sliced green onions, cheese, beaten egg and pepper. Mix well. Spoon into a greased baking dish. Bake at 375° for 40 minutes. Top with remaining cheese. Bake an additional 5 minutes. 6 servings.

Complete Menu

Beef Stroganoff
- Orange Carrots, 41
- Baked Mashed Potatoes, 86
- Buttermilk Salad, 246

Potato Puff

6 potatoes
1/2 cup milk
1 (8-ounce) package cream cheese
2 tablespoons minced onion
2 tablespoons flour
2 eggs
1/2 teaspoon salt
dash of pepper
1 cup French fried onions

Peel and cube potatoes. Cook in salted, boiling water until tender. Drain. Add milk and mash. Add cream cheese to hot mashed potatoes and allow to soften. Whip until smooth. Stir in onion, flour, eggs, salt and pepper. Mix well. Pour into a greased baking dish. Top with French fried onions. Bake at 300° for 35 minutes. 8 servings.

Complete Menu

Chicken and Mushrooms
- Potato Puff, 87
- Sweet and Sour Salad, 166
- Sweet and Sour Dressing, 275

For delicious flavor, substitute chive and onion flavored cream cheese for the plain cream cheese.

Golden Fried Potatoes

6 potatoes
2 tablespoons canola oil
1 onion, sliced
1 1/2 teaspoons salt
1/4 teaspoon pepper
2 tablespoons butter

Peel and slice potatoes 1/4-inch thick. Cook in salted, boiling water until almost tender. Drain. Heat oil in a heavy skillet. Combine potatoes and onion in skillet. Sprinkle with salt and pepper. Dot top with butter. Cover and cook over medium heat for 15 minutes. Uncover and cook, turning once, until potatoes are brown. 6 servings.

Complete Menu

Skillet BBQ Pork Chops
- Golden Fried Potatoes, 88
- Bacon Corn, 48
- German Cole Slaw, 204

The secrets to successful **Golden Fried Potatoes** are a heavy skillet, even heat and the patience to not turn the potatoes until they are brown!

Potato Skins

4 potatoes
oil for deep-frying
1 cup shredded Cheddar cheese
1/2 cup sour cream
4 slices bacon
1 tablespoon sliced green onion

Wrap potatoes in foil and bake at 350° for 60 to 90 minutes until tender. Unwrap and cut potatoes in half lengthwise. Carefully scoop out centers of potato leaving 1/4-inch shell. Heat oil to 375° in electric skillet or deep-fryer. Deep-fry potato shells for 2 or 3 minutes until golden brown. Drain on paper towels. Place on baking sheet. Sprinkle with shredded Cheddar cheese. Broil until cheese begins to melt. Remove from oven. Spread sour cream over each. Top with crumbled bacon and sliced green onion. 8 servings.

Complete Menu

Country Barbequed Ribs
- Potato Skins, 89
- Apple Salad, 226
- Apple Cider Biscuits, 322

Twice Baked Potatoes

4 baking potatoes
1/2 cup cream
1/4 cup butter
1/2 teaspoon salt
dash of pepper
1/2 cup diced ham
1 cup shredded Cheddar cheese

Wrap potatoes with foil and bake at 350° for 60 to 90 minutes, until tender. Increase oven temperature to 400°. Unwrap potatoes and cut a slit in the top of each. Carefully scoop out centers of potato, leaving a thin shell. Mash potatoes with cream, butter, salt and pepper, adding more cream if necessary. Stir in diced ham. Stuff each shell with mashed potato filling. Sprinkle with cheese. Bake uncovered until filling is golden, about 20 minutes. 4 servings.

Complete Menu

Smothered Steak
- Herbed Corn, 47
- Twice Baked Potatoes, 90
- Deep Fried Zucchini, 97

To Freeze: Stuff potatoes. Do not top with cheese. Do not bake. Wrap each stuffed potato tightly with plastic wrap. Place wrapped potatoes in freezer bag. Label and freeze.

To Serve: Thaw. Unwrap and bake at 400° for 30 minutes. Top with cheese and bake for an additional 10 minutes until golden.

Garden Stuffed Baked Potatoes

4 baking potatoes
2 tablespoons butter
1/4 cup chopped onion
1 (10-ounce) package frozen chopped broccoli
1/2 cup **Ranch Dressing** (page 264)
1 tablespoon canola oil
2 teaspoons dried parsley flakes

Wrap potatoes with foil and bake at 350° for 60 to 90 minutes until tender. Increase oven temperature to 400°. Unwrap potatoes and cut a slit in the top of each. Carefully scoop out centers of potato, leaving a thin shell. Mash potatoes in a medium bowl. Melt butter in a small skillet. Add onion. Cook and stir until onion is tender but not brown. Stir onion into mashed potatoes. Thaw and drain broccoli. Squeeze to remove excess moisture. Stir broccoli and Ranch Dressing into mashed potatoes. Spoon potato mixture into shells. Brush outside of potato skins with oil. Place on a baking sheet. Bake at 425° for about 15 minutes, until heated through. Sprinkle with parsley. Add salt and pepper to taste. 4 servings.

Complete Menu

Mock Filet Mignon
- Garden Stuffed Baked Potatoes, 91
- Tomato Wedges, 101
- Batter Fried Shrimp, 388
- Cocktail Sauce, 305

To Freeze: Stuff potatoes. Do not bake. Wrap each stuffed potato tightly with plastic wrap. Place wrapped potatoes in freezer bag. Label and freeze.

To Serve: Thaw. Unwrap. Brush outside of potato skins with oil. Bake at 425° for 25 minutes. Sprinkle with parsley. Add salt and pepper to taste.

Hawaiian Baked Potatoes

6 baking potatoes
1 (12-ounce) jar processed American cheese
1 (20-ounce) can crushed pineapple
1 cup diced ham
1/4 cup minced green bell pepper
1 bunch green onion, sliced

Wrap potatoes with foil and bake at 350° for 60 to 90 minutes until tender. Unwrap potatoes and cut a slit in the top of each. Fluff potato with a fork. Heat cheese in microwave safe bowl. Drain pineapple and stir into cheese. Stir in ham, bell pepper and green onion. Split open potatoes and generously top each potato with filling. 6 servings.

Complete Menu

Ham Loaf with Pineapple Sauce
- Hawaiian Baked Potatoes, 92
- Glazed Carrots, 40
- Pineapple Cole Slaw, 205

Baked Sweet Potatoes

2 pounds sweet potatoes
1/2 cup milk
1/2 cup sugar
1 teaspoon salt
1/4 cup melted butter
2 eggs, lightly beaten
1 teaspoon vanilla
2/3 cup packed brown sugar
1/3 cup flour
3 tablespoons butter
1/2 cup chopped pecans
1/2 cup sweetened flaked coconut

Cook whole sweet potatoes in boiling water until tender. Drain. Peel and cut into chunks. Return to pan. Mash with milk, sugar, salt, melted butter, eggs and vanilla. In a small bowl, combine brown sugar and flour. Cut in butter with pastry blender or fork until crumbly. Stir in pecans and coconut. Place half the mashed sweet potatoes in a greased baking dish. Top with half of the sugar pecan mixture. Add remaining potatoes and top with remaining topping. Bake uncovered at 350° for 30 minutes. 6 servings.

Complete Menu

Chicken and Dressing
• Baked Sweet Potatoes, 93
• Broccoli with Mustard Sauce, 32
• Sweet Potato Biscuits, 320

Maple Glazed Sweet Potatoes

2 pounds sweet potatoes
2/3 cup maple syrup
4 tablespoons melted butter
1 tablespoon cornstarch
1/2 teaspoon salt

Cook whole sweet potatoes in boiling water until tender. Peel and cut into one inch slices. Arrange sweet potato slices in greased, shallow baking dish. Combine maple syrup, melted butter, cornstarch and salt. Whisk until smooth. Pour over sweet potatoes. Bake uncovered at 375° for 35 to 40 minutes, until sauce is thickened. Baste frequently. 6 servings.

Complete Menu

Turkey and Stuffing Roll-Ups
• Maple Glazed Sweet Potatoes, 94
• Cranberry Pineapple Salad, 250
• Orange Cream Cheese Muffins, 325

Orange Candied Sweet Potatoes

2 (18-ounce) cans sweet potatoes, drained
1 1/4 cups packed brown sugar
2 tablespoons cornstarch
3/4 cup orange juice
2 tablespoons lemon juice
1/4 cup melted butter

Arrange drained sweet potatoes in greased, shallow baking dish. In a separate bowl, combine brown sugar and cornstarch. Stir in orange juice and lemon juice. Mix well. Stir in butter. Pour over sweet potatoes. Bake uncovered at 375° for 40 to 45 minutes, until sauce is thickened. Baste often. 6 servings.

Complete Menu

Turkey Dressing Pie
• Orange Candied Sweet Potatoes, 95
• Cranberry Sauce, 302

Pecan Stuffed Acorn Squash

1 cup chicken broth
2 small acorn squash
1/3 cup butter
1 tablespoon packed brown sugar
2/3 cup chicken broth
2 cups seasoned dry stuffing mix
1/4 cup pecan pieces

Pour chicken broth in shallow baking dish. Cut squash in half, remove seeds. Place cut sides down in broth. Bake at 400° for 25 minutes. In a medium saucepan, over medium heat, heat butter, brown sugar and chicken broth until butter melts. Stir in stuffing mix and pecans. Turn squash over and divide stuffing among the 4 squash halves. Return stuffed squash to oven for 20 minutes longer, basting with broth after 10 minutes.
4 servings.

Complete Menu

Stuffing Meat Loaves
- Pecan Stuffed Acorn Squash, 96
- Fresh Cranberry Salad, 247

Deep Fried Zucchini

3 cups sliced zucchini
1/2 cup flour
2 eggs, beaten
1 1/2 cups Italian seasoned bread crumbs
oil for deep-frying

Coat zucchini slices with flour. Dip in beaten egg, then coat with bread crumbs. Deep-fry until tender and golden brown. Serve immediately with **Buttermilk Ranch Dressing** (page 263). 6 servings.

Complete Menu

Smothered Steak
- Herbed Corn, 47
- Twice Baked Potatoes, 90
- Deep Fried Zucchini, 97

Parmesan Zucchini

3 cups sliced zucchini
1/4 cup sour cream
1 tablespoon softened butter
3/4 cup shredded fresh Parmesan cheese
1/2 teaspoon salt
2 eggs, beaten
1/2 cup dry bread crumbs
2 tablespoons melted butter
1/4 cup shredded fresh Parmesan cheese

Boil sliced zucchini in salted water for 7 minutes. Drain. In a bowl, combine sour cream, butter, Parmesan cheese, salt and eggs. Mix well. Stir in drained zucchini. Pour into a greased baking dish. Combine dry bread crumbs and melted butter. Top zucchini with buttered bread crumbs and Parmesan cheese. Bake uncovered at 375° for 20 minutes. 8 servings.

Complete Menu

Smoky Maple Chicken
• Bacon Pilaf, 118
• Parmesan Zucchini, 98
• Triple Orange Salad, 242

For buttered bread crumbs, place 1 slice of bread in a food processor. Process for a few seconds until small crumbs form. Melt 1 tablespoon of butter. Drizzle over crumbs. Stir to coat all crumbs.

Zucchini Rounds

3 eggs, beaten
1/3 cup shredded fresh Parmesan cheese
1/4 teaspoon salt
1/4 teaspoon baking powder
1/3 cup flour
2 cups shredded zucchini
1/4 cup butter

In a mixing bowl, combine beaten eggs, cheese, salt, baking powder and flour. Mix well. Stir in shredded zucchini. Melt butter in a large skillet. Drop 1/4 cup portions in hot melted butter. Cook over medium heat for about 2 to 3 minutes per side, or until browned. Delicious served with chili. 8 servings.

Complete Menu

Slow Cooked Chili
- Zucchini Rounds, 99
- Corn Meal Bread, 335

To Freeze: Arrange cooked rounds in a single layer on a baking sheet. Cover and place in freezer until rounds are frozen. Transfer frozen zucchini rounds to a freezer bag. Label and freeze.

To Serve: Thaw. Heat briefly in microwave. For crisper rounds, heat briefly in toaster oven.

Zucchini and Tomatoes

1/4 cup butter
1 teaspoon minced garlic
4 cups thinly sliced zucchini
3 tomatoes
1/2 cup water
1 (1.25-ounce) envelope onion soup mix

In a large skillet, cook garlic and zucchini in butter for about 5 minutes. Peel tomatoes. Coarsely chop tomato and add to skillet with zucchini. Combine water with onion soup mix. Add onion soup mixture to zucchini. Bring to a boil, reduce heat and simmer for about 10 minutes. Zucchini should be tender and coated with thickened sauce. 6 servings.

Complete Menu

Cornflake Chicken
- Zucchini and Tomatoes, 100
- Wild Rice Salad, 258
- Onion Rings, 62

To easily peel tomatoes, dip each tomato in boiling water for 30 seconds. Dip immediately into cold water. Skins should slip off easily.

1 (14.5-ounce) can stewed tomatoes may be substituted for the 3 tomatoes. Omit 1/2 cup water. Drain tomatoes, reserving 1/2 cup juice. Combine reserved juice with onion soup mix.

Tomato Wedges

6 tomatoes
1 bunch green onions
1/4 cup apple cider vinegar
2/3 cup canola oil
1 clove garlic
2 tablespoons mayonnaise
1 teaspoon dill weed
1 teaspoon basil
1 teaspoon salt
1/4 teaspoon pepper
1/8 teaspoon oregano

Cut tomatoes into wedges. Place in serving bowl. Thinly slice green onions and sprinkle over tomatoes. Place vinegar, oil and garlic in a blender. Process until well blended and garlic is chopped fine. Add mayonnaise, dill weed, basil, salt, pepper and oregano. Process on high until smooth. Pour over tomatoes and toss gently. 6 servings.

Complete Menu

Mock Filet Mignon
- Garden Stuffed Baked Potatoes, 91
- Tomato Wedges, 101
- Batter Fried Shrimp, 388
- Cocktail Sauce, 305

Tomatoes and Cucumbers

2 tomatoes
1 sweet onion
1 cucumber
1/3 cup white vinegar
1/2 cup sugar
1/3 cup canola oil
1/2 teaspoon salt
1 teaspoon minced garlic

Cut tomatoes into wedges. Slice onion and separate into rings. Peel and slice cucumber. Place tomatoes, onion and cucumber in a medium bowl. In a small bowl, combine vinegar and sugar. Stir until sugar dissolves. Stir in oil, salt and garlic. Mix well. Pour over tomatoes. Chill several hours. 6 servings.

Complete Menu

Biscuit Beef Bake
- Tomatoes and Cucumbers, 102
- Club Salad, 153
- Roquefort Dressing, 273

Cucumber Stuffed Tomatoes

6 tomatoes
1 cup peeled, sliced, quartered cucumber
1/3 cup mayonnaise
1 teaspoon minced garlic
1 tablespoon snipped fresh parsley
1 tablespoon sugar
1/4 teaspoon salt
dash of pepper

Remove stem ends from tomatoes. Cut thin slice from bottom of each tomato to prevent tipping. Carefully scoop pulp from tomatoes. Drain and

Complete Menu

Beef and Broccoli
• Cucumber Stuffed Tomatoes, 103

reserve pulp. Invert tomatoes on paper towels and refrigerate for about 2 hours. Meanwhile, finely chop tomato pulp. Drain. Add cucumber to tomato pulp. In a small bowl, combine mayonnaise, garlic, parsley, sugar and salt. Mix well. Add to cucumber and tomato mixture. Cover and refrigerate for about 2 hours. To serve, fill tomato shells with cucumber mixture. Sprinkle with pepper. 6 servings.

Fried Green Tomatoes

3 green tomatoes
1/2 cup flour
1/4 cup corn meal
1/4 cup canned Parmesan cheese
1/2 teaspoon salt
1/8 teaspoon pepper
oil for cooking

Cut tomatoes into 1/2-inch slices. In shallow dish, combine flour, corn meal, cheese, salt and pepper. Dip tomato slices in flour mixture. In a skillet over medium heat, cook tomato slices in hot oil for 2 minutes on each side. Tomatoes should be tender and lightly browned. Drain on paper towels before serving. 6 servings.

Complete Menu

Cowboy Barbeque
• Fried Green Tomatoes, 104

Chinese Green Peppers

1 tablespoon peanut oil
1 teaspoon minced garlic
1 teaspoon minced ginger
1 cup ground pork
1 green onion, minced
1/2 cup minced celery
4 green bell peppers

In a skillet, over medium heat, stir-fry garlic in oil until lightly browned. Reduce heat and add ginger and pork. Stir-fry 2 minutes or until pork is no longer pink. Add green onion and celery. Mix and cook for another 30 seconds. Remove from heat and allow to cool slightly. Cut peppers into quarters (lengthwise) and remove core and seeds. Divide filling among the peppers. Press filling down into the cavities of each pepper piece. Arrange the filled peppers in a greased baking dish. Bake at 400° for 25 minutes, until tender. 16 pieces.

Complete Menu

Waikiki Turkey
- Fried Rice, 111
- Chinese Green Peppers, 105

To Freeze: Arrange cooked peppers in a single layer on a baking sheet. Cover and place in freezer. When peppers are frozen, transfer to freezer bag. Label and freeze.

To Serve: Heat briefly in microwave.

Rice

Rice makes a wonderful accompaniment to a wide range of meals. Some rice dishes are so delicious and filling that they could be served as a main dish.

Freezing Rice

Even though most varieties of rice can be prepared quickly and easily, there are certainly some situations that would benefit greatly from having the rice already prepared. Therefore, the instructions for freezing rice have been included with each recipe.

Most rice recipes can be frozen very conveniently and easily. A plastic resealable freezer bag may be the best method for freezing rice since virtually all the air can be squeezed from the bag before sealing. Rice that is completely protected from freezer burn will keep for 2 or 3 months in the freezer.

Freeze rice in the serving sizes that are convenient and useful to you. A single serving of rice will freeze just as effectively as an entire recipe. When the rice is thawed it will separate easily. If you desire the ability to dip some rice from a bag of frozen rice, simply massage the bag a few times as it freezes to ensure that it does not completely stick together.

Reheating Rice

There are a few options for reheating rice:

1. Place rice (frozen or thawed) in a glass dish in the microwave. Heat just until hot throughout. Sprinkle rice with a few drops of water if the rice starts to dry out. Fluff with a fork and serve.

2. Place rice in a saucepan with just enough water to produce a little steam. Place the pan over low heat and stir, being careful to not allow the rice to stick to the bottom of the pan.

3. Place rice in a colander and pour about 2 quarts of boiling water over it. The boiling water serves to heat the rice and make it moist and wonderful while not allowing it to get mushy. This only works with plain rice since you would not want to wash off seasonings or vegetables that may be cooked into some rice dishes.

4. Stir-fry rice dishes may be reheated in the microwave. Alternately they may be thawed and briefly stir-fried in a skillet. You may need to add a small amount of oil to the skillet to prevent the rice from sticking.

Whether you choose to prepare and serve your rice on the same day or prepare it ahead of time and freeze for convenient use later, rice dishes add delicious variety and are well worth any effort required to serve them as part of a fabulous meal.

Rice Recipes

Oven Steamed Rice

1 cup uncooked rice
2 cups boiling water
1 teaspoon salt

Mix rice, boiling water and salt in ungreased 1 quart baking dish. Cover and bake at 350° for 25 to 30 minutes, or until liquid is absorbed. 6 servings.

Complete Menu

Sweet and Sour Chicken
• Oven Steamed Rice, 109
• Egg Rolls, 384

To Freeze: Cool and place in freezer bag. Label and freeze.

To Serve: Heat rice, fluff with a fork and serve.

For delicious flavored rice, substitute 2 cups boiling broth (any flavor including beef, chicken, vegetable, etc.) for the boiling water.

Rice Ring

2 cups uncooked rice

Cook rice according to package instructions. Lightly press warm rice into a well greased 4 cup ring mold. Keep hot until serving. Invert serving plate onto mold. Holding tightly together, turn plate covered ring mold over. Remove ring mold. 8 servings.

Complete Menu

Hawaiian Meatballs
- Rice Ring, 110
- Crispy Wonton, 382
- Red Sauce, 303

 To add beauty, interest and flavor to your **Rice Ring** try these optional stir-ins:
- 2 tablespoons snipped fresh parsley
- 1 tablespoon dried parsley flakes
- 1/2 cup sliced mushrooms cooked in 2 tablespoons butter
- 1/2 cup frozen peas
- 1/2 cup shredded carrots
- 1/2 cup shredded zucchini
- 1/2 cup sweetened dried cranberries
- 1/2 cup sweetened dried cherries

 It may not be practical to freeze the assembled rice ring since it is bulky in the freezer, and it may be difficult to heat without drying out the rice. However, you can use previously frozen rice to make the **Rice Ring**. Be sure to heat the rice before pressing into the ring mold. Cover and keep warm in oven until serving.

For a beautiful presentation, spoon meatballs or other main dish into center of Rice Ring.

 Any variety of rice, including rice cooked in broth may be used.

Fried Rice

3/4 cup uncooked rice
2 tablespoons peanut oil
2 green onions, minced
1 teaspoon minced garlic
1 cup diced ham
2 tablespoons soy sauce
2 eggs
1/4 teaspoon salt
1/8 teaspoon pepper
1 cup bean sprouts

Cook rice according to package instructions. In large skillet, heat oil until very hot. Add green onion and garlic and stir-fry for 2 minutes. Add the cooked rice and stir. Cook, stirring constantly as rice heats through. Stir in the ham and soy sauce. Beat the eggs with salt and pepper. While constantly stirring, pour the eggs into the rice mixture in a thin stream. Add the bean sprouts and continue cooking and stirring until hot throughout and the eggs are set. 6 servings.

Complete Menu

Waikiki Turkey
• Fried Rice, 111
• Chinese Green Peppers, 105

To Freeze: Cool and place in freezer bag. Label and freeze.

To Serve: Heat rice in microwave and fluff with a fork or briefly stir-fry thawed rice in skillet, stirring to separate rice. Serve immediately.

Confetti Fried Rice

2 cups uncooked rice
1 tablespoon butter
1 egg
3 tablespoons peanut oil
1/2 cup shredded carrots
1 teaspoon minced garlic
1/2 cup chopped onion
1 (20-ounce) can pineapple tidbits, drained
1 cup diced ham
1/2 cup frozen petite peas
1/4 cup soy sauce
1 teaspoon sugar

Cook rice according to package instructions. Melt butter in a skillet over low heat. Beat egg until frothy. Pour into hot butter. Swirl egg around into a 6-inch circle until egg is set but not brown. Turn pan upside down onto a plate. Cut egg into thin strips. Heat peanut oil over high heat in same skillet. Add carrots, garlic and onion to hot oil. Stir-fry for about 1 minute. Add rice, stirring until grains separate. Reduce heat to medium. Stir in pineapple, ham and peas. Mix sugar into soy sauce. Increase heat to high and stir in soy sauce. Cook and stir until heated through. Remove from heat and gently stir in egg strips. 6 servings.

Complete Menu

Hawaiian Chicken
• Confetti Fried Rice, 112
• Mandarin Salad, 174
• Mandarin Dressing, 300

To Freeze: Cool and place in freezer bag. Label and freeze.

To Serve: Heat rice in microwave and fluff with a fork or briefly stir-fry thawed rice in skillet, stirring to separate rice. Serve immediately.

New Year Fried Rice

2 cups uncooked rice
4 slices bacon
1 bunch green onions, sliced
2 small mushrooms, sliced
1/4 cup diced red bell pepper
1/3 cup frozen petite peas, thawed
1 egg, beaten
2 tablespoons soy sauce
1 teaspoon sugar

Cook rice according to package instructions. Allow to cool. Cut bacon into 1/4-inch strips. Cook in large skillet until almost crisp. Add green onion, mushrooms and bell pepper. Cook for 2 minutes but do not brown. Pour in beaten egg and scramble. Stir in cooled rice and stir to separate grains. Stir in soy sauce and sugar. Cook and stir until heated through.
6 servings.

Complete Menu

Sweet and Sour Meatballs
- New Year Fried Rice, 113
- Coconut Shrimp, 387
- Marmalade Sauce, 304

To Freeze: Cool and place in freezer bag. Label and freeze.

To Serve: Heat rice in microwave and fluff with a fork or briefly stir-fry thawed rice in skillet, stirring to separate rice. Serve immediately.

Monterey Rice

2 cups water
1 cup uncooked rice
1 tablespoon chicken bouillon
2 cups sour cream
1 cup shredded Colby cheese
1 cup shredded Monterey Jack cheese
1 (4-ounce) can diced green chiles
1/2 cup diced red bell pepper
1/8 teaspoon pepper
1/2 cup shredded Monterey Jack cheese

In a medium saucepan, combine water, rice and bouillon. Bring to a boil. Reduce heat. Cover and simmer for 15 minutes. In large bowl, combine cooked rice, sour cream, Colby cheese, Monterey Jack cheese, green chiles, red bell pepper and pepper. Mix well. Place in buttered baking dish. Bake at 350° for 25 minutes. Top with Monterey Jack cheese. Bake additional 3 minutes, or until cheese melts. 6 servings.

Complete Menu

Nacho Meat Loaf
- Monterey Rice, 114
- Honey Glazed Stir-Fry, 18
- Chili Cheddar Biscuits, 317

To Freeze: Prepare rice and bake but do not top with cheese. Cool and place in freezer bag. Label and freeze.

To Serve: Thaw and heat rice. Top hot rice with cheese and bake for 3 to 5 minutes until cheese melts.

Lemon Rice

1 cup rice
1 teaspoon butter
1 teaspoon minced garlic
1 teaspoon grated lemon peel
1/4 teaspoon black pepper
2 cups chicken broth
2 teaspoons dried parsley flakes

Combine rice, butter, garlic, lemon peel, pepper and broth in a medium saucepan. Bring to a boil. Reduce heat. Cover and simmer 15 minutes until rice is tender and liquid is absorbed. Stir in parsley. 6 servings.

Complete Menu

Honey Lime Chicken
• Lemon Rice, 115
• Lime Vegetables, 16

To Freeze: Cool and place in freezer bag. Label and freeze.

To Serve: Heat rice, fluff with a fork and serve.

Pepper Rice

1 1/2 cups uncooked rice
1 tablespoon peanut oil
1 teaspoon hot chili oil
1/2 cup diced yellow onion
1/3 cup diced green bell pepper
1/3 cup diced red bell pepper
1/3 cup diced yellow bell pepper
1 teaspoon minced garlic
1/8 teaspoon pepper
1/2 teaspoon garlic salt

Cook rice according to package instructions. Heat peanut oil and hot chili oil in large skillet. Add onion, peppers and garlic. Cook over medium heat until tender but not browned. Stir in rice, pepper and garlic salt. Cook and stir until well mixed and very hot. 6 servings.

Complete Menu

Pineapple Meatballs
• Pepper Rice, 116
• Pineapple Salad, 182

To Freeze: Cool and place in freezer bag. Label and freeze.

To Serve: Heat rice, fluff with a fork and serve.

Oriental Rice Pilaf

1 cup uncooked rice
1 3/4 cups beef broth
1 teaspoon minced garlic
1/2 cup chopped onion
1 tablespoon soy sauce
1 tablespoon sesame oil
1/4 teaspoon crushed red pepper flakes
1 bunch green onions, sliced
1/4 cup minced red bell pepper

In medium saucepan, combine rice, beef broth, garlic, chopped onion, soy sauce, oil and red pepper flakes. Bring to a boil. Reduce heat. Cover and cook for 15 minutes until rice is tender and liquid is absorbed. Stir in green onions and red bell pepper. 6 servings.

Complete Menu

Teriyaki Beef
- Oriental Rice Pilaf, 117
- Chinese Dumplings, 381

To Freeze: Cool and place in freezer bag. Label and freeze.

To Serve: Heat rice, fluff with a fork and serve.

Bacon Pilaf

1/4 cup diced onion
2 tablespoons butter
8 slices bacon
2 tomatoes, diced
2 cups water
1 cup uncooked rice
1 teaspoon chicken bouillon

In a large saucepan, cook onion in butter until tender but not brown. In a skillet, cook bacon until almost crisp. Cut bacon into 1-inch pieces. Set aside half of the bacon pieces. Add the other half of the bacon to the saucepan. Add tomatoes, water, rice and chicken bouillon to the saucepan. Bring to boil. Reduce heat and cover. Simmer for 15 minutes or until liquid is absorbed. Stir in remaining bacon. 6 servings.

Complete Menu

Smoky Maple Chicken
- Bacon Pilaf, 118
- Parmesan Zucchini, 98
- Triple Orange Salad, 242

To Freeze: Cool and place in freezer bag. Label and freeze.

To Serve: Heat rice, fluff with a fork and serve.

Carrot Rice

1 cup uncooked rice
2 cups chicken broth
1/2 teaspoon salt
1/4 teaspoon pepper
2 tablespoons butter
3/4 cup shredded carrots
1/2 cup chopped onion

In a large saucepan, combine rice, chicken broth, salt and pepper. Bring to a boil. Stir rice and reduce heat to Low. Cover and simmer for 15 minutes, until rice is tender. Melt butter in a skillet. Cook carrots and onion in butter over medium heat until tender but not brown. Stir rice into skillet and stir gently to combine with carrots. 6 servings.

To Freeze: Cool and place in freezer bag. Label and freeze.

To Serve: Heat rice, fluff with a fork and serve.

Complete Menu

<u>Cantonese Meatballs</u>
- Carrot Rice, 119
- Sweet and Sour Vegetables, 17
- Lettuce Wraps, 386

Coconut Rice

1 1/4 cups uncooked rice
2 (10-ounce) cans coconut milk
1/2 teaspoon salt
1/2 cup sweetened flaked coconut

In a large saucepan, combine rice, coconut milk and salt. Bring to a boil. Stir rice and reduce heat to Low. Cover and simmer for 15 minutes, until rice is tender. Gently stir in flaked coconut and serve. 6 servings.

Complete Menu

Peachy Chicken
- Coconut Rice, 120
- Walnut Broccoli, 37
- Layered Peach Salad, 239

To Freeze: Cool and place in freezer bag. Label and freeze.

To Serve: Heat rice, fluff with a fork and serve.

 Coconut milk can usually be found on the beverage isle at most grocery stores.

Shrimp Rice

1 cup uncooked rice
3 tablespoons butter
3 tablespoons milk
1/2 cup cooked salad shrimp
1/2 teaspoon salt
1/8 teaspoon pepper

Cook rice according to package instructions. Melt butter in a large skillet. Stir in milk and cooked rice. Mix well. Add shrimp, salt and pepper. Cook and stir until heated through.
6 servings.

Complete Menu

Polynesian Pork Roast
- Shrimp Rice, 121
- Carrot Pineapple Salad, 248
- Sweet Potato Rolls, 364

To Freeze: Stir together ingredients but do not heat. Place in freezer bag. Label and freeze.

To Serve: Thaw and heat just until hot throughout, being careful not to overcook shrimp. Serve.

Baked Mushroom Rice

1/4 cup butter
1 cup sliced mushrooms
2 cups uncooked rice
1 (10.75-ounce) can cream of mushroom soup
1 1/2 cups chicken broth
1/2 cup chopped onion
1/2 teaspoon salt
pepper

Melt butter in a skillet. Cook and stir mushrooms in butter until soft. In a large bowl, combine rice, soup and broth. Mix well. Stir in onion, salt and pepper. Stir in mushrooms and butter. Pour into a greased baking dish. Cover. Bake at 400° for 35 to 40 minutes. 10 servings.

Complete Menu

Beef and Pork Chop Suey
- Baked Mushroom Rice, 122
- Green Beans and Bean Sprouts, 58

To Freeze: Cool and place in freezer bag. Label and freeze.

To Serve: Heat rice, stir and serve.

For delicious **Baked Chicken Mushroom Rice**, substitute cream of chicken soup for the cream of mushroom soup.

Baked Rice

6 tablespoons butter
1/2 cup chopped onion
1 cup uncooked rice
2 cups chicken broth
1 teaspoon chicken bouillon
1/8 teaspoon pepper

In a skillet, melt butter. Add onion. Cook and stir until onion is tender but not browned. Add uncooked rice. Cook and stir for 2 minutes. Stir in chicken broth, bouillon and pepper. Simmer 5 minutes. Transfer to a greased baking dish. Cover and bake at 350° for 30 minutes. 6 servings.

Complete Menu

Meatballs in Sour Cream Sauce
- Baked Rice, 123
- Snow Pea Stir-Fry, 27
- Potato Rolls, 363

To Freeze: Cool and place in freezer bag. Label and freeze.

To Serve: Heat rice, fluff with a fork and serve.

Substitute beef broth and beef bouillon for the chicken broth and chicken bouillon for delicious beef flavored **Baked Rice**.

Cheesy Broccoli Rice

1 cup uncooked rice
1 (16-ounce) package frozen chopped broccoli
1 (10.75-ounce) can cream of mushroom soup
1/2 cup processed American cheese
1 cup French fried onions

Cook rice according to package instructions. Thaw broccoli and drain. Combine cooked rice, broccoli, cream of mushroom soup and cheese. Pour into greased baking dish. Bake uncovered at 350° for 45 minutes. Top with French fried onions and bake 10 minutes longer. 6 servings.

Complete Menu

Scalloped Pork Chops
• Cheesy Broccoli Rice, 124
• Melon Cucumber Salad, 220

 To use fresh broccoli, substitute 4 cups fresh broccoli florets for the frozen chopped broccoli.

Pasta

Pasta makes the perfect accompaniment to so many different meals. Pasta recipes can be so delicious and filling that they can be served as main dishes. They also make beautiful pairings with other main dishes.

Cooking Pasta

Cooking perfect pasta is easy if you follow a few simple rules:

1. Cook the pasta in plenty of water. You should be able to stir the pasta and have it move freely. Add salt to water if you desire. (About 1 teaspoon to 1 tablespoon to cook 8 to 16 ounces of pasta.) Salted water gives the pasta a pleasant taste without making it salty.

2. Add pasta to rapidly boiling water. Stir as soon as pasta has been added to the water so it does not stick together. It will usually only need to be stirred at the beginning. When adding long pasta to boiling water, hold onto the pasta as it softens and you are able to bend it until it will all go into the water. Stir it to assure that all strands separate.

3. Start timing the pasta as soon as the water resumes boiling after the pasta has been added. Every pasta package has a recommended cooking time. (This is usually a 2 minute spread.) If you are serving the pasta on the day you prepare it, cook it to the doneness you desire. If you desire to freeze the pasta and it has a light coating of sauce or no sauce, cook the pasta only to the shortest recommended cooking time. If you are going to freeze pasta in a dish that includes a quantity of sauce, shorten the cooking time to 2 minutes less than the shortest recommended cooking time. The pasta will continue to absorb moisture from the sauce as it cools, freezes, thaws and is heated.

4. Drain pasta with a colander as soon as the cooking time is over. If you are going to serve it immediately or mix it with sauce right away, there is no need to rinse. However, if you are not going to use it immediately or if you are going to use it in a cold recipe, you will need to rinse the pasta. Rinsing stops the cooking and helps prevent it from sticking together.

Freezing Pasta
Most varieties of pasta cook very rapidly and are easy to prepare. This is good news since pasta can be fussy to freeze. Generally, the larger pastas freeze better than the small or thin types. Some recipes containing pasta can be frozen successfully but a recipe that is mainly pasta is probably better served the same day it is prepared.

Since all the recipes in this chapter are mainly pasta, freezing instructions have not been included for each recipe. This does not mean they cannot be frozen. If you desire to freeze pasta, freeze only a small test portion first. Wait a few days and try it. If you like it, it is freezer worthy and you can confidently freeze an entire recipe.

Some (perhaps all) of the recipes in this chapter could be frozen but it is certainly a matter of personal taste. If you desire to freeze pasta be sure to place it in an airtight container. A freezer bag is the surest way to make it airtight since you can press all the air from the bag before sealing. Pasta is especially susceptible to freezer burn. It becomes brittle and disintegrates rapidly if exposed to air. If you choose to put pasta into a freezer container, be sure to press plastic wrap on top of the pasta before attaching the lid to help prevent freezer burn. Even a half inch of air space at the top of the freezer container can allow freezer burn.

Reheating Pasta

To reheat cooked pasta there are a few options. The one you choose will depend on the pasta and recipe.

1. To reheat plain cooked pasta just place it in boiling water for about 60 seconds, drain and serve.

2. To reheat plain cooked pasta or other dish containing pasta, place it in the microwave and heat just until hot throughout. You may need to stir it at intervals to ensure even heating. If so, be sure to stir gently so you don't break the pasta into unappealing pieces. You may need to add some moisture compatible with the recipe (milk, cream, broth, etc.) and stir gently.

3. To reheat pasta or pasta dishes in the oven, be sure to cover the dish with a lid or foil so that the pasta does not dry out. You may need to add some moisture compatible with the recipe (milk, cream, broth, etc.) and stir gently.

Pasta is a winner whether you prepare it on the day you desire to serve it or prepare and freeze it for convenient future use. There are so many options that make it easy to add variety and beautiful presentation to even the simplest meal.

Pasta Recipes

Pasta Ring

1 (8-ounce) package wide noodles
3 tablespoons butter

Cook noodles in boiling, salted water according to package directions. Drain. Stir in butter. Press noodles in buttered 1 1/2 quart ring mold. Place ring mold in pan of 1-inch deep hot water. Bake at 375° for 20 minutes. Invert serving plate over mold. Turn over. Remove ring mold. 6 servings.

Complete Menu

Swedish Meatballs
- Pasta Ring, 129
- Fruit and Lettuce Salad, 181
- Apple Carrot Muffins, 324

 To add beauty, interest and flavor to your **Pasta Ring** try these optional stir-ins:
  - 2 tablespoons snipped fresh parsley
  - 1 tablespoon dried parsley flakes
  - 1/2 cup sliced mushrooms, cooked in 2 tablespoons butter
  - 1/2 cup frozen peas
  - 1/2 cup shredded carrots
  - 1/2 cup shredded zucchini
  - 2 teaspoons poppy seed

 For interesting **Pasta Ring** variations, substitute other pasta shapes for the wide egg noodles.

 For a beautiful presentation, spoon meatballs or other main dish into center of **Pasta Ring**.

Homemade Egg Noodles

2 cups flour
3 egg yolks
1 egg
2 teaspoons salt
1/4 to 1/2 cup water

Place flour in a mixing bowl. Make a well in center of flour. Add egg yolks, egg and salt. Mix thoroughly. Mix in water, 1 tablespoon at a time, until

Complete Menu

Chicken Stroganoff
• Homemade Egg Noodles, 130
• 24 Hour Fruit Salad, 227

dough is stiff but easy to roll. Divide dough into 4 equal parts. Roll dough, one part at a time, into a very thin rectangle on a well floured cloth. Keep remaining dough covered. Loosely fold rectangle lengthwise into thirds. Cut crosswise into desired width of noodles. Shake out strips and place on towel until stiff and dry, about 2 hours. To cook noodles, drop into boiling salted water and cook for 15 to 25 minutes or until tender. About 6 cups noodles.

 Dry noodles can be covered and stored for up to 1 month.

Bacon Fettuccine Alfredo

1 (12-ounce) package fettuccine
1 pound bacon
1 tomato
2 cups cream
1/4 cup butter
1/2 teaspoon salt
1/4 teaspoon pepper
1 cup shredded fresh Parmesan cheese

Cook fettuccine in boiling, salted water according to package directions. Drain. Cut bacon into 1-inch pieces and cook until almost crisp.

Complete Menu

Chicken Ham Roll-Ups
• Bacon Fettuccine Alfredo, 131
• Strawberry Romaine Salad, 188

Dice tomato. In medium saucepan, combine cream, butter, salt and pepper. Cook over medium heat until bubbly. Stir in Parmesan cheese and stir until cheese is melted. Pour sauce over pasta. Stir in bacon and tomato. 6 servings.

 For plain **Fettuccine Alfredo** omit bacon and tomato.

Noodles Romanoff

1 (8-ounce) package wide noodles
2 cups sour cream
1/4 cup shredded fresh Parmesan cheese
1 teaspoon salt
1/8 teaspoon pepper
1 teaspoon minced garlic
2 tablespoons butter
1/4 cup shredded fresh Parmesan cheese

Cook noodles in boiling, salted water according to package directions. Drain. Combine sour cream, Parmesan cheese, salt, pepper and garlic. Stir butter into hot noodles. Stir in sour cream mixture. Transfer to platter or bowl. Sprinkle with Parmesan cheese. 6 servings.

Complete Menu

Slow Cooked Goulash
- Noodles Romanoff, 132
- Wilted Salad, 165
- Cloverleaf Rolls, 362

Tortellini Primavera

1 cup sliced mushrooms
1/2 cup chopped onion
1 teaspoon minced garlic
2 tablespoons butter
1 (10-ounce) package frozen chopped spinach
1 (8-ounce) package cream cheese, softened
1 tomato, chopped
1/4 cup milk
1/4 cup shredded fresh Parmesan cheese
1 teaspoon basil
1/4 teaspoon salt
1/4 teaspoon pepper
1 (16-ounce) package frozen cheese filled tortellini

Cook and stir mushrooms, onion and garlic in butter in a large skillet. Thaw spinach. Squeeze out moisture. Cook tortellini according to package instruc-tions. Add softened cream cheese, tomato, milk, Parmesan cheese, basil, salt and pepper to skillet. Cook and stir gently just until mixture starts to boil. Stir in tortellini. Continue to cook until thoroughly heated and tortellini is well coated. 8 servings.

Complete Menu

Beef and Cheese Rolls
- Tortellini Primavera, 133
- Broiled Garlic Rolls, 366

Pasta Primavera

1 (16-ounce) package fettuccine
1/4 cup butter
1/2 cup chopped onion
1 teaspoon minced garlic
2 cups sliced mushrooms
1 cup sliced zucchini
1/2 cup sliced carrots
1 cup half-and-half
1/2 cup water
1 teaspoon chicken bouillon
1 tablespoon flour
1 teaspoon basil
3/4 cup shredded fresh Parmesan cheese

Cook fettuccine in boiling, salted water according to package directions. Drain. Melt butter in large skillet. Add onion, garlic, mushrooms, zucchini and carrots. Cook over medium heat for about 5 minutes, until vegetables are crisp tender. Increase heat to high. Combine half-and-half, water, bouillon, flour and basil. Add to skillet. Allow mixture to boil, stirring constantly until thickened. In serving bowl, combine fettuccine and sauce. Top with cheese. 8 servings.

Complete Menu

Chicken Cacciatore
- Pasta Primavera, 134
- Spinach Slaw, 203

Press garlic through a garlic press for instantly and uniformly minced garlic. For an even easier method, buy a small bottle of minced garlic, usually found in the produce department at the grocery store.

Garlic Pasta

1 (16-ounce) package linguine
8 cloves garlic, peeled and sliced
1/2 cup olive oil
4 teaspoons oregano
1 tablespoon dried parsley flakes
1 teaspoon salt
1/4 teaspoon pepper

Cook pasta in boiling, salted water according to package directions. Drain. Meanwhile, cook garlic in olive oil 2 minutes or until golden brown. Remove from heat and add oregano, parsley, salt and pepper. Add hot pasta and toss. 8 servings.

Complete Menu

Italian Meat Sauce
- Garlic Pasta, 135
- Lime Avocado Salad, 187
- Cheesy Texas Toast, 343

 To easily peel garlic, roll one clove at a time back and forth on counter top with the palm of your hand. Peeling will slip right off.

 Substitute any shape of pasta for the linguine.

Zucchini Garlic Bow Ties

1 (16-ounce) package bow tie pasta
1 pound bacon
4 teaspoons minced garlic
1/2 cup chopped onion
3 tablespoons butter
2 cups sliced zucchini
1/2 teaspoon salt
1/4 teaspoon pepper
1/2 cup shredded fresh Parmesan cheese

Cook pasta in boiling, salted water according to package directions. Drain. Cut bacon into 1-inch pieces. In a large skillet, cook bacon until almost crisp. Drain on paper towels. Remove all but 3 tablespoons bacon drippings. Add garlic and onion to skillet. Cook in drippings until onion is tender but not brown. Add butter to skillet and stir until melted. Add zucchini, salt and pepper. Cook until tender. Add pasta and bacon. Transfer to serving bowl or platter. Sprinkle with cheese. 10 servings.

Complete Menu

Tomato Stroganoff
- Zucchini Garlic Bow Ties, 136
- Apple Lettuce Salad, 184

 Press garlic through a garlic press for instantly and uniformly minced garlic. For an even easier method, buy a small bottle of minced garlic, usually found in the produce department at the grocery store.

 Substitute any shape of pasta for the bow ties.

Corkscrew Broccoli

1 (16-ounce) package corkscrew pasta
1 quart half-and-half
1/2 cup butter
1 teaspoon minced garlic
1/2 cup spaghetti sauce
2 cups fresh broccoli florets
1 cup sliced mushrooms
1/2 teaspoon salt
1/8 teaspoon pepper
1 cup shredded fresh Parmesan cheese

Cook pasta in salted water for half the recommended cooking time. Drain. Return pasta to pan. Add half-and-half, butter, garlic, spaghetti sauce, broccoli, mushrooms, salt and pepper. Bring to a boil and cook until pasta is tender. Remove from heat and stir in cheese. 10 servings.

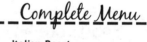

Complete Menu

Italian Roast
- Corkscrew Broccoli, 137
- Caesar Salad, 155
- Caesar Salad Dressing, 296

 Substitute any shape of pasta for the corkscrew pasta.

Tangy Linguine

1 (8-ounce) package linguine
1/4 cup **Italian Dressing** (page 284)

Cook linguini in boiling, salted water according to package directions. Drain. Toss hot noodles with dressing. 6 servings.

Complete Menu

Spaghetti Sauce
- Tangy Linguini, 138
- Italian Broccoli Salad, 211
- Italian Dressing, 284
- Italian Twists, 347

 Substitute any shape of pasta for the linguine.

Italian Fettuccine

1 (8-ounce) package fettuccine
1/2 cup melted butter
2 teaspoons basil
2 teaspoons lemon juice
1 1/4 garlic powder
3/4 teaspoon Italian seasoning
1/2 teaspoon salt
1/8 teaspoon pepper

Cook fettuccine in boiling, salted water according to package directions. Drain. In a large bowl, combine butter, basil, lemon juice, garlic powder, Italian seasoning, salt and pepper. Add drained pasta and mix to coat. 6 servings.

Complete Menu

Chicken with Mushroom Gravy
- Italian Fettuccine, 139
- Crunchy Spinach Mushroom Salad, 192
- Honey Dressing, 270
- Cheddar Biscuits, 316

Asparagus Linguine

1 (8-ounce) package linguine
1/4 cup butter
1/2 cup chopped onion
1 tablespoon minced garlic
2 cups fresh asparagus, cut in 1/2-inch pieces
2 tablespoons chicken broth
1/4 cup shredded fresh Parmesan cheese
3/4 cup shredded Mozzarella cheese

Cook linguine in boiling, salted water according to package directions. Drain. In a large skillet, melt butter. Cook onion and garlic until soft but not brown. Add asparagus and cook for about 3 minutes, until tender. Add chicken broth and continue cooking and stirring for another minute. Season with salt and pepper. Toss with pasta and Parmesan cheese. Pour onto serving platter. Top with Mozzarella cheese. 6 servings.

Complete Menu

Continental Chicken
- Asparagus Linguine, 140
- Strawberry, Kiwi, Spinach Salad, 202
- Strawberry Dressing, 301

Lemon Garlic Angel Hair Pasta

1 (16-ounce) package angel hair pasta
1 teaspoon basil
1/2 cup shredded fresh Parmesan cheese
2 tablespoons olive oil
6 teaspoons minced garlic
1 1/4 cups chicken broth
1/2 cup fresh lemon juice
2 1/2 cups chopped tomato
2 tablespoons sugar
1 teaspoon salt
1/4 teaspoon pepper

Cook pasta in boiling, salted water according to package directions. Drain. Place in a large bowl. Add basil and Parmesan cheese. Toss lightly. In a large skillet, heat olive oil and garlic just until garlic begins to change color. Remove from heat and add chicken broth. Return to heat and cook for 2 minutes. Stir in lemon juice, tomato and sugar. Remove from heat. Pour hot lemon and tomato mixture over pasta in serving bowl. Season with salt and pepper. Toss gently. 8 servings.

Complete Menu

Cola Chicken
• Lemon Garlic Angel Hair Pasta, 141
• Broccoli Raisin Salad, 207

  For quick and easy fresh lemon juice, heat a lemon in the microwave in a glass bowl until the lemon bursts (about 1 minute). Immediately stop the microwave and allow lemon to cool briefly. Juice can then be squeezed easily from the hole made by the escaping steam.

  For easy minced garlic see page 136 .

Broccoli Fettuccine

1 (8-ounce) package fettuccine
1/4 cup olive oil
3 teaspoons minced garlic
2 1/2 cups fresh broccoli florets
1/8 teaspoon crushed red pepper flakes
1/3 cup shredded fresh Parmesan cheese

Cook fettuccine in boiling, salted water according to package directions. Heat oil in a large skillet. Cook and stir garlic, broccoli and red pepper flakes until broccoli is crisp tender. Add fettuccine. Toss to coat. Sprinkle with cheese. Toss lightly. 6 servings.

Complete Menu

Tuna Stroganoff
• Broccoli Fettuccine, 142
• Taffy Apple Salad, 229

Chow Mein

1 (16-ounce) package Chinese egg noodles
1 (4-ounce) pork chop
4 tablespoons peanut oil, divided
1 cup chunked onion
1/2 cup snow peas
1/2 cup frozen French green beans
1/4 cup fresh bean sprouts
3 green onions, sliced
2 tablespoons soy sauce
1 tablespoon chili sauce

Cook Chinese noodles in boiling, salted water for the shortest recommended cooking time on package directions. Do not overcook. Drain and rinse under cold running water.

Complete Menu

Beefy Chinese Rice
• Chow Mein, 143

Set aside. Bake pork chop for about 20 minutes or until cooked through. Cool and cut into thin strips. In large skillet, heat 3 tablespoons oil. Add onion, pork strips, snow peas, green beans and bean sprouts. Stir-fry for about 1 minute. Remove from pan. Heat the remaining oil in the same pan. Add the green onions and noodles. Stir in about half the pork and vegetable mixture. Add soy sauce and stir-fry for about 1 minute. Transfer to large serving dish. Pour the remaining pork and vegetable mixture on the top of the noodles. Sprinkle with chili sauce and serve. 8 servings.

 Substitute spaghetti for the Chinese egg noodles.

Oriental Noodles

1 (12-ounce) package thin spaghetti
1/4 cup peanut oil
1 teaspoon minced garlic
1 cup julienned carrots
3/4 cup sliced mushrooms
1 cup broccoli florets
1 onion, sliced
1 cup bean sprouts
1/2 cup teriyaki sauce
1 bunch green onions, sliced

Cook thin spaghetti in boiling, salted water according to package directions. Drain and rinse under hot water. Heat oil in skillet or wok. Add garlic. Cook and stir to flavor oil. Add carrots, mushrooms, broccoli, onion and bean sprouts. Stir-fry until crisp tender. Add noodles, adding more oil if necessary, and mix with vegetables. Add teriyaki sauce and stir to coat. Sprinkle with green onions. 6 servings.

Complete Menu

Teriyaki Chicken
• Oriental Noodles, 144
• Pot Stickers, 380

For the 1/2 cup teriyaki sauce, use the sauce from **Teriyaki Chicken (*Dinner is Ready*)** recipe. Delicious served together.

Fried Noodles

1 (16-ounce) package fettuccine
1 (4-ounce) pork chop
1 boneless skinless chicken breast half
3 celery stalks
3 cups spinach
2 tablespoons peanut oil
1 teaspoon minced garlic
1/2 teaspoon minced ginger
2 tablespoons soy sauce
1 teaspoon sugar
3 green onions, minced

Cook fettuccine in boiling, salted water for the shortest recommended cooking time on package directions. Do not overcook. Drain and rinse with cold water. Bake pork chop and chicken for about 20 minutes or until cooked through. Cut pork chop into thin strips and shred the chicken. Slice the celery diagonally and shred the spinach. In large skillet, heat the oil until very hot. Add the garlic and ginger. Stir-fry for 1 minute. Add the pork and chicken and stir-fry for 2 minutes. Mix the sugar into the soy sauce until sugar dissolves. Add noodles to pan and stir in soy sauce. Stir-fry for about 3 minutes. Pile onto serving platter. Sprinkle with minced green onion. 8 servings.

Complete Menu

Maple Almond Beef
- Fried Noodles, 145
- Cream Cheese Wonton, 383

For easy minced ginger, buy a small bottle at the grocery store. Minced ginger is usually found in the produce department, right next to the fresh ginger.

Salad

One of the most beautiful accompaniments to almost any meal is a salad. The variety of greens and vegetables, mixed or topped with the myriad simple to elaborate ingredients, and served with one or more of the scores of fabulous dressings, makes for endless combinations for delicious salads.

Most salads can be prepared in a very short time. This is good news since salad ingredients prepared very long in advance tend to brown on the edges and become sadly limp. Most ingredients can be prepared up to 24 hours ahead of time, but unless the recipe calls for advance preparation, you'll probably be happier with the results if you toss the ingredients together just before serving.

This is especially true for tomatoes. The juice from cut tomatoes can add too much liquid to the salad and can thin the dressing. Consider serving tomatoes on the side, as a garnish and certainly at the last minute. Better yet, use grape tomatoes or cherry tomatoes in salads.

Salad greens range from crisp and strong to very delicate. When dressing a salad, consider that heavier dressings can weigh down the greens, causing your salad to collapse and appear limp. Unless the recipe calls for advance preparation, be sure to add the dressing at the last minute or serve it on the side.

It is not practical to freeze a salad made from fresh lettuces and vegetables. Freezing causes the water in the plant cells to expand, which bursts the cells and causes the lettuce or vegetables to become soft. There is no way to prevent this from happening, consequently there is no way to freeze a salad and maintain its crisp delicious crunch. Green salads and vegetable salads should always be served fresh, the day they were prepared if possible.

There are, however, other types of salads that can be frozen. These salads are usually made with fruit, whipped cream, cream cheese, etc. When freezing these salads be sure to package them properly for the freezer. A covered dish or container will work if the salad is going to be used with a few days. A longer freezing time will require more care to be taken to prevent freezer burn. Press plastic to the top of the salad and replace the cover. Any air, even trapped air, can allow freezer burn.

Whether simple or elaborate, sweet or savory, fresh or frozen, salad can be a beautiful and satisfying meal complement. In many cases, with very few additions, the salad can become the main event. The unmatched variety of choices makes this category a sure winner.

Salad Recipes

continued...

Green Salad

6 cups salad greens
1 tablespoon butter
1/2 cup chopped onion
1/2 cup chopped green bell pepper
4 slices deli ham
1 tomato, chopped
1/4 teaspoon onion powder
1/8 teaspoon garlic powder
1/8 teaspoon pepper
1/4 teaspoon salt
Thousand Island Dressing (page 291)

Place salad greens in a large salad bowl. Melt butter in a medium skillet. Cook onion and green bell pepper in butter until soft. Allow to cool. Add to salad bowl. Cut ham into thin strips. Add to salad bowl. Top with chopped tomato. Sprinkle with the onion powder, garlic powder, pepper and salt. Toss to mix. Pour on enough salad dressing to coat, toss again and serve. 6 servings.

Complete Menu

Simply Lasagna
- Green Salad, 151
- Thousand Island Dressing, 291
- Buttery French Bread, 339

Red, White and Green Salad

4 cups torn leaf lettuce
1 cup grape or cherry tomatoes
1 cup fresh cauliflower florets
1 cup fresh broccoli florets
Creamy Italian Dressing (page 286)

In a large salad bowl, combine lettuce, tomatoes, cauliflower and broccoli. Pour dressing over all. Toss to coat. 6 servings.

Complete Menu

Chicken Stuffed Manicotti
- Red, White and Green Salad, 152
- Creamy Italian Dressing, 286
- Mushroom Puffs, 370

Club Salad

3 cups torn Iceberg lettuce
3 cups torn leaf lettuce
1 tomato
1 cup julienned, cooked turkey
1 cup julienned ham
8 slices bacon
Roquefort Dressing (page 273)

In a large salad bowl, combine Iceberg and leaf lettuce. Cut tomato into wedges and fan in a circle in the center of the salad. Arrange the turkey in a circle around the tomato. Arrange the ham in a circle around the turkey. Cook bacon until crisp. Cut bacon in pieces and sprinkle over top of salad. Serve with **Roquefort Dressing**. 6 servings.

Complete Menu

Biscuit Beef Bake
- Tomatoes and Cucumbers, 102
- Club Salad, 153
- Roquefort Dressing, 273

Purchase the ham and the turkey from the deli counter at the grocery store. Ask for a 1/2-inch thick slice of each.

Elegant Salad

2 1/2 cups torn Iceberg lettuce
2 1/2 cups torn Romaine lettuce
1 cup cooked salad shrimp
1/2 cup quartered and sliced zucchini
1 cup frozen corn, thawed
1/3 cup diced red bell pepper
1 bunch green onion, thinly sliced
Simple Caesar Dressing (page 297)

In a large bowl, combine lettuce, shrimp, zucchini, corn, red bell pepper and green onion. Pour dressing over salad and toss gently to coat. 6 servings.

Complete Menu

Cheesy Lasagna
- Elegant Salad, 154
- Simple Caesar Salad Dressing, 297
- Vegetable Cheese Texas Toast, 342

Caesar Salad

6 cups torn Romaine lettuce
8 anchovy filets, chopped
Caesar Salad Dressing (page 296)
1/2 lemon
1/2 cup shredded fresh Parmesan cheese
1/8 teaspoon pepper
1/2 cup croutons

Place lettuce in a large serving bowl. Add cut up anchovy filets. Pour dressing over Romaine and toss. Squeeze lemon juice over all. Sprinkle with shredded Parmesan cheese and pepper. Top with croutons. Serve immediately. 6 servings.

Complete Menu

Italian Roast
- Corkscrew Broccoli, 137
- Caesar Salad, 155
- Caesar Salad Dressing, 296

To easily squeeze a lemon, heat the lemon in the microwave in a glass bowl until the lemon bursts (about 1 minute). Immediately stop the microwave and allow the lemon to cool enough to handle. Juice can then be squeezed easily from the hole made by the escaping steam.

For Caesar Croutons, trim crusts from 4 slices of white bread. Generously butter both sides of the bread slices. Sprinkle with lemon pepper and garlic powder. Cut into 1/2-inch cubes. Arrange cubes on an ungreased baking sheet. Bake at 400° for 10 to 15 minutes, stirring occasionally, until golden brown and crisp.

BLT Salad

4 cups torn Romaine lettuce
4 cups torn curly leaf lettuce
1 pound bacon
3 plum tomatoes
2 cups shredded Swiss cheese
Ranch Dressing (page 264)

Arrange Romaine and curly leaf lettuce in a large salad bowl. Cook bacon until almost crisp. Cut into pieces. Cut tomatoes into thick slices. Cut slices in half. Add bacon and tomatoes to lettuce. Sprinkle cheese over top. Pour dressing over salad and toss to coat. 8 servings.

Complete Menu

Bacon Meat Loaf
- Cheesy Bacon Potatoes, 72
- BLT Salad, 156
- Ranch Dressing, 264

Bleu Cheese Salad

6 cups torn Romaine lettuce
3 hard boiled eggs
Bleu Cheese Dressing (page 298)
1 cup croutons
1/2 cup crumbled bleu cheese

Place lettuce in a large salad bowl. Peel and dice eggs. Add to lettuce. Pour dressing over salad and toss. Top with croutons and crumbled bleu cheese. 6 servings.

Complete Menu

Lasagna
• Bleu Cheese Salad, 157
• Bleu Cheese Dressing, 298
• Bread Sticks, 348

For Onion Croutons, trim crusts from 4 slices of white bread. Cut slices into 1/2-inch cubes. Arrange cubes on a baking sheet. Drizzle melted butter over cubes. Toss to coat. Sprinkle with onion powder and dried parsley flakes. Toss again. Bake at 300° for 30 to 35 minutes, stirring occasionally, until dry, crisp and golden brown.

Swiss Salad

4 cups torn Iceberg lettuce
1 cup shredded Swiss cheese
1/4 cup sliced pimento stuffed olives
2 hard boiled eggs
1/4 cup salad dressing
1/4 cup mayonnaise
2 tablespoons half-and-half
1 teaspoon ground mustard
1/2 teaspoon salt
1/4 teaspoon pepper

In a salad bowl, combine lettuce, cheese and olives. Peel and chop eggs. Arrange on top of salad. In a small bowl, combine salad dressing, mayonnaise and half-and-half. Mix well. Stir in ground mustard, salt and pepper. Mix well and pour over salad. Toss to coat. 4 servings.

Complete Menu

Chicken Cordon Bleu
- Mustard Red Potatoes, 66
- Cheddar Vegetables, 19
- Swiss Salad, 158

Curly Red Salad

8 cups torn curly red lettuce
2 (11-ounce) cans Mandarin oranges, drained
1 cup grape tomatoes
1/4 cup sweetened dried cranberries
Creamy French Dressing (page 268)

In a large salad bowl, combine curly red lettuce, orange segments, tomatoes and dried cranberries. Pour dressing over salad and toss to coat.
8 servings.

Complete Menu

Chicken and Ham Dinner
• Curly Red Salad, 159
• Creamy French Dressing, 268

California Salad

8 curly red lettuce leaves
2 peaches, sliced
2 kiwi, peeled, quartered and sliced
1 cup sliced strawberries
1 cup cubed cantaloupe
1 cup Brie cheese
1 cup cooked salad shrimp
1/2 cup frozen pineapple-orange juice concentrate
1/3 cup honey
1 teaspoon grated lime peel
1 1/2 tablespoons lime juice

Arrange lettuce leaves on serving platter. Arrange sliced peaches, kiwi, strawberries and cantaloupe over lettuce leaves. Add cheese and shrimp. In a small bowl, whisk together juice concentrate, honey, lime peel and lime juice. Serve over fruit. 8 servings.

Complete Menu

Chicken and Broccoli
- Potato Bake, 70
- California Salad, 160

Sweet and Sour Lettuce

4 cups torn curly leaf lettuce
4 cups torn red curly leaf lettuce
1/2 cup half-and-half
3 tablespoons apple cider vinegar
1 tablespoon sugar
1/4 teaspoon salt

Arrange green and curly red lettuce in a large salad bowl. In a small bowl, combine half-and-half, vinegar, sugar and salt. Pour over lettuce and toss to coat. 8 servings.

Complete Menu

Steak and Vegetable Pie
• Sweet and Sour Lettuce, 161

Green and Gold Salad

3 cups torn leaf lettuce
1 (10-ounce) package frozen petite peas
1/2 cup shredded Cheddar cheese
2 tablespoons minced onion
1/4 cup salad dressing
2 teaspoons mustard
1 teaspoon sugar
1/2 teaspoon salt
1/8 teaspoon pepper

Place lettuce in a salad bowl. Run peas under cold water to separate. Drain. Add peas to lettuce. Add cheese and onion. In a small bowl, combine salad dressing, mustard, sugar, salt and pepper. Pour over salad. 6 servings.

Complete Menu

Beefy Macaroni
• Green and Gold Salad, 162
• Onion Poppy Seed Rolls, 374

Petite peas are younger, smaller and more tender than regular peas. Using petite peas rather than regular peas makes a delicious difference in this salad.

Red and Orange Salad

8 cups torn red curly leaf lettuce
2 oranges, peeled and sectioned
1 small red onion, sliced
4 small white mushrooms, sliced
Honey French Dressing (page 269)

In a large bowl, combine lettuce, orange sections, onion and mushrooms. Pour dressing over salad and toss to coat.
8 servings.

Complete Menu

Onion Soup Meat Loaf
- Onion Roasted Potatoes, 78
- Red and Orange Salad, 163
- Honey French Dressing, 269

Parmesan Pimento Salad

6 cups torn Romaine lettuce
6 cups torn Iceberg lettuce
2 tomatoes
2 small red onions
1 (4-ounce) jar diced pimentos, drained
1 cup shredded fresh Parmesan cheese
Parmesan Dressing (page 276)

Place lettuce in a large salad bowl. Cut tomatoes in wedges and arrange on top of lettuce. Slice onions and separate into individual rings. Scatter onion rings and pimentos over all. Top with cheese. Pour dressing over salad and toss. 12 servings.

Complete Menu

Spaghetti and Meatballs
- Parmesan Pimento Salad, 164
- Parmesan Dressing, 276
- Toasted Garlic French Bread, 341

Wilted Salad

6 cups torn leaf lettuce
1 small red onion, sliced
4 small white mushrooms, sliced
3 radishes, sliced
6 slices bacon
2 tablespoons apple cider vinegar
1 teaspoon packed brown sugar
1/4 teaspoon ground mustard
1/4 teaspoon salt
1/8 teaspoon pepper

Toss lettuce, onion, mushrooms and radishes in a salad bowl. Dice bacon. In a skillet, cook bacon until crisp. Remove bacon. Add vinegar, brown sugar, mustard, salt and pepper to bacon drippings in skillet. Cook and stir until bubbly. Immediately pour over lettuce and toss. Top salad with bacon and serve. 6 servings.

Complete Menu

Slow Cooked Goulash
- Noodles Romanoff, 132
- Wilted Salad, 165
- Cloverleaf Rolls, 362

Sweet and Sour Salad

1 (12-ounce) package bacon
1/2 (16-ounce) package square wonton wraps
oil for deep-frying
1 cup red grapes
1 large carrot
6 cups torn Iceberg lettuce
3 cups baby spinach leaves
Sweet and Sour Dressing (page 275)

Cut bacon into half-inch strips. Cook until almost crisp. Drain on paper towels. Cut wonton wraps into 1/4-inch strips. Deep-fry in hot oil until golden and crispy. Drain on paper towels. Cut each grape in half. Peel carrot. Use a vegetable peeler to cut carrot into thin flat strips. In a large serving bowl, place lettuce, baby spinach leaves, bacon, grapes, and carrot strips. Add fried wonton strips and dressing just before serving. Mix gently. 8 servings.

Complete Menu

Chicken and Mushrooms
• Potato Puff, 87
• Sweet and Sour Salad, 166
• Sweet and Sour Dressing, 275

Italian Salad

6 cups torn Iceberg lettuce
2 bunches green onion, thinly sliced
1/2 cup sliced celery
1 cup shredded Mozzarella cheese
1 (2.25-ounce) can sliced black olives, drained
1 tomato, cut into wedges
Simple Italian Dressing (page 285)
2 tablespoons shredded fresh Parmesan cheese
Italian seasoned croutons

In a large bowl, combine lettuce, onion, celery, Mozzarella cheese, olives and tomato. Pour dressing over salad and toss to coat. Top with Parmesan cheese and croutons. 6 servings.

Complete Menu

Almost Ravioli
- Italian Salad, 167
- Simple Italian Dressing, 285
- French Loaves, 338

For Italian Croutons, trim crusts from 4 slices of white bread. Generously butter both sides of the bread slices. Sprinkle with Italian seasoning. Cut into 1/2-inch cubes. Arrange cubes on an ungreased baking sheet. Bake at 400° for 10 to 15 minutes, stirring occasionally, until golden brown and crisp.

Mexican Salad

8 cups salad greens
1 bunch green onions, sliced
2 tomatoes, diced
1 (2.25-ounce) can sliced black olives, drained
2 cups corn chips
Garlic Tomato Dressing (page 278)

Place lettuce, onions, tomatoes, olives and chips in a large salad bowl. Pour dressing over salad. Toss to coat. 8 servings.

Complete Menu

Chicken Enchiladas
• Mexican Salad, 168
• Garlic Tomato Dressing, 278

Chicken Fajitas Salad

1 pound chicken tenders
1 tablespoon canola oil
1 (1.4-ounce) envelope dry fajitas seasoning
1/4 cup water
4 cups shredded Iceberg lettuce
1 bunch green onion, sliced
1/2 green bell pepper, thinly sliced
1/2 red bell pepper, thinly sliced
1 tomato, halved and thinly sliced
1 avocado, sliced
Salsa Dressing (page 279)

Brown chicken in oil. Add fajitas seasoning and water. Blend and simmer for about 5 minutes. Shred chicken. Place shredded lettuce in a serving bowl. Arrange onion, peppers, tomato and avocado in rings on top of lettuce. Place chicken in center. Pour dressing over salad. Toss just before serving. 6 servings.

Complete Menu

Taco Pie
• Chicken Fajitas Salad, 169
• Salsa Dressing, 279

 After chicken is cooked through, cook onion and peppers until crisp-tender, if desired.

 For Steak Fajitas Salad, substitute 1 pound sirloin steak for the chicken. Also delicious with a combination of steak and chicken.

Mexican Avocado Salad

6 cups torn Iceberg lettuce
2 avocados
2 tablespoons lemon juice
1 tomato
1 (2.25-ounce) can sliced black olives, drained
1 1/2 cups shredded Monterey Jack cheese
1 1/2 cups tortilla chips
Avocado Dressing (page 280)

Place lettuce in a large salad bowl. Peel and slice avocados. Sprinkle avocado slices with lemon juice and arrange over lettuce. Cut tomato into chunks and arrange with avocado. Add black olives and cheese. Just before serving, add coarsely crushed tortilla chips. Pour dressing over all and toss. 6 servings.

Complete Menu

Mexican Lasagna
• Mexican Avocado Salad, 170
• Avocado Dressing, 280

To peel and slice an avocado, using a sharp knife, cut avocado in half lengthwise, down to the seed. Gently twist and pull halves apart. Tap the seed with the edge of a knife and lift the seed out. Slide a spoon just under the thick skin to remove the avocado. Place avocado, cut side down, on a flat surface. Cut lengthwise into thin slices.

Piñata Salad

6 cups torn Iceberg lettuce
1 tomato
1 avocado
1 (2.25-ounce) can sliced black olives, drained
1 (15-ounce) can garbanzo beans, drained
1/2 cup sliced celery
1/2 cup sliced jicama
1 1/2 cups shredded Cheddar cheese
Chile Dressing (page 283)

Place lettuce in a large salad bowl. Cut tomato into chunks. Peel and slice avocado. Arrange tomato and avocado over lettuce. Add black olives, beans, celery, jicama and cheese over top. Toss with **Chile Dressing** just before serving. Or place lettuce in a salad bowl and the other ingredients in separate bowls for a choice of toppings. Serve dressing on the side. 6 servings.

Complete Menu

Chili Beef and Rice
- Piñata Salad, 171
- Chile Dressing, 283
- Nachos, 389

Jicama is like a crisp white turnip that tastes more like a radish. Substitute radish, if you desire.

Gazpacho Salad

3 cups torn red curly leaf lettuce
3 cups torn Iceberg lettuce
1/4 cup diced red onion
1 avocado, diced
1/2 green bell pepper, cut in thin strips
1/2 red bell pepper, cut in thin strips
1/2 cup diced cucumber
1 tomato, diced
2 flour tortillas
oil for deep-frying
Gazpacho Dressing (page 282)

Place lettuce in a large salad bowl. Arrange onion, avocado, bell pepper strips, cucumber and tomato over top. Cut tortillas in very thin strips about 4 inches long. Heat oil and deep-fry tor-tilla strips until just barely crisp. Arrange over salad. Toss with **Gazpacho Dressing** just before serving. 6 servings.

Complete Menu

Navajo Tacos
• Gazpacho Salad, 172
• Gazpacho Dressing, 282

Guacamole Salad

6 cups torn curly leaf lettuce
2 tomatoes, chunked
1 bunch green onions, sliced
1 (2.25-ounce) can sliced black olives, drained
1 1/2 cups shredded Cheddar cheese
1 1/2 cups corn chips, divided
Guacamole Dressing (page 281)

In a large salad bowl, combine lettuce, tomatoes, onions, olives, cheese and 1 cup corn chips. Pour dressing over salad and mix gently to coat. Top with remaining 1/2 cup corn chips. 6 servings.

Complete Menu

Tortilla Chicken
• Guacamole Salad, 173
• Guacamole Dressing, 281

Mandarin Salad

1/4 cup sliced almonds
2 tablespoons sugar
3 cups torn Iceberg lettuce
3 cups torn Romaine lettuce
2 stalks celery, sliced
2 green onions, sliced
1 (11-ounce) can Mandarin oranges, drained
Mandarin Dressing (page 300)

Cook almonds and sugar over low heat, stirring constantly, until sugar is melted and almonds are coated. Cool and break apart. Place lettuce and Romaine lettuce in a salad bowl. Add celery, onions and oranges. Pour dressing over salad and stir gently to coat. Top with sugared almonds. 6 servings.

Complete Menu

Hawaiian Chicken
- Confetti Fried Rice, 112
- Mandarin Salad, 174
- Mandarin Dressing, 300

 Save the drained juice from the Mandarin oranges to make **Mandarin Dressing**.

Oriental Salad

4 cups torn Romaine lettuce
2 cups shredded red cabbage
2 cups shredded Napa cabbage
1 carrot, julienned
1 (8-ounce) can Mandarin oranges, drained
1 bunch green onions, sliced
3/4 cup chow mein noodles
Chinese Salad Dressing (page 299)

In a large bowl, toss together lettuce and cabbage. Add carrots, oranges and onions. Add chow mein noodles. Serve dressing on the side. 8 servings.

Complete Menu

Tuna Chow Mein
- Oriental Salad, 175
- Chinese Salad Dressing, 299

Chow mein noodles are especially delicious toasted. Spread them in a thin layer on a baking sheet. Place under broiler for about 30 seconds, until golden and sizzling.

Bacon Cauliflower Salad

3 cups torn Romaine lettuce
8 slices bacon
2 cups fresh cauliflower florets
1/4 cup sliced radishes
Sweet Dijon Salad Dressing (page 287)
1/2 cup French fried onions

Place lettuce in a salad bowl. Cook bacon and cut into pieces. Add bacon, cauliflower and radishes to salad bowl. Pour dressing over salad and mix to coat. Sprinkle with French fried onions. 6 servings.

Complete Menu

Cheesy Meat Loaf
- Saucy Vegetables, 21
- Bacon Cauliflower Salad, 176
- Sweet Dijon Salad Dressing, 287

Layered Red and White Salad

6 cups torn Iceberg lettuce
1 small red onion
3 cups fresh cauliflower florets
1 cup cherry tomatoes
1 pound bacon
2 cups salad dressing
1/2 cup sugar
1/2 cup shredded fresh Parmesan cheese

Place lettuce in a large clear glass bowl with straight sides. Slice onion and separate into rings. Arrange rings on top of lettuce. Arrange cauliflower on top of onion. Top with cherry tomatoes. Cook bacon until almost crisp. Drain on paper towels. Cut into small strips. Place bacon on top of cauliflower layer. Spread salad dressing over top. Sprinkle sugar on top of salad dressing. Sprinkle with Parmesan cheese. Refrigerate overnight. 8 servings.

Complete Menu

Ham Primavera
- Layered Red and White Salad, 177
- Strawberry Bavarian Salad, 252

 Use dressing such as Miracle Whip®, for the salad dressing.

Asparagus Salad

3 cups salad greens
1 cup fresh asparagus
1/2 pound deli honey ham
1 (8-ounce) can pineapple tidbits, drained
Buttermilk Ranch Dressing (page 263)
1/2 cup chow mein noodles

Place salad greens in a salad bowl. Trim asparagus and cut into 1-inch pieces. Cook in salted, boiling water for 3 minutes. Drain and allow to cool. Arrange ham, pineapple and asparagus over greens. Top with chow mein noodles. Serve with dressing. 4 servings.

Complete Menu

Ham and Noodles
- Asparagus Salad, 178
- Buttermilk Ranch Dressing, 263

Banana Salad

6 cups torn Iceberg lettuce
2 bananas
2/3 cup salad dressing
6 tablespoons milk
2 teaspoons apple cider vinegar
2 teaspoons sugar
1/8 teaspoon celery seed
1/8 teaspoon celery salt
salt
pepper

Place torn lettuce in a large bowl. Slice bananas and arrange over salad. In a small bowl, combine salad dressing, milk, vinegar, sugar, celery seed and celery salt. Whisk until smooth. Add salt and pepper to taste. Pour over salad and mix well. 6 servings.

Complete Menu

Chicken and Rice
• Broccoli and Mushrooms, 33
• Banana Salad, 179

Orange Tossed Salad

1 (11-ounce) can Mandarin oranges, drained
6 cups torn lettuce
1/2 cup sliced celery
1/2 cup julienned carrots
Sweet Honey Mustard Dressing (page 271)

Toss together oranges, lettuce, celery and carrots. Pour dressing over salad and toss to coat.
6 servings.

Complete Menu

California Dip Meat Loaf
- Monterey Potatoes, 75
- Garlic Green Beans, 53
- Orange Tossed Salad, 180
- Sweet Honey Mustard Dressing, 271

Fruit and Lettuce Salad

5 cups torn Iceberg lettuce
5 cups torn Bibb lettuce
2 cups fresh orange sections
2 cups sliced fresh strawberries
1 (20-ounce) can pineapple chunks, drained
1/4 cup pineapple juice
1/4 cup orange juice
1/4 cup grapefruit juice
2 teaspoons cornstarch
1/4 cup white vinegar
1 teaspoon minced garlic
2 tablespoons sugar
1 teaspoon mustard
1/2 teaspoon salt

In a large salad bowl, toss lettuce and fruit. In a small saucepan, stir pineapple juice, orange juice and grapefruit juice together. Stir in cornstarch until smooth. Bring to a boil over medium heat. Cool to room temperature. Stir in vinegar, minced garlic, sugar, mustard and salt. Pour over salad and toss. 10 servings.

Complete Menu

Swedish Meatballs
- Pasta Ring, 129
- Fruit and Lettuce Salad, 181
- Apple Carrot Muffins, 324

Pineapple Salad

1/4 cup pecans
2 tablespoons sugar
3 cups torn curly leaf lettuce
3 cups torn red curly leaf lettuce
1 cup sliced celery
2 green onions, sliced
1 (13.25-ounce) can pineapple chunks
2 tablespoons apple cider vinegar
1 tablespoon sugar
1 tablespoon snipped mint leaves
1/2 teaspoon salt
dash pepper
1/4 cup olive oil

Cook pecans and sugar over low heat, stirring constantly, until sugar is melted and pecans are coated. Cool and break apart. Place lettuces in a salad bowl. Add celery and onions. Drain pineapple, reserving juice. Add pineapple to salad. In a small bowl, combine vinegar, sugar and reserved pineapple juice. Whisk together until sugar dissolves. Whisk in mint, salt and pepper. Whisk in oil. Pour over salad and toss gently to coat. Top with sugared pecans. 6 servings.

Complete Menu

Pineapple Meatballs
• Pepper Rice, 116
• Pineapple Salad, 182

Blueberry Salad

4 cups baby spinach leaves
4 cups torn curly leaf lettuce
1/2 cup crumbled bleu cheese
1 cup fresh blueberries
1/4 cup white vinegar
3 tablespoons blueberry syrup
2 teaspoons Dijon mustard
1/2 teaspoon salt
1/2 cup canola oil

Place spinach and lettuce in a large salad bowl. Sprinkle cheese and blueberries over top. In a small bowl, whisk together vinegar, syrup, mustard and salt. Add oil and mix well. Pour dressing over salad and toss gently. 8 servings.

Complete Menu

Swiss Steak and Gravy
- Home-Style Potatoes, 64
- Blueberry Salad, 183
- Blueberry Muffins, 323

Apple Lettuce Salad

1/4 cup apple juice
2 tablespoons apple cider vinegar
1 tablespoon packed brown sugar
1/2 teaspoon mustard
1/8 teaspoon salt
dash of cinnamon
1 tablespoon canola oil
1 apple, chopped
3 cups torn curly leaf lettuce
3 cups torn red curly leaf lettuce

In a large salad bowl, whisk together apple juice, vinegar and brown sugar until sugar dissolves. Whisk in mustard, salt and cinnamon. Whisk in oil. Add chopped apple and mix well to coat. Cover and refrigerate. Add lettuce and toss just before serving. 6 servings.

Complete Menu

Tomato Stroganoff
- Zucchini Garlic Bow Ties, 136
- Apple Lettuce Salad, 184

Dried Cherry Salad

6 cups torn curly leaf lettuce
1 small red onion
4 white mushrooms
1/2 cup sweetened dried cherries
Poppy Seed Dressing (page 289)

Place lettuce in a serving bowl. Slice onion and separate rings. Slice mushrooms. Add onion rings, sliced mushrooms and dried cherries to salad. Toss all. Just before serving drizzle with dressing. 6 servings.

Complete Menu

Chicken a'la King
- Puff Bowls, 367
- Dried Cherry Salad, 185
- Poppy Seed Dressing, 289

Fresh Pear Salad

4 cups salad greens
2 pears
1 cup red grapes
1/3 cup toasted pecans
1/2 cup crumbled bleu cheese
Ginger Dressing (page 294)

Place salad greens in a large salad bowl. Slice pears and arrange over salad greens. Cut each grape in half and scatter over pears. Sprinkle with pecans and cheese. Drizzle with dressing. 6 servings.

Complete Menu

Meatball Spaghetti
- Fresh Pear Salad, 186
- Ginger Dressing, 294
- Cheese-Onion Bread Sticks, 349

Lime Avocado Salad

4 cups torn red curly leaf lettuce
3 avocados
1 tablespoon lime juice
2 grapefruit
2 oranges
1 (20-ounce) can pineapple rings
1/4 cup lime juice
2 tablespoons powdered sugar
2 tablespoons olive oil
1/4 teaspoon salt

Place lettuce in a large salad bowl. Peel and cut avocados into 1/2-inch pieces. Sprinkle avocado with lime juice. Peel and section grapefruit and oranges. Remove most of the skin and any seeds from each section. Drain pineapple, reserving syrup. Cut pineapple rings in half. In a small bowl, combine 1/3 cup reserved pineapple juice, lime juice and powdered sugar. Whisk until sugar is dissolved. Whisk in oil and salt. Toss avocado pieces with pineapple, grapefruit and orange sections. Place on lettuce. Pour dressing over all. Toss to combine. 8 servings.

Complete Menu

Italian Meat Sauce
- Garlic Pasta, 135
- Lime Avocado Salad, 187
- Cheesy Texas Toast, 343

To peel and dice an avocado, using a sharp knife, cut avocado in half lengthwise, down to the seed. Gently twist and pull halves apart. Tap the seed with the edge of a knife and lift the seed out. Slide a spoon just under the thick skin to remove the avocado. Place avocado, cut side down, on a flat surface. Cut lengthwise into slices. Holding all slices together, turn and slice again to cut into cubes.

Strawberry Romaine Salad

6 cups torn Romaine lettuce
2 cups sliced fresh strawberries
1 small red onion
1 (11-ounce) can Mandarin oranges
1 cup mayonnaise
2 tablespoons Maraschino cherry juice
2 tablespoons honey
1 teaspoon poppy seeds
1/8 teaspoon white vinegar

In a large bowl, mix the Romaine lettuce and strawberries. Slice the red onion and separate into individual rings. Arrange onion and Mandarin oranges over salad. In a separate bowl, whisk together mayonnaise, cherry juice, honey, poppy seeds and vinegar. Pour over the salad. Toss gently to coat and serve. 6 servings.

Complete Menu

Chicken Ham Roll-Ups
• Bacon Fettuccine Alfredo, 131
• Strawberry Romaine Salad, 188

Use an egg slicer to quickly, easily and evenly slice strawberries. Hull the strawberries and place each on its side in the egg slicer. Press down and wow! Beautiful perfect strawberry slices!

Dried Cranberry Salad

6 cups torn curly leaf lettuce
2 tablespoons sliced green onion
4 white mushrooms
1/2 cup sweetened dried cranberries
1/4 cup toasted slivered almonds
Celery Seed Dressing (page 290)

Place lettuce in a serving bowl. Sprinkle with sliced green onion. Slice mushrooms. Add mushrooms, dried cranberries and slivered almonds. Toss all. Drizzle with dressing. 6 servings.

Complete Menu

Cranberry Chicken
- Dried Cranberry Salad, 189
- Celery Seed Dressing, 290
- Honey Cranberry Muffins, 328

Spinach Salad

1 (12-ounce) bag spinach leaves
1/3 cup sweetened dried cranberries
1/3 cup sliced almonds
3/4 cup sliced white mushrooms
1/2 cup raspberry vinaigrette

Tear spinach into bite-sized pieces. Place in a serving bowl. Sprinkle with dried cranberries, sliced almonds and sliced mushrooms. Drizzle with raspberry vinaigrette. Toss all together just before serving. 6 servings.

Complete Menu

Cheese Manicotti
• Spinach Salad, 190
• Layered Pineapple Carrot Salad, 240

Simple Spinach Salad

4 cups torn spinach leaves
1 cup shredded Monterey Jack cheese
12 butter crackers
Buttermilk Dressing (page 265)

Place torn spinach in a salad bowl. Sprinkle with Monterey Jack cheese. Coarsely crush crackers and scatter over top of salad. Drizzle dressing over all. 4 servings.

Complete Menu

Meatballs in Gravy
- Garlic Mashed Potatoes, 81
- Simple Spinach Salad, 191
- Buttermilk Dressing, 265
- Potato Bread, 357

Crunchy Spinach Mushroom Salad

6 cups torn spinach
2 cups torn Iceberg lettuce
1 1/2 cups sliced white mushrooms
2 cups fresh bean sprouts
1 (8-ounce) can sliced water chestnuts, drained
8 slices bacon
Honey Dressing (page 270)

In a large salad bowl, combine torn spinach and lettuce. Slice mushrooms. Add mushrooms, bean sprouts and water chestnuts to salad bowl. Cook bacon until almost crisp. Cut into pieces and add to salad. Pour dressing over salad. Toss to coat. 8 servings.

Complete Menu

Chicken with Mushroom Gravy
• Italian Fettuccine, 139
• Crunchy Spinach Mushroom Salad, 192
• Honey Dressing, 270
• Cheddar Biscuits, 316

Bacon Spinach Salad

8 cups baby spinach leaves
2 cups fresh bean sprouts
10 slices bacon
4 hard boiled eggs
1 small red onion
Brown Sugar Dressing (page 295)

Combine spinach and bean sprouts in a large bowl. Cook bacon and cut into bite-sized pieces. Peel and slice eggs. Slice onion and separate into individual rings. Arrange sliced eggs, onion and bacon over salad. Pour dressing over salad and mix gently. 8 servings.

Complete Menu

Italian Shells
- Bacon Spinach Salad, 193
- Brown Sugar Dressing, 295
- Three Cheese Bread, 356

Swiss Spinach Salad

8 cups torn Iceberg lettuce
4 cups baby spinach leaves
1/2 pound bacon
1 small red onion
1 1/2 cups sliced white mushrooms
1 1/2 cups shredded Swiss cheese
1 cup cottage cheese
Simple Thousand Island Dressing (page 292)

In a large bowl, combine lettuce and spinach. Cook bacon and cut into small pieces. Slice onion and separate into individual rings. Add bacon, onion, mushrooms and Swiss cheese to salad bowl. Toss lightly. Sprinkle cottage cheese over top of salad. Pour dressing over all. Mix gently. 10 servings.

Complete Menu

Swiss Ham and Noodles
- Swiss Spinach Salad, 194
- Simple Thousand Island Dressing, 292
- Cherry Freeze, 234

Almond Spinach Salad

6 cups torn spinach
1/3 cup toasted sliced almonds
6 slices bacon
1 small red onion
1/2 cup white vinegar
1 1/2 teaspoons salt
1/4 teaspoon pepper
1/2 teaspoon ground mustard
1 teaspoon minced garlic
1 cup canola oil

Place spinach in a large salad bowl. Cook bacon until crisp and crumble over salad. Slice onion and separate into individual rings. Arrange on top of salad. In a small bowl, whisk together vinegar, salt, pepper, ground mustard and garlic. Mix well. Add oil and whisk until blended. Drizzle dressing over salad. 6 servings.

Complete Menu

Creamy Chicken and Pasta
• Lemon Pepper Vegetables, 25
• Almond Spinach Salad, 195

Spinach Bean Sprout Salad

1 (10-ounce) bag baby spinach
1 cup bean sprouts
1 (8-ounce) can sliced water chestnuts, drained
Russian Dressing (page 288)
1/2 cup shredded fresh Parmesan cheese
Parmesan croutons

In a salad bowl, combine spinach, bean sprouts and water chestnuts. Pour dressing over salad. Top with croutons. 6 servings.

Complete Menu

Mayonnaise Chicken
• Spinach Bean Sprout Salad, 196
• Russian Dressing, 288
• Sour Cream Croissants, 371

For Parmesan croutons, trim crusts from 4 slices of white bread. Generously butter both sides of the bread slices. Sprinkle with canned Parmesan cheese. Cut into 1/2-inch cubes. Arrange cubes on an ungreased baking sheet. Bake at 400° for 10 to 15 minutes, stirring occasionally, until golden brown and crisp.

Spinach Raspberry Salad

8 cups baby spinach leaves
3/4 cup sliced white mushrooms
1/2 small red onion
6 slices bacon
1/2 cup frozen red raspberries, thawed
1 cup plain yogurt
2 tablespoons cream

Place spinach leaves in a salad bowl. Arrange sliced mushrooms over top. Slice onion and separate into rings. Add onion rings to salad bowl. Cook bacon and cut into pieces. Add to salad. In a small bowl, combine raspberries, yogurt and cream. Stir and break up some of the raspberries. Serve dressing with salad. 8 servings.

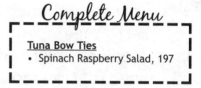

Complete Menu

Tuna Bow Ties
• Spinach Raspberry Salad, 197

Spinach Cran-Apple Salad

1/3 cup canola oil
1 tablespoon apple cider vinegar
1/2 cup frozen cranberry juice concentrate
1/4 teaspoon salt
4 cups chopped apples
2 cups pecans
1 cup sugar
3 cups torn curly leaf lettuce
5 cups torn spinach
1 cup sweetened dried cranberries

In a medium bowl, combine oil, vinegar, cranberry juice concentrate and salt. Stir in chopped apples. Mix to coat all apples. Cover and refrigerate for 3 or 4 hours. Cook pecans and sugar over low heat, stirring constantly, until sugar is melted and pecans are coated. Cool and break apart. In a large salad bowl, combine leaf lettuce and torn spinach. Add sweetened dried cranberries. Add apples including juice marinade. Gently toss salad. Top with sugared pecans. 10 servings.

Complete Menu

Broccoli Chicken and Rice
• Spinach Cran-Apple Salad, 198

 Spinach Cran-Apple Salad is best with tart apples, such as Granny Smith or Jonathan.

Strawberry Spinach Salad

4 slices bacon
1/2 cup sliced fresh strawberries
6 cups baby spinach leaves
2 cups chopped apples
Onion Dressing (page 293)

Cook bacon until crisp. Break or cut into small pieces. Place spinach, strawberries and apples in a large serving bowl. Add bacon. Pour dressing over salad and toss. 6 servings.

Complete Menu

French Onion Soup
• Strawberry Spinach Salad, 199
• Onion Dressing, 293
• Stuffed Crescent Rolls, 373

 Strawberry Spinach Salad is best with tart apples, such as Granny Smith or Jonathan.

Blackberry Spinach Salad

3 cups baby spinach leaves
2 cups fresh blackberries
3/4 cup crumbled feta cheese
2 cups cherry tomatoes
1 green onion, sliced
1/4 cup finely chopped walnuts
1/2 cup fresh blackberries
1 cup vanilla yogurt
2 tablespoons cream

Place spinach in a salad bowl. Scatter blackberries and feta cheese over spinach. Cut each cherry tomato in half. Add tomatoes, green onion and walnuts. Place blackberries, yogurt and cream in blender. Pulse a few times to break up berries and combine. Pour over salad. 6 servings.

Complete Menu

Tuna Fettuccine
• Blackberry Spinach Salad, 200

Orange Cauliflower Salad

4 cups baby spinach leaves
2 (11-ounce) cans Mandarin oranges
2 cups fresh cauliflower florets
1/4 cup chopped green bell pepper
French Dressing (page 267)

Place baby spinach leaves in a salad bowl. Add drained oranges, cauliflower and bell pepper. Pour dressing over salad. Toss to coat. 6 servings.

Complete Menu

Tuna Broccoli Au Gratin
- Orange Cauliflower Salad, 201
- French Dressing, 267

Strawberry, Kiwi and Spinach Salad

8 cups torn spinach
1/2 cup chopped walnuts
2 cups sliced strawberries
2 kiwis, peeled, quartered and sliced
Strawberry Dressing (see note on page 301)

Place spinach in a large salad bowl. Arrange walnuts, strawberries and kiwi over spinach. Drizzle dressing over salad. 8 servings.

Complete Menu

Continental Chicken
- Asparagus Linguine, 140
- Strawberry, Kiwi, Spinach Salad, 202
- Strawberry Dressing, 301

For a nifty way to peel a kiwi, cut off both ends of the kiwi. Slide a spoon just under the skin and carefully slide the spoon around the kiwi. The skin will come off all in one piece.

To make slicing strawberries a breeze, use an egg slicer. Hull the strawberries and place each on its side in the egg slicer. Press down to cut the berry into perfect, even slices.

Spinach Slaw

5 cups shredded spinach
6 cups shredded lettuce
4 cups shredded red cabbage
4 cups shredded cabbage
1 cup mayonnaise or salad dressing
1/3 cup honey
1 teaspoon garlic powder
1/2 teaspoon salt
1/4 teaspoon pepper

Toss shredded spinach, lettuce and cabbage in a large salad bowl. In a small bowl, combine mayonnaise or salad dressing, honey, garlic powder, salt and pepper. Pour over salad and mix well. 12 servings.

Complete Menu

Chicken Cacciatore
- Pasta Primavera, 134
- Spinach Slaw, 203

German Coleslaw

8 cups shredded cabbage
1 bunch green onions, sliced
3/4 cup sugar
3/4 cup apple cider vinegar
1 1/2 teaspoons celery seed
1 1/2 teaspoons salt
3/4 cup canola oil

Place cabbage and onions in a large serving bowl. Mix sugar and vinegar in small saucepan. Stir until sugar dissolves. Add celery seed and salt. Bring to a boil. Add oil. Return to boiling. Pour over cabbage and toss to coat. Serve warm or cold. 10 servings.

Complete Menu

Skillet BBQ Pork Chops
- Golden Fried Potatoes, 88
- Bacon Corn, 48
- German Cole Slaw, 204

Pineapple Coleslaw

4 cups shredded cabbage
1 (8-ounce) can pineapple tidbits, drained
3/4 cup salad dressing
2 tablespoons apple cider vinegar
2 tablespoons sugar
2 tablespoons milk
1/2 teaspoon salt

Place cabbage and pineapple in a large salad bowl. In a small bowl, combine salad dressing, vinegar, sugar, milk and salt. Mix until smooth. Pour over cabbage and pineapple. Toss to coat. 6 servings.

Complete Menu

Ham Loaf with Pineapple Sauce
- Hawaiian Baked Potatoes, 92
- Glazed Carrots, 40
- Pineapple Cole Slaw, 205

Cranberry Cabbage Slaw

3/4 cup fresh or frozen cranberries
1/3 cup sugar
1 cup green grapes
6 cups shredded cabbage
1/2 cup sliced celery
1/4 cup orange juice
2 tablespoons cranberry juice
1/4 cup mayonnaise
1/2 teaspoon salt

Cut cranberries in half and toss with sugar in a small bowl. Cut grapes in half. Place cabbage, celery and grapes in a large bowl. Gently add sugar and cranberries. Combine orange juice, cranberry juice, mayonnaise and salt. Pour over salad and mix gently. 6 servings.

Complete Menu

Beef Stuffing Bake
- Sweet Potato Salad, 219
- Cranberry Cabbage Slaw, 206

Fresh cranberries are only available for a few months of the year. Purchase them while available and freeze them to use later.

Broccoli Raisin Salad

2 pounds fresh broccoli
8 slices bacon
1/4 cup minced onion
1 cup raisins
1 cup mayonnaise
1 tablespoon apple cider vinegar
1/4 cup sugar
1/4 teaspoon salt
1/4 teaspoon pepper

Cut broccoli into bite-sized pieces. Cook bacon and break or cut into bite-sized pieces. In a salad bowl, combine broccoli, bacon, onion and raisins. In a small bowl, combine mayonnaise, vinegar, sugar, salt and pepper. Pour over broccoli and mix well. Refrigerate before serving. 8 servings.

Complete Menu

Cola Chicken
- Lemon Garlic Angel Hair Pasta, 141
- Broccoli Raisin Salad, 207

Layered Salad

2 cups julienned carrots
2 cups shredded red cabbage
2 cups sliced mushrooms
2 cups shredded cabbage
2 cups sliced zucchini
1 small red onion
1 cup shredded Cheddar cheese
Catalina Dressing (page 266)

In a large clear glass bowl with straight sides, layer vegetables starting with carrots. Top with red cabbage, then mushrooms, green cabbage and then zucchini. Slice onion and separate into individual rings. Add onion to bowl. Top with cheese. Pour dressing over salad and serve. Do not toss. 10 servings.

Complete Menu

Bacon Chicken
- Mashed Red Potatoes, 82
- Company Peas, 28
- Layered Salad, 208
- Catalina Dressing, 266

Broccoli and Cheddar Salad

8 slices bacon
4 cups fresh broccoli florets
1 cup shredded Cheddar cheese
1 bunch green onions, sliced
1 cup mayonnaise
1/2 cup sugar
2 tablespoons apple cider vinegar

Cook bacon until almost crisp. Drain on paper towels. Cut or tear into bite-sized pieces. In a large bowl, combine broccoli, cheese, onions and bacon. In a small bowl, combine mayonnaise, sugar and vinegar. Stir until sugar dissolves. Pour over broccoli and toss to coat. 6 servings.

Complete Menu

Cream Cheese Chicken
- Candied Carrots, 38
- Whipped Potatoes, 80
- Broccoli and Cheddar Salad, 209

Broccoli Tomato Salad

3 cups torn Iceberg lettuce
2 tomatoes
2 cups fresh broccoli florets
1/2 pound bacon
Green Goddess Dressing (page 277)

Arrange lettuce on serving platter. Cut tomatoes in wedges. Arrange tomatoes in a ring on lettuce. Place broccoli florets in center of tomato ring. Cut bacon into 1/2-inch strips. Cook until almost crisp. Sprinkle over tomatoes and broccoli. Drizzle with dressing. 6 servings.

Complete Menu

Corkscrew Chicken
- Broccoli Tomato Salad, 210
- Green Goddess Dressing, 277
- Hawaiian Sweet Bread, 353

Italian Broccoli Salad

4 cups fresh broccoli florets
1 pound bacon
4 cups torn Iceberg lettuce
1/4 cup sliced green onion
1 cup **Italian Dressing** (page 284)
1 cup mayonnaise
3/4 cup shredded fresh Parmesan cheese

In a saucepan, cook broccoli in salted, boiling water for 8 minutes. Drain and rinse with cold water. Cook bacon until almost crisp. Cut into 1-inch pieces. Place lettuce, broccoli, bacon and onions in a large salad bowl.
In a small bowl, combine Italian dressing, mayonnaise and Parmesan cheese. Mix well. Pour over salad and toss to coat. 10 servings.

Complete Menu

Spaghetti Sauce
• Tangy Linguini, 138
• Italian Broccoli Salad, 211
• Italian Dressing, 284
• Italian Twists, 347

Asparagus Bacon Salad

8 slices bacon
1 pound fresh asparagus
2 mushrooms
1/3 cup apple cider vinegar
2 tablespoons sugar
1/2 teaspoon ground mustard
1/4 teaspoon pepper
4 cups salad greens
1/2 cup sliced toasted almonds
2 hard boiled eggs

Cut bacon into 1-inch pieces. Cook bacon in a skillet until crisp. Drain on paper towels. Remove all but 3 tablespoons drippings from skillet. Trim asparagus and cut into 1-inch pieces. Slice mushrooms. Add asparagus and mushrooms to skillet and cook in drippings until crisp-tender. Add vinegar, sugar, mustard, pepper and bacon. Cook and stir for about 1 minute. In a large bowl, combine the salad greens and almonds. Add the asparagus mixture and toss gently. Peel and slice eggs. Arrange on top of salad. 6 servings.

Complete Menu

Chicken and Biscuits
- Asparagus Bacon Salad, 212
- Creamy Frozen Apricots, 238

Shrimp Salad

1 (16-ounce) bag frozen petite peas
1 cup cashews
1 cup sliced celery
1 cup cooked salad shrimp
1 (8-ounce) can sliced water chestnuts, drained
1 cup mayonnaise
1 teaspoon curry powder
1/2 teaspoon garlic salt

In a bowl, combine thawed peas, cashews, celery, shrimp and water chestnuts. In a small bowl, combine mayonnaise, curry powder and garlic salt. Mix well. Pour over salad. Stir to coat. 6 servings.

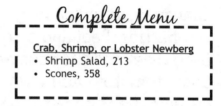

Complete Menu

Crab, Shrimp, or Lobster Newberg
• Shrimp Salad, 213
• Scones, 358

Petite peas are younger, smaller and more tender than regular peas. Using petite peas rather than regular peas makes a delicious difference in this salad.

Raspberry Avocado Salad

2 1/2 cups shredded Napa cabbage
1 1/2 cups shredded red cabbage
1 cup fresh raspberries
1 avocado
1 cucumber
2 tomatoes
Raspberry Dressing (page 301)

In a salad bowl, combine Napa cabbage and red cabbage. Add raspberries. Peel and dice avocado. Peel and slice cucumber. Dice tomato. Add avocado, cucumber and tomato to salad bowl. Drizzle dressing over salad. 6 servings.

Complete Menu

Cheesy Chicken and Rice
• Baked Broccoli, 36
• Raspberry Avocado Salad, 214
• Raspberry Dressing, 301

To peel and dice an avocado, using a sharp knife, cut avocado in half lengthwise, down to the seed. Gently twist and pull halves apart. Tap the seed with the edge of a knife and lift the seed out. Slide a spoon just under the thick skin to remove the avocado. Place avocado, cut side down, on a flat surface. Cut lengthwise into slices. Holding all slices together, turn and cut again into cubes.

Corn Bread Salad

1 pound bacon
5 cups cubed corn bread
2 tomatoes
1 small sweet onion
1 sweet pickle
1 cup diced green bell pepper
1/2 cup mayonnaise
1/2 cup salad dressing
1/4 cup sweet pickle juice
1/4 teaspoon salt
1/8 teaspoon pepper

Cook bacon until mostly crisp and cut into bite-sized pieces. In a large bowl, combine bacon and corn bread. Dice tomatoes, onion and pickle. Add tomatoes, onion, pickle and bell pepper to the bowl. In a small bowl, combine mayonnaise, salad dressing, pickle juice, salt and pepper. Mix well. Pour over corn bread mixture and toss gently. 6 servings.

Complete Menu

Country Style BBQ Ribs
- Baked Beans, 60
- Pasta Fruit Salad, 255
- Corn Bread Salad, 215

For the sweet onion, choose Vidalia or Walla Walla. These onions are sweeter than regular yellow or white onions. Other onions may be substituted but none is as sweet and delicious in this salad as a Vidalia or Walla Walla onion.

Bacon Potato Salad

8 cups cubed potatoes
1 cup diced onion
1 cup sliced celery
1/4 cup julienned carrots
8 slices bacon
1 cup mayonnaise
1 cup salad dressing
1 tablespoon mustard
2 tablespoons apple cider vinegar
1 tablespoon sugar
1/2 teaspoon salt
pepper

Cook potatoes in boiling, salted water just until tender. Drain. Place potatoes in a large bowl. Add onion, celery and carrots. Cook bacon until crisp. Break into small pieces. Add bacon to bowl. Combine mayonnaise, salad dressing, mustard, vinegar, sugar, salt and pepper. Whisk to combine. Pour over potato mixture and toss to coat. 10 servings.

Complete Menu

Slow Cooked Short Ribs
• Bacon Potato Salad, 216
• Apricot Salad, 243

Bacon and Egg Potato Salad

6 slices bacon
5 potatoes
4 hard boiled eggs
1 bunch green onions, sliced
1/3 cup lemon juice
1/3 cup water
1 1/2 teaspoons celery salt
1 teaspoon Worcestershire sauce
1/2 teaspoon ground mustard
1/4 teaspoon pepper

Cook bacon until crisp. Break into small pieces. Cook potatoes in boiling, salted water until tender. Drain, peel and cube. Place potatoes in a large bowl. Peel and dice eggs. Add bacon, eggs and onions to potatoes. In a small saucepan, combine lemon juice, water, celery salt, Worcestershire sauce, ground mustard and pepper. Bring to a boil. Remove from heat and pour over potato mixture. Mix well. Cover and refrigerate. Best refrigerated 8 hours or overnight. Remove from refrigerator 30 minutes before serving. 6 servings.

Complete Menu

Calico Beans
- Bacon and Egg Potato Salad, 217
- Vegetable Kabobs, 26

For easy fresh lemon juice, heat lemon in the microwave in a glass bowl until the lemon bursts (about 1 minute). Immediately stop microwave and allow lemon to cool enough to handle. Juice can then be squeezed easily from the hole made by the escaping steam.

German Potato Salad

8 potatoes
6 slices bacon
1/2 cup chopped onion
2 tablespoons flour
1 1/3 cups water
2/3 cup apple cider vinegar
1/3 cup sugar
1/2 teaspoon salt
1/8 teaspoon pepper

Cook potatoes in boiling, salted water until tender. Drain, cool, peel and slice potatoes. Cook bacon and drain, reserving 2 tablespoons drippings. Break or cut bacon into bite-sized pieces. Place potatoes and bacon in a serving bowl. Cook onion in bacon drippings until tender. Stir in flour, blend well. Add water and vinegar. Cook and stir until bubbly and slightly thick. Add sugar, salt and pepper. Stir until dissolved. Pour over potatoes and bacon. Serve warm. 10 servings.

Complete Menu

Corned Beef and Cabbage
• German Potato Salad, 218
• Sour Cream and Chive Biscuits, 318

Sweet Potato Salad

3 pounds sweet potatoes
1 cup diced red bell pepper
1/2 cup diced onion
1 1/4 cups mayonnaise
1 tablespoon sugar
1 tablespoon white vinegar
1 1/2 teaspoons salt
1/8 teaspoon pepper

Cook sweet potatoes boiling, salted water until tender. Drain, cool, peel and dice potatoes. Add red bell pepper and onion. In a small bowl, combine mayonnaise, sugar, vinegar, salt and pepper. Whisk until smooth. Pour over potato mixture and toss gently to coat. 10 servings.

Complete Menu

Beef Stuffing Bake
- Sweet Potato Salad, 219
- Cranberry Cabbage Slaw, 206

Melon Cucumber Salad

1 cup sliced cucumber
2 cups cubed watermelon
2 tablespoons apple cider vinegar
1 tablespoon sugar
1/2 teaspoon salt
dash of pepper
1/4 cup canola oil
4 lettuce leaves

Mix cucumber slices and melon cubes in a bowl. In a small bowl, whisk together vinegar, sugar, salt and pepper until sugar dissolves. Whisk in oil. Pour over cucumber and melon. Toss to coat. Cover and refrigerate. To serve, stir then remove with a slotted spoon and arrange on lettuce leaves. 4 servings.

Complete Menu

Scalloped Pork Chops
• Cheesy Broccoli Rice, 124
• Melon Cucumber Salad, 220

Five Fruit Salad

6 lettuce leaves
1 (8.25-ounce) can pineapple rings, drained
1 banana
1 tablespoon lemon juice
1 orange, peeled and sectioned
1 cup green grapes
1 cup melon cubes
Honey Lime Dressing (page 272)

Arrange lettuce leaves on a serving platter. Arrange pineapple rings on lettuce. Slice banana and dip in lemon juice to prevent darkening. Mix banana, orange, grapes and melon cubes. Arrange on pineapple. Drizzle dressing over fruit. 6 servings.

Complete Menu

Country Chicken and Vegetables
- Five Fruit Salad, 221
- Honey Lime Dressing, 272
- Easy Yeast Rolls, 359

Honey Lime Fruit Salad

2 kiwi
1 cup green grapes
1 cup fresh raspberries
1 cantaloupe
1 honeydew melon
1/2 cup honey
1/3 cup lime juice
1/4 teaspoon coriander
1/4 teaspoon nutmeg

Peel, quarter and slice kiwi. Peel and cube the melons. Toss kiwi, grapes, raspberries, cantaloupe and honeydew in a large bowl. Whisk together honey, lime juice, coriander and nutmeg. Pour over fruit and toss to coat. 10 servings.

Complete Menu

Pizza Meat Loaf
• Italian Scalloped Potatoes, 65
• Honey Lime Fruit Salad, 222

To easily peel a kiwi, cut off both ends of the kiwi. Slide a spoon just under the skin and carefully slide the spoon around the kiwi. The skin will come off all in one piece.

Fruit Salad

1 (29-ounce) can sliced peaches, drained
1 (20-ounce) can pineapple chunks, drained
1 (11-ounce) can Mandarin oranges, drained
1/4 cup Maraschino cherries
1 cup sugar
2 tablespoons cornstarch
1 cup water
3 tablespoons peach gelatin (from a 3-ounce box)

Toss peaches, pineapple, Mandarin oranges and cherries in a large bowl. Combine sugar and cornstarch in a small saucepan. Stir in water until smooth. Bring to a boil over medium heat. Remove from heat and stir in gelatin until dissolved. Pour over fruit and toss to coat. Sauce will thicken as it cools. 6 servings.

Complete Menu

BBQ Beef and Biscuits
• California Vegetables, 22
• Fruit Salad, 223

Speedy Fruit Salad

1 (11-ounce) can Mandarin oranges, drained
1 (20-ounce) can pineapple chunks, drained
1 (16-ounce) can fruit cocktail, drained
2 bananas, sliced
1 1/2 cups miniature marshmallows
1 (8-ounce) container frozen whipped topping, thawed
1/2 cup sweetened flaked coconut

In a large serving bowl, combine oranges, pineapple, fruit cocktail and bananas. Stir in marshmallows. Fold in whipped topping. Sprinkle coconut over top. Stir in just before serving. 8 servings.

Complete Menu

Skillet BBQ Chicken
- Crisp New Potatoes, 69
- Speedy Fruit Salad, 224
- Western Zucchini, 346

Fresh Fruit Salad

1 red apple
1 yellow apple
1 tart green apple (Granny Smith)
1 pineapple
1 cantaloupe
2 cups red grapes
2 cups green grapes
2 cups strawberries
2 cups blueberries
3 kiwi
1 banana
1 (3-ounce) package cream cheese
1/2 cup powdered sugar
1 teaspoon lemon juice
1 (8-ounce) container frozen whipped topping, thawed

Cube the apples. Peel and cube the pineapple and cantaloupe. Hull and cut each strawberry in half. Peel, slice and quarter the kiwi. Slice the banana. Place apples, pineapple, cantaloupe, grapes, strawberries, blueberries, kiwi and banana in a large serving bowl. In a small bowl, beat cream cheese until smooth. Gradually add powdered sugar and lemon juice and mix well. Fold in whipped topping. Spread over fruit. 12 servings.

Complete Menu

Honey Barbequed Ribs
- Potato Pancakes, 76
- Fresh Fruit Salad, 225
- Southern Corn Muffins, 331

To easily peel a kiwi, cut off both ends of the kiwi. Slide a spoon just under the skin and carefully slide the spoon around the kiwi. The skin will come off all in one piece.

Apple Salad

3 apples
1 (8-ounce) can pineapple tidbits, drained
1 cup green grapes
1/2 cup julienned carrots
1 cup sliced celery
3/4 cup sour cream
1 tablespoon sugar
1 tablespoon pineapple juice

Dice the apples and place in a salad bowl. Add pineapple, grapes, carrots and celery. In a small bowl, combine sour cream, sugar and pineapple juice. Stir until sugar dissolves. Pour over salad and mix well. 6 servings.

Complete Menu

Country Barbequed Ribs
• Potato Skins, 89
• Apple Salad, 226
• Apple Cider Biscuits, 322

24 Hour Fruit Salad

1 (20-ounce) can pineapple chunks
2 (11-ounce) cans Mandarin oranges, drained
1 (17-ounce) can pitted sweet cherries, drained
1 cup miniature marshmallows
2 eggs, beaten
2 tablespoons sugar
2 tablespoons apple cider vinegar
1 tablespoon butter
dash of salt
3/4 cup cream

Drain pineapple and reserve 2 tablespoons syrup. In a bowl, combine pineapple, oranges, cherries and marshmallows. In a small saucepan, combine reserved pineapple syrup, eggs, sugar, vinegar, butter and salt. Heat to boiling, stirring constantly. Allow to cool. In a small bowl, beat cream until stiff. Fold in egg mixture. Pour over fruit and toss to coat. Refrigerate at least 8 hours but not more than 24 hours. 10 servings.

Complete Menu

Chicken Stroganoff
• Homemade Egg Noodles, 130
• 24 Hour Fruit Salad, 227

Creamy Apple Salad

3 apples
2 bananas
1 (16-ounce) can fruit cocktail, drained
1 (11-ounce) can Mandarin oranges, drained
1 (8-ounce) can crushed pineapple
3/4 cup miniature marshmallows
1/2 cup sweetened flaked coconut
1/2 cup raisins
1/2 cup Maraschino cherries
1 (4-ounce) box instant vanilla pudding
1 (8-ounce) container frozen whipped topping, thawed

Peel and dice the apples. Slice the bananas. In a large bowl, combine apple, banana, fruit cocktail, orange segments and undrained pineapple. Add marshmallows, coconut, raisins and cherries. Stir to combine. Sprinkle dry pudding mix over top. Gently stir in whipped topping. Chill. 10 servings.

Complete Menu

Pork Chops and Potatoes
• Bacon Carrots, 42
• Creamy Apple Salad, 228

Taffy Apple Salad

1 (20-ounce) can pineapple tidbits
1 egg, beaten
1 tablespoon flour
1 1/2 tablespoons apple cider vinegar
1/2 cup sugar
2 apples
2 cups miniature marshmallows
1 (8-ounce) container frozen whipped topping, thawed

Drain pineapple and reserve juice. In saucepan, combine reserved pineapple juice, egg, flour, vinegar and sugar. Stir over medium heat until bubbly and thickened. Remove from heat. Allow to cool completely. Dice apples. Stir in pineapple, apples and marshmallows. Mix well. Gently stir in whipped topping. 6 servings.

Complete Menu

Tuna Stroganoff
• Broccoli Fettuccine, 142
• Taffy Apple Salad, 229

Taffy Apple Salad is best with tart apples, such as Granny Smith or Jonathan.

Frog Eye Salad

1 cup Acini de Pepe pasta
1 cup sugar
2 tablespoons flour
3 eggs
1 (20-ounce) can crushed pineapple
1 (11-ounce) can Mandarin oranges
1 cup miniature marshmallows
1 (8-ounce) container frozen whipped topping, thawed

Cook pasta in boiling water for 10 minutes. Drain and rinse. Drain juice from pineapple and oranges into a saucepan. Add sugar and flour to juice in pan. Mix well. Add eggs. Cook over medium heat, stirring constantly until mixture thickens. Allow to cool. In a salad bowl, combine cooked mixture with pasta. Stir in pineapple and orange segments. Add marshmallows and whipped topping. Mix gently. 10 servings.

Complete Menu

Pork Chops, Carrots and Gravy
- Cream Cheese Mashed Potatoes, 85
- Frog Eye Salad, 230
- Buttermilk Oatmeal Muffins, 327

To Freeze: Place in covered bowl. Label and freeze.

To Serve: Remove from freezer at least 15 minutes before serving. Serve thawed or frozen.

Frozen Fruit Salad

1 (4-ounce) box instant vanilla pudding mix
2 cups milk
1 cup whipped topping
1 (11-ounce) can Mandarin oranges, drained
1 (16-ounce) can fruit cocktail, drained
3 bananas, sliced

Prepare pudding mix with milk as directed on package. Stir in whipped topping. Stir in oranges, fruit cocktail and bananas. Pour into a serving dish. Cover and freeze. Remove from freezer 1 hour before serving. 10 servings.

Complete Menu

Candied Chicken
- Cheese Potatoes, 71
- Baked Corn, 46
- Frozen Fruit Salad, 231

Frozen Peach Salad

1 (3-ounce) package cream cheese, softened
1 cup mayonnaise
1 cup drained crushed pineapple
1 (16-ounce) can sliced peaches, drained
1/2 cup Maraschino cherries
1 cup cream

Combine cream cheese and mayonnaise until smooth. Stir in pineapple, peaches and cherries. Whip the cream. Gently stir in whipped cream. Spoon into mold or dish. Cover and freeze until firm. Cut in squares and serve on salad greens. 6 servings.

Complete Menu

Porcupine Meatballs
- Au Gratin Potatoes, 68
- Broccoli with Cheese Sauce, 31
- Frozen Peach Salad, 232

Frozen Strawberry Salad

1 (8-ounce) package cream cheese, softened
2/3 cup sugar
1 (10-ounce) package frozen strawberries, thawed
1 (20-ounce) can crushed pineapple, drained
1 (12-ounce) container frozen whipped topping, thawed

In a large bowl, combine cream cheese and sugar. Mix in strawberries. Stir in pineapple and whipped topping. Pour into a serving dish. Cover and freeze until firm. Remove from freezer 15 minutes before serving. 8 servings.

Complete Menu

Brown Sugar Pork Ribs
- Oriental Noodle Salad, 257
- Baked Hash Browns, 63
- Frozen Strawberry Salad, 233

Cherry Freeze

1 (3-ounce) package cream cheese, softened
1 cup crushed pineapple, drained
2 cups miniature marshmallows
1 (16-ounce) can pitted sweet cherries, drained
1/3 cup Maraschino cherries, halved
1 cup cream, whipped

Combine cream cheese and pineapple. Add marshmallows and cherries. Fold in whipped cream. Pour into a serving dish. Cover and freeze. Remove from freezer 15 minutes before serving. 6 servings.

Complete Menu

Swiss Ham and Noodles
- Swiss Spinach Salad, 194
- Simple Thousand Island Dressing, 292
- Cherry Freeze, 234

Frozen Raspberry Salad

1 (8-ounce) package cream cheese, softened
1/4 cup honey
1 banana, sliced
1 (10-ounce) package frozen raspberries
1 cup cream
2 cups miniature marshmallows

Whip softened cream cheese with electric mixer. Add honey and mix well. Gently stir in bananas and raspberries. Whip the cream. Gently fold into fruit mixture. Stir in marshmallows. Pour into a serving dish. Cover and freeze until firm. Remove from freezer 15 minutes before serving. 8 servings.

Complete Menu

Cheesy Ham and Potatoes
• Cheesy Green Beans, 51
• Frozen Raspberry Salad, 235

Make great popsicle salads by spooning the salad into individual paper cups. Place a popsicle stick or a spoon in each. When frozen, tear off the paper cup.

Frozen Fruit Cocktail

1 (8-ounce) package cream cheese, softened
1 cup mayonnaise
1 (30-ounce) can fruit cocktail, drained
2 cups miniature marshmallows
1/3 cup Maraschino cherries, halved
1 cup cream, whipped

Combine cream cheese and mayonnaise until smooth. Stir in fruit cocktail, marshmallows and cherries. Fold in whipped cream. Pour into buttered shallow serving dish. Cover and freeze. Remove from freezer 15 minutes before serving. 12 servings.

Complete Menu

Ham and Chicken Roll-Ups
- Swiss Green Beans, 54
- Frozen Fruit Cocktail, 236

Frozen Sour Cream Fruit Salad

2 cups sour cream
3/4 cup sugar
1 tablespoon lemon juice
1 (30-ounce) can fruit cocktail, drained
2 bananas, sliced
1 (10-ounce) jar Maraschino cherries, drained

Mix sour cream, sugar and lemon juice. Stir in fruit cocktail, bananas and cherries. Pour into a dish, cover and freeze. Remove from freezer 15 minutes before serving. 8 servings.

Complete Menu

Pizza in a Dish
- Frozen Sour Cream Fruit Salad, 237
- Garlic Cheese Bread, 344

Creamy Frozen Apricots

1 (8-ounce) package cream cheese, softened
1 cup sour cream
1/4 cup sugar
1 (8-ounce) can crushed pineapple, drained
1 (17-ounce) can apricot halves, drained
1 (16-ounce) can pitted sweet cherries, drained
1 1/2 cups miniature marshmallows

In mixing bowl, beat cream cheese until smooth. Mix in sour cream and sugar. Stir in pineapple, apricots, cherries and marshmallows. Pour into dish or mold. Freeze at least 8 hours. Remove from freezer 15 minutes before serving. 8 servings.

Complete Menu

Chicken and Biscuits
- Asparagus Bacon Salad, 212
- Creamy Frozen Apricots, 238

Layered Peach Salad

1 (16-ounce) can sliced peaches, drained
1/4 cup sliced celery
3/4 cup boiling water
1 (3-ounce) box raspberry gelatin
1 cup ice cubes

Arrange sliced peaches and celery in bottom of bread pan. In blender, combine boiling water and gelatin. Blend on low speed until gelatin is dissolved. Add water to fill one cup measure of ice cubes. Add to gelatin and stir until ice is partially melted. Blend on high speed for 30 seconds. Pour over peaches. Chill until firm. Salad layers as it chills. 6 servings.

Complete Menu

Peachy Chicken
- Coconut Rice, 120
- Walnut Broccoli, 37
- Layered Peach Salad, 239

Layered Pineapple Carrot Salad

1 (8-ounce) can pineapple rings
1/4 cup shredded carrot
3/4 cup boiling water
1 (3-ounce) box orange gelatin
1 cup ice cubes

Drain pineapple and reserve juice. Cut pineapple rings in half. Arrange pineapple and carrots in bottom of a bread pan. In blender, combine boiling water and gelatin.

Complete Menu

Cheese Manicotti
• Spinach Salad, 190
• Layered Pineapple Carrot Salad, 240

Blend on low speed until gelatin is dissolved. Add reserved pineapple juice to fill one cup measure of ice cubes. Add to gelatin and stir until ice is partially melted. Blend on high speed for 30 seconds. Pour over pineapple. Chill until firm. Salad layers as it chills. 6 servings.

 Substitute 1 (8-ounce) can crushed pineapple for the pineapple rings, if desired.

Pretzel Salad

2 cups coarsely crushed pretzels
3 tablespoons sugar
3/4 cup melted butter
1 (8-ounce) package cream cheese
1 cup sugar
1 (8-ounce) container frozen whipped topping, thawed
2 (3-ounce) boxes strawberry gelatin
2 cups boiling water
1 (16-ounce) package frozen strawberries

In a 9 x 13-inch serving dish, combine pretzels, sugar and melted butter. Mix well and press onto bottom of dish. Bake at 400° for 5 minutes. Cool. In a mixing bowl, combine cream cheese and sugar. Stir in whipped topping. Spread over pretzel crust. Combine gelatin and boiling water. Stir until gelatin is dissolved. Stir in frozen strawberries. Pour over top of cream cheese layer. Refrigerate until firm. Cut in squares. 12 servings.

Complete Menu

Creamed Corn and Beef
- Lemon Glazed Asparagus and Carrots, 23
- Pretzel Salad, 241

Triple Orange Salad

1 (20-ounce) can pineapple chunks
1 (6-ounce) package orange gelatin
1 pint orange sherbet
2 (11-ounce) cans Mandarin oranges, drained
1 cup sweetened flaked coconut
1 cup miniature marshmallows
1 cup sour cream

Drain pineapple and reserve syrup. Measure syrup and add water to equal 2 cups liquid. Bring liquid to boil. Pour boiling liquid on gelatin in a bowl. Stir until gelatin is dissolved. Add orange sherbet. Stir until melted. Stir in 1 can oranges. Pour into a 6-cup ring mold. Refrigerate until firm. In a separate bowl, mix remaining oranges, pineapple, coconut and marshmallows. Fold in sour cream. Refrigerate 3 hours. Unmold ring and fill center with fruit mixture. 12 servings.

Complete Menu

Smoky Maple Chicken
- Bacon Pilaf, 118
- Parmesan Zucchini, 98
- Triple Orange Salad, 242

To unmold gelatin, dip *container only* into hot water for about 20 seconds. Place a serving plate over top. Hold carefully and turn container upside down on plate to release gelatin.

Apricot Salad

2 cups boiling water
1 (6-ounce) box orange gelatin
1 (30-ounce) can apricot halves
1 (20-ounce) can crushed pineapple
3/4 cup miniature marshmallows
1/4 cup sugar
1 tablespoon flour
1 egg, beaten
1 cup cream
1/2 cup sweetened flaked coconut, toasted

Pour boiling water on gelatin in a large bowl. Stir until gelatin is dissolved. Drain apricots and pineapple and reserve syrup. Mix apricot and pineapple syrups. Set aside 1 cup of syrup. Measure remaining syrup and add

Complete Menu

Slow Cooked Short Ribs
• Bacon Potato Salad, 216
• Apricot Salad, 243

enough water to measure 1 cup. Stir syrup-water mixture into gelatin mixture. Refrigerate until slightly thickened, about 1 hour. Stir apricots, pineapple and marshmallows into gelatin mixture. Pour into a serving dish. Refrigerate until firm, about 3 hours. Mix sugar and flour in a saucepan. Stir in reserved apricot-pineapple syrup and the egg. Heat to boiling over low heat, stirring constantly. Boil and stir for about one minute. Allow to cool. Beat cream in chilled small mixing bowl until soft peaks form. Fold into fruit syrup mixture. Spread evenly over gelatin layer. Sprinkle toasted coconut over the top. 12 servings.

 To toast coconut, spread it in a thin layer on a baking sheet. Bake at 325° for about 10 minutes, stirring frequently.

Lime Pear Salad

1 (3-ounce) box lemon gelatin
1 cup boiling water
1 cup pear juice
1 cup crushed pears
2 (3-ounce) packages cream cheese
1 cup cream, whipped
1 (3-ounce) package lime gelatin

Combine lemon gelatin with boiling water until gelatin is dissolved. Stir in pear juice. Pour into dish and refrigerate until thickened but not firm, about 1 hour. Combine thickened gelatin, pears, cream cheese and whipped cream. Return to refrigerator until firm. Prepare lime gelatin according to package directions. Pour lime gelatin over first layer. Refrigerate until firm. 6 servings.

Complete Menu

Ground Beef Stroganoff
- Mashed Cauliflower, 44
- Honey Mustard Vegetables, 24
- Lime Pear Salad, 244

Lime Sour Cream Salad

1 (8-ounce) can crushed pineapple
1 (3-ounce) box lime gelatin
1/2 cup green grapes
1 1/2 cups sour cream, divided
1 banana
2 tablespoons packed brown sugar
1 teaspoon lemon juice

Drain pineapple, reserving syrup. Add enough water to reserved syrup to measure 1 cup. Heat liquid just to boiling. Stir gelatin into hot syrup until dissolved. Refrigerate until slightly thickened. Stir in pineapple, grapes and 1 cup sour cream. Pour into clear glass dish. Refrigerate until firm. In blender, combine remaining 1/2 cup sour cream, banana, brown sugar and lemon juice. Blend until smooth. Pour over firm lime salad. 6 servings.

Complete Menu

Cheesy Ham and Noodles
- Green Beans and Carrots, 57
- Lime Sour Cream Salad, 245

Buttermilk Salad

1 (20-ounce) can crushed pineapple
2 tablespoons sugar
2 (3-ounce) packages lime gelatin
2 cups buttermilk
1 (8-ounce) package whipped cream

Heat and sir pineapple and sugar until sugar dissolves. Stir in lime gelatin until dissolved. Remove from heat and stir in buttermilk. Stir in whipped cream. Pour into dish and refrigerate until firm. 10 servings.

Complete Menu

Beef Stroganoff
- Orange Carrots, 41
- Baked Mashed Potatoes, 86
- Buttermilk Salad, 246

Fresh Cranberry Salad

2 cups water
2 cups sugar
1 pound fresh cranberries
2 cups pineapple juice
1 (6-ounce) box orange gelatin
1 cup crushed pineapple
1 (11-ounce) can Mandarin oranges, drained

In saucepan, combine water and sugar. Boil 5 minutes. Stir in cranberries. Cook until cranberries pop. Pour into a serving dish. Bring pineapple juice to a boil. Stir in orange gelatin. Stir until dissolved. Add to cranberries. Add pineapple and oranges. Mix well. Refrigerate until firm. 8 servings.

Complete Menu

Stuffing Meat Loaves
• Pecan Stuffed Acorn Squash, 96
• Fresh Cranberry Salad, 247

Carrot Pineapple Salad

2 1/2 cups orange juice, divided
1 (6-ounce) box orange gelatin
1 cup shredded carrots
1 cup crushed pineapple
1/2 cup sugar
2 tablespoons flour
1 egg
2 tablespoons butter
1 cup whipped cream

Heat 1 1/2 cups orange juice. Dissolve orange gelatin in warm juice. Pour into 9 x 13-inch serving dish. Chill until partially thickened. Stir in carrots and undrained pineapple. Chill until firm. In a small saucepan, combine remaining 1 cup orange juice, sugar, flour and egg. Heat to boiling, stirring constantly. Cook one minute. Remove from heat and add butter. Allow to cool. Stir in whipped cream. Pour on top of chilled salad. 12 servings.

Complete Menu

Polynesian Pork Roast
• Shrimp Rice, 121
• Carrot Pineapple Salad, 248
• Sweet Potato Rolls, 364

Lemonade Salad

1 (3-ounce) box lemon gelatin
1 cup boiling water
1/2 cup sugar
3/4 cup frozen lemonade concentrate
1/8 teaspoon salt
1 cup frozen whipped topping, thawed

Dissolve gelatin in boiling water. Stir in sugar, lemonade concentrate and salt. Allow to cool. Stir in whipped topping. Place in mold or dish. Chill until firm. 6 servings.

Complete Menu

Meat Loaf and Potatoes
• Bacon Green Beans, 50
• Lemonade Salad, 249

·This salad is beautiful molded in a ring mold and served with fresh mixed berries, such as raspberries, blueberries and strawberries, mounded in the center.

Cranberry Pineapple Salad

2 (3-ounce) boxes cherry gelatin
1 cup boiling water
1 cup pineapple juice
1 tablespoon lemon juice
1 (16-ounce) can whole berry cranberry sauce
1 cup sliced celery
1 cup crushed pineapple
1 (11-ounce) can Mandarin oranges, drained

Dissolve gelatin in boiling water. Stir in pineapple juice and lemon juice. Chill until slightly thickened. Add cranberry sauce, celery, pineapple and orange segments. Chill until firm. 12 servings.

Complete Menu

Turkey and Stuffing Roll-Ups
- Maple Glazed Sweet Potatoes, 94
- Cranberry Pineapple Salad, 250
- Orange Cream Cheese Muffins, 325

Raspberry Ribbon Salad

2 (3-ounce) boxes raspberry gelatin
1 1/2 cups boiling water
1 (10-ounce) package frozen raspberries
1 (20-ounce) can crushed pineapple, drained
1 banana, sliced
1 cup sour cream

Dissolve gelatin in boiling water. Add raspberries and stir until thawed. Stir in pineapple and banana. Pour half of the gelatin and fruit mixture into a serving dish. Chill until set. Spread sour cream over gelatin. Spoon remaining gelatin and fruit mixture over sour cream. Chill until firm, at least 2 hours. 9 servings.

Complete Menu

Chicken Fried Steak
- Mashed Potatoes, 79
- Confetti Corn, 49
- Raspberry Ribbon Salad, 251

Strawberry Bavarian Salad

1 cup boiling water
1 (3-ounce) box strawberry gelatin
1 (16-ounce) package frozen sweetened sliced strawberries
1 1/2 cups miniature marshmallows
1/2 cup cream, whipped

In a bowl, dissolve gelatin in boiling water. Stir in strawberries. Stir in marshmallows and whipped cream. Pour into serving dish. Cover and refrigerate at least 4 hours. 6 servings.

Complete Menu

Ham Primavera
- Layered Red and White Salad, 177
- Strawberry Bavarian Salad, 252

Tortellini Spinach Salad

1 cup frozen cheese filled tortellini
6 cups baby spinach leaves
1/2 cup shredded fresh Parmesan cheese
Creamy Cheese Dressing (page 274)

Cook tortellini according to package directions. Drain. In a salad bowl, combine baby spinach leaves and tortellini. Top with Parmesan cheese. Pour dressing over all and toss to coat. 6 servings.

Complete Menu

Baked Chicken in Gravy
- Mushroom Pie, 61
- Tortellini Spinach Salad, 253
- Creamy Cheese Dressing, 274

Paradise Pasta Salad

1 (16-ounce) box bow tie pasta
1 (20-ounce) can pineapple chunks
2 (11-ounce) cans Mandarin oranges, drained
2 kiwi
1 cup red grapes
1 small bunch green onions
1/2 cup sweetened dried cranberries
1/2 cup cashews
1 (16-ounce) bottle cole slaw dressing
1/2 cup mayonnaise

Cook pasta in boiling, salted water according to package directions. Drain and cool. Drain pineapple and reserve 1/4 cup juice. Drain oranges. Peel kiwi, quarter and slice. Slice onions. Place pasta in a large serving bowl. Add pineapple, oranges, kiwi, grapes, onions, dried cranberries and cashews. Combine the cole slaw dressing, mayonnaise and the reserved pineapple juice. Pour dressing over all. Mix gently. 12 servings.

Complete Menu

New England Baked Beans
• Paradise Pasta Salad, 254
• Sweet Braided Bread, 354

For a nifty way to peel a kiwi, cut off both ends of the kiwi. Slide a spoon just under the skin and carefully slide the spoon around the kiwi. The skin will come off all in one piece.

Salad dressing may be substituted for the mayonnaise.

Turn this salad into a main dish by adding 2 cups of cooked, chopped chicken.

Pasta Fruit Salad

1 1/2 cups small uncooked sea shell pasta
1 tablespoon cornstarch
2 tablespoons sugar
1 (30-ounce) can fruit cocktail
1 1/2 tablespoons lemon juice
1/2 cup cream
1 tablespoon sugar
1/4 cup halved Maraschino cherries

Cook pasta in boiling, salted water according to package directions. Drain. In small saucepan, combine cornstarch and sugar. Drain fruit cocktail, reserving 1/2 cup syrup. Stir reserved syrup into cornstarch mixture. Mix well. Stir in lemon juice. Cook over medium heat, stirring constantly, until mixture thickens and boils. Stir into drained pasta. Cover and refrigerate for at least 4 hours. Just before serving, beat cream with sugar until stiff. Fold whipped cream, fruit cocktail and Maraschino cherries into pasta mixture. 6 servings.

Complete Menu

Country Style BBQ Ribs
• Baked Beans, 60
• Pasta Fruit Salad, 255
• Corn Bread Salad, 215

Apple Pasta Salad

2 cups uncooked rotini pasta
1 (8-ounce) container plain nonfat yogurt
1 (8-ounce) can crushed pineapple
1/4 teaspoon garlic powder
1/2 teaspoon salt
1/4 teaspoon ground mustard
1 tablespoon honey
1/2 cup shredded carrots
1 cup sliced celery
1/4 cup sliced green onions
1/4 cup raisins
3 apples, unpeeled and diced

Cook pasta in boiling, salted water according to package directions. Drain. Rinse with cold water and drain again. Place in a serving bowl. In a small bowl, combine yogurt, pineapple, garlic powder, salt, ground mustard and honey. Whisk until mostly smooth. Add carrots, celery, green onions, raisins and apples to bowl of pasta. Pour dressing over all. Stir to coat. Chill thoroughly before serving. 8 servings.

Complete Menu

Manhattan Clam Chowder
- Apple Pasta Salad, 256
- Dinner Rolls, 360

Oriental Noodle Salad

1 package uncooked ramen noodles, crumbled
2 green onions, minced
4 cups finely shredded cabbage
1/4 cup rice vinegar
1/2 cup sugar
1/4 teaspoon pepper
1/2 teaspoon salt
1 teaspoon Accent®
1/2 cup canola oil

In a large bowl, combine dry crumbled noodles, onions and shredded cabbage. In a small bowl, whisk together vinegar and sugar until sugar dissolves. Whisk in contents of seasoning packet from ramen noodles, pepper, salt and Accent®. Whisk in oil. Pour over salad and mix well. 8 servings.

Complete Menu

Brown Sugar Pork Ribs
• Oriental Noodle Salad, 257
• Baked Hash Browns, 63
• Frozen Strawberry Salad, 233

 Turn this salad into a main dish by adding 2 cups cooked, shredded chicken.

Any flavor of ramen noodles may be used. This salad is especially good with Teriyaki Chicken or Oriental flavored ramen noodles.

Wild Rice Salad

1 (6-ounce) package long and wild rice mix
1 3/4 cups chicken broth
1/2 cup chopped green bell pepper
1/2 cup chopped red onion
1/2 cup sliced celery
6 lettuce leaves
2/3 cup olive oil
1 cup chicken broth
1/3 cup lemon juice
2 tablespoons sugar
1 1/2 teaspoons ground mustard
salt
pepper

In a medium saucepan, combine rice, seasoning packet and 1 3/4 cups chicken broth. Cover and cook for 30 minutes. Allow to cool. Combine cooled rice, green pepper, onion and celery. Cover bottom of serving plate with lettuce leaves. Spoon rice mixture over top. Or line individual serving plates with lettuce leaf. Top with about 2/3 cup of rice. In a small bowl, combine oil, chicken broth, lemon juice, sugar, ground mustard, salt and pepper. Whisk until blended. Drizzle dressing over rice. 6 servings.

Complete Menu

Cornflake Chicken
- Zucchini and Tomatoes, 100
- Wild Rice Salad, 258
- Onion Rings, 62

For easy fresh lemon juice, heat a lemon in the microwave in a glass bowl until the lemon bursts (about 1 minute). Immediately stop microwave and allow lemon to cool enough to handle. Juice can then be squeezed easily from the hole made by the escaping steam.

Dressings and Sauces

How delicious are homemade salad dressings and sauces! Store bought dressings, while convenient, can be much more expensive and not nearly as good as the dressings you can make at home, in just a few minutes and for a fraction of the cost.

Most salad dressings are very simple to make. There are several different ways to mix dressings and the methods can be interchangeable in many recipes. In all salad dressings, there are several ingredients to be incorporated. Following is a brief explanation of the different methods of mixing dressing:

1. Stir - the simplest method, usually mixing ingredients that mix together easily. Usually all ingredients are smooth, no lumps.

2. Whisk - necessary to mix together ingredients that require a bit of extra mixing to get them to blend thoroughly, such as oil.

3. Jar with a tight-fitting lid (add dressing ingredients and shake, shake, shake) - a different method to achieve the same results as using a whisk.

4. Blender - necessary to turn lumpy ingredients, such as chopped vegetables, into a smooth dressing. Also makes blending oil a breeze.

A great dressing can make the difference between a good salad and truly fabulous salad. An added bonus of great dressings is they can often be used for more than just a dressing for salad. For example, use dressing:

- as a spread for sandwiches or burgers instead of other condiments.
- as a dip for egg rolls or wonton.
- as a dip for fresh, raw vegetables. When serving a vegetable tray, offer 2 or 3 different choices of dips.
- as a dip for cooked or deep fried vegetables, such as **Deep Fried Zucchini** or **Fried Green Tomatoes**.
- as a dip for chicken strips or nuggets.

While many dressings taste great as soon as they are prepared, some taste better when served chilled. Others taste best after chilling for 24 hours or more. This is generally a matter of personal preference, although a few recipes will give you a recommendation.

All dressings should be stored in a covered container in the refrigerator. Most salad dressings and sauces do not freeze well, but if stored properly, will keep for several weeks. Prepare several kinds and serve a variety. After preparing and serving these dressings, you'll wonder why you ever settled for that other stuff!

Dressing and Sauce Recipes

continued...

Buttermilk Ranch Dressing

1/2 cup buttermilk
1 cup mayonnaise
1 teaspoon dried parsley flakes
1/2 teaspoon pepper
1/2 teaspoon Accent®
1/2 teaspoon salt
1/4 teaspoon garlic powder
1/4 teaspoon onion powder
pinch thyme

In a medium bowl, combine buttermilk and mayonnaise. Whisk until smooth. Add parsley flakes, pepper, Accent®, salt, garlic powder, onion powder and thyme. Whisk until smooth. Cover and refrigerate. Shake before serving. 1 1/2 cups.

Complete Menu

Ham and Noodles
- Asparagus Salad, 178
- Buttermilk Ranch Dressing, 263

Spread this dressing on your sandwich in place of mayonnaise. It also makes a great dip for just about anything, especially carrots sticks, chicken nuggets or deep fried zucchini.

Ranch Dressing

1/2 cup milk
1 tablespoon apple cider vinegar
1 cup mayonnaise
1 teaspoon garlic salt
1 teaspoon pepper
1 teaspoon sugar

In a medium bowl, combine milk and vinegar. Stir. Add mayonnaise and whisk until smooth. Add garlic salt, pepper and sugar. Whisk until smooth. Cover and refrigerate. Shake before serving. 1 1/2 cups.

Complete Menu

Bacon Meat Loaf
• Cheesy Bacon Potatoes, 72
• BLT Salad, 156
• Ranch Dressing, 264

A simpler version of the favorite and most used dressing! Especially useful when you don't have buttermilk on hand. Great as a dip for almost anything.

Buttermilk Dressing

1 cup buttermilk
1/4 cup salad dressing
1/4 cup sugar
1/4 cup apple cider vinegar

In a medium bowl, combine buttermilk and salad dressing. Whisk until smooth. Add sugar and vinegar. Whisk until smooth. Allow to rest for about 5 minutes to allow the sugar to dissolve. Whisk again. Cover and refrigerate. Shake before serving. 1 1/2 cups.

Complete Menu

Meatballs in Gravy
- Garlic Mashed Potatoes, 81
- Simple Spinach Salad, 191
- Buttermilk Dressing, 265
- Potato Bread, 357

Use dressing such as Miracle Whip® for the salad dressing.

Catalina Dressing

1/2 cup sugar
1/4 cup apple cider vinegar
1 teaspoon salt
dash paprika
1/4 teaspoon chili powder
1/4 teaspoon celery seed
1/4 teaspoon ground mustard
1 teaspoon onion
1/3 cup ketchup
1/2 cup canola oil

In a medium bowl, whisk together sugar and vinegar until sugar is dissolved. Stir in salt, paprika, chili powder, celery seed and ground mustard. Press onion through garlic press. Add to bowl. Stir in ketchup and oil. Whisk until smooth. Cover and refrigerate. Chill at least 30 minutes and shake before serving. 1 1/2 cups.

Complete Menu

Bacon Chicken
- Mashed Red Potatoes, 82
- Company Peas, 28
- Layered Salad, 208
- Catalina Dressing, 266

French Dressing

3/4 cup sugar
1 cup red wine vinegar
2 tablespoons onion
1 1/2 teaspoons salt
1 1/2 teaspoons ground mustard
1 (12-ounce) bottle chili sauce
1 cup canola oil

In a medium bowl, whisk together vinegar and sugar until sugar dissolves. Press onion through garlic press and add to bowl. Whisk in salt and mustard. Add chili sauce and mix well. Whisk in oil. Cover and refrigerate. Shake before serving. 4 cups.

Complete Menu

Tuna Broccoli Au Gratin
• Orange Cauliflower Salad, 201
• French Dressing, 267

Creamy French Dressing

1/3 cup red wine vinegar
1/2 cup packed brown sugar
1 (10.75-ounce) can tomato soup
1 cup olive oil
1 cup mayonnaise
1 teaspoon ground mustard
1 teaspoon garlic salt
1/2 teaspoon onion salt
1/2 teaspoon celery salt
1/4 teaspoon Worcestershire sauce
1/4 teaspoon paprika
dash cayenne pepper

In a medium bowl, combine vinegar and brown sugar. Whisk until sugar is dissolved. Add tomato soup, oil and mayonnaise. Whisk until smooth. Add ground mustard, garlic salt, onion salt, celery salt, Worcestershire sauce, paprika and cayenne pepper. Whisk until thoroughly mixed and very smooth. Cover and refrigerate. Shake before serving. 4 cups.

Complete Menu

Chicken and Ham Dinner
• Curly Red Salad, 159
• Creamy French Dressing, 268

Honey French Dressing

1/2 cup honey
1/2 cup red wine vinegar
1/2 cup chili sauce
1/2 cup olive oil
1/2 teaspoon onion
1/2 teaspoon celery seed

In a small bowl, combine honey, vinegar, chili sauce and oil. Whisk until well blended. Press onion through a garlic press. Add onion and celery seed. Mix well. Cover and refrigerate. Shake before serving. 2 cups.

Complete Menu

Onion Soup Meat Loaf
- Onion Roasted Potatoes, 78
- Red and Orange Salad, 163
- Honey French Dressing, 269

Great as a dip for chicken nuggets or wonton.

Honey Dressing

1/3 cup honey
1/3 cup apple cider vinegar
2 teaspoons lemon juice
1 teaspoon onion
2/3 cup sugar
1 teaspoon ground mustard
1 teaspoon celery seed
1/4 teaspoon salt
1 cup canola oil

In a small mixing bowl, combine honey, vinegar and lemon juice. Press onion through garlic press and add to bowl. Whisk in sugar, ground mustard, celery seed and salt. Add oil and whisk thoroughly. Cover and refrigerate. Shake before serving. Serve over lettuce or fruit. 2 cups.

Complete Menu

Chicken with Mushroom Gravy
- Italian Fettuccine, 139
- Crunchy Spinach Mushroom Salad, 192
- Honey Dressing, 270
- Cheddar Biscuits, 316

Sweet Honey Mustard Dressing

1 cup canola oil
1/2 cup sugar
1/4 cup apple cider vinegar
1/4 cup honey
2 tablespoons mustard
1 teaspoon onion powder
1 teaspoon salt
1 teaspoon celery seed
1 teaspoon paprika

In a saucepan, combine oil, sugar, vinegar, honey and mustard. Whisk in onion powder, salt, celery seed, and paprika. Cook and stir until well combined and sugar is dissolved. Remove from heat. Allow to cool. Cover and refrigerate. Shake before serving. 2 cups.

Complete Menu

California Dip Meat Loaf
- Monterey Potatoes, 75
- Garlic Green Beans, 53
- Orange Tossed Salad, 180
- Sweet Honey Mustard Dressing, 271

 Great as a dip for chicken or fresh vegetables.

Honey Lime Dressing

1/3 cup lime juice
1/2 teaspoon grated lime peel
1/3 cup honey
1/2 cup canola oil
1 teaspoon ground mustard
1/2 teaspoon salt
dash pepper

In a small bowl, combine lime juice, lime peel, honey and oil. Whisk until well blended. Add ground mustard, salt and pepper. Mix well. Cover and refrigerate. Shake before serving. 1 1/2 cups.

Complete Menu

Country Chicken and Vegetables
• Five Fruit Salad, 221
• Honey Lime Dressing, 272
• Easy Yeast Rolls, 359

To easily juice a lime, heat lime in the microwave in a glass bowl until the lime bursts (about 1 minute). Immediately stop microwave and allow lime to cool enough to handle. Juice can then be squeezed easily from the hole made by the escaping steam.

Roquefort Dressing

1/4 cup mayonnaise
1/4 cup salad dressing
1 cup sour cream
1 teaspoon apple cider vinegar
1 teaspoon lemon juice
1 teaspoon Worcestershire sauce
1/2 teaspoon salt
1 teaspoon onion
1 teaspoon minced garlic
1 (4-ounce) package crumbled Roquefort cheese
dash cayenne pepper

In a small bowl, whisk together mayonnaise, dressing, sour cream, vinegar, lemon juice, Worcestershire and salt. Press onion through garlic press. Stir in onion and garlic. Whisk all together. Stir in crumbled cheese. Add cayenne pepper. Cover and refrigerate. Stir before serving. 2 cups.

Complete Menu

Biscuit Beef Bake
- Tomatoes and Cucumbers, 102
- Club Salad, 153
- Roquefort Dressing, 273

Creamy Cheese Dressing

1/4 cup milk
1 1/2 tablespoons apple cider vinegar
1 1/2 cups mayonnaise
1 teaspoon sugar
1/4 teaspoon pepper
1 teaspoon minced garlic
1/4 cup shredded fresh Parmesan cheese
1/4 cup shredded fresh Romano cheese

In a small bowl, combine milk and vinegar. Add mayonnaise and sugar. Whisk until well blended. Allow to sit for about 5 minutes to allow sugar to dissolve. Add pepper. Press garlic through a garlic press. Add to bowl. Whisk until well combined. Add fresh Parmesan and fresh Romano cheeses. Mix well. Cover and refrigerate. Best served chilled. Stir before serving. 2 cups.

Complete Menu

Baked Chicken in Gravy
- Mushroom Pie, 61
- Tortellini Spinach Salad, 253
- Creamy Cheese Dressing, 274

Fresh cheese makes a huge difference in this dressing. Using the dry, previously grated cheese or cheese substitute that comes in a can makes a much different dressing.

Sweet and Sour Dressing

1 1/2 cups sugar
1 cup apple cider vinegar
1/2 teaspoon salt
1/2 teaspoon chili powder
1/2 teaspoon ground mustard
1/4 teaspoon crushed red pepper flakes
1 tablespoon onion
1/2 cup corn syrup
1 cup canola oil

In a small bowl, combine sugar and vinegar. Stir until sugar is dissolved. Add salt, chili powder, mustard and red pepper flakes. Mix well. Press onion through garlic press. Add to dressing. Add corn syrup and mix well. Whisk in oil until smooth and glossy. Cover and refrigerate. Shake before serving. 3 1/2 cups.

Complete Menu

Chicken and Mushrooms
- Potato Puff, 87
- Sweet and Sour Salad, 166
- Sweet and Sour Dressing, 275

This delicious dressing makes a great dip for wonton or egg rolls.

Parmesan Dressing

1/2 cup mayonnaise
1/2 cup shredded fresh Parmesan cheese
1 tablespoon onion
3 tablespoons cream
1 1/2 teaspoons dill weed
1 1/2 teaspoons lemon-pepper seasoning

In a small bowl, mix together mayonnaise and cheese. Press onion through garlic press and add to bowl. Mix in cream, dill and lemon pepper. Combine thoroughly. Cover and refrigerate. Stir before serving. 1 cup.

Complete Menu

Spaghetti and Meatballs
- Parmesan Pimento Salad, 164
- Parmesan Dressing, 276
- Toasted Garlic French Bread, 341

Green Goddess Dressing

1 cup salad dressing
1/2 cup sour cream
3 tablespoons finely minced green onion
3 tablespoons finely snipped fresh parsley
3 tablespoons minced anchovy filets
3 tablespoons white wine vinegar
1 tablespoon lemon juice
1/4 teaspoon salt
1/8 teaspoon pepper

Place salad dressing and sour cream in a blender. Add green onion, parsley, anchovies, vinegar, lemon juice, salt and pepper. Process for about 30 seconds or until smooth. Cover and refrigerate. Stir before serving. 2 cups.

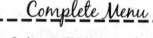

Complete Menu

Corkscrew Chicken
- Broccoli Tomato Salad, 210
- Green Goddess Dressing, 277
- Hawaiian Sweet Bread, 353

Great as a dip for fresh vegetables.

Use dressing such as Miracle Whip® for the salad dressing.

Garlic Tomato Dressing

2 tomatoes
1 cup mayonnaise
1 cup salad dressing
1 teaspoon apple cider vinegar
1 teaspoon minced garlic

Place tomatoes in boiling water for 30 seconds. Remove from water and place under cold running water and remove skin and core. Skin should slip off easily. Place tomatoes, mayon-naise, dressing, vinegar and garlic in blender. Blend on high until very smooth. Cover and refrigerate. Stir before serving. 3 cups.

Complete Menu

Chicken Enchiladas
- Mexican Salad, 168
- Garlic Tomato Dressing, 278

Press garlic through a garlic press for instantly and uniformly minced garlic. For an even easier method, buy a small bottle of minced garlic, usually found in the produce department at the grocery store.

Use dressing such as Miracle Whip® for the salad dressing.

Salsa Dressing

2 tablespoons red wine vinegar
2 tablespoons lime juice
2 tablespoons sugar
1/4 cup olive oil
1 1/2 cups chunky tomato salsa

In a medium bowl, combine vinegar, lime juice and sugar. Whisk until sugar is dissolved. Whisk in oil. Mix until well blended. Stir in salsa. Cover and refrigerate. Shake before serving. 2 cups.

Complete Menu

Taco Pie
• Chicken Fajitas Salad, 169
• Salsa Dressing, 279

 For quick fresh lime juice, place a lime in the microwave in a glass bowl. Heat until the lime bursts (about 1 minute). Immediately stop microwave and allow lime to cool enough to handle. Juice can then be squeezed easily from the hole made by the escaping steam.

Avocado Dressing

1 large avocado
1/2 cup sour cream
2 teaspoons lemon juice
1 tablespoon onion
1 tablespoon water
1/4 teaspoon salt
1/4 teaspoon cayenne pepper

Peel avocado and mash in a mixing bowl. Stir in sour cream and lemon juice. Press onion through garlic press. Stir into avocado mixture. Add water, salt and cayenne pepper. Mix well. Cover and refrigerate. Stir before serving. 1 1/2 cups.

Complete Menu

Mexican Lasagna
- Mexican Avocado Salad, 170
- Avocado Dressing, 280

To peel an avocado, using a sharp knife, cut avocado in half lengthwise, down to the seed. Gently twist and pull halves apart. Tap the seed with the edge of a knife and lift the seed out. Slide a spoon just under the thick skin to remove the avocado.

Guacamole Dressing

1 cup mashed avocado
2 tablespoon lemon juice
1 teaspoon minced garlic
2/3 cup olive oil
1 cup sour cream
1 tablespoon sugar
1 teaspoon chili powder
1/2 teaspoon salt
1/8 teaspoon pepper

In a blender, combine avocado, lemon juice, garlic, oil, sour cream, sugar, chili powder, salt and pepper. Process until smooth. Cover and refrigerate. Stir before serving. 2 cups.

Complete Menu

Tortilla Chicken
- Guacamole Salad, 173
- Guacamole Dressing, 281

Gazpacho Dressing

1/2 cup olive oil
1/4 cup apple cider vinegar
3 green onions, minced
3/4 cup diced tomato
1/4 cup diced green bell pepper
1 teaspoon minced garlic
3 tablespoons chopped cilantro
1 teaspoon salt
1/4 teaspoon cayenne pepper

In a jar with a tight fitting lid, combine olive oil and vinegar. Add green onion, tomato, bell pepper, garlic, cilantro, salt and cayenne pepper. Shake for about 1 minute or until well combined. Cover and refrigerate. Shake before serving. 2 cups.

Complete Menu

For a less chunky dressing, you may want to press the garlic through a garlic press and mince the green bell pepper.

For a smooth dressing, place all ingredients in a blender. Process for about 30 seconds or until smooth.

Chile Dressing

1 cup mayonnaise
1/4 cup sour cream
1 teaspoon sugar
1/4 teaspoon salt
1/8 teaspoon pepper
1 (4-ounce) can diced green chiles

Place mayonnaise and sour cream in a blender. Add sugar, salt and pepper. Process for about 15 seconds or until smooth. Add about 1/2 the can of green chiles. Process for about 15 seconds or until mostly smooth. Add remaining green chiles. Pulse the food processor several times to slightly blend the green chiles but leave most in chunks. Cover and refrigerate. Stir before serving. 2 cups.

Complete Menu

Chili Beef and Rice
- Piñata Salad, 171
- Chile Dressing, 283
- Nachos, 389

For a chunky dressing, combine mayonnaise, sour cream, sugar, salt and pepper in a bowl. Whisk until smooth and the sugar is dissolved. Add green chiles and mix well.

Italian Dressing

1 cup olive oil
1/4 cup white wine vinegar
1/4 cup lemon juice
2 teaspoons minced garlic
1 teaspoon salt
2 teaspoons sugar
1/2 teaspoon ground mustard
1/2 teaspoon paprika
1/2 teaspoon onion salt
1/2 teaspoon oregano

In a small bowl, combine oil, vinegar, lemon juice and garlic. Whisk until well blended. Add salt, sugar, ground mustard, paprika, onion salt and oregano seasoning. Whisk until smooth. Cover and refrigerate. Shake before serving. 1 1/2 cups.

Complete Menu

Spaghetti Sauce
- Tangy Linguini, 138
- Italian Broccoli Salad, 211
- Italian Dressing, 284
- Italian Twists, 347

Press garlic through a garlic press for instantly and uniformly minced garlic. For an even easier method, buy a small bottle of minced garlic, usually found in the produce department at the grocery store.

Simple Italian Dressing

1/2 cup red wine vinegar
2 tablespoons sugar
1 cup olive oil
1 teaspoon Italian seasoning
1 teaspoon garlic salt
1/8 teaspoon pepper

In a small bowl, combine vinegar and sugar. Stir until sugar is
dissolved. Add oil, Italian seasoning, garlic salt and pepper.
Whisk until well blended. Cover
and refrigerate. Shake before
serving. 1 1/2 cups.

Almost Ravioli
- Italian Salad, 167
- Simple Italian Dressing, 285
- French Loaves, 338

A great tasting, yet simpler version of the traditional Italian dressing.

Creamy Italian Dressing

3/4 cup sour cream
1/3 cup mayonnaise
1/4 cup milk
1 (.7-ounce) envelope Italian dressing mix
2 tablespoons sugar
1/8 teaspoon salt

In a small bowl, combine sour cream, mayonnaise and milk. Mix well. Stir in Italian dressing mix, sugar and salt. Stir until well combined. Chill to blend flavors. Cover and refrigerate. Stir before serving. 1 1/4 cups.

Complete Menu

Chicken Stuffed Manicotti
• Red, White and Green Salad, 152
• Creamy Italian Dressing, 286

Sweet Dijon Salad Dressing

1/4 cup apple cider vinegar
1/4 cup sugar
1/4 cup Dijon mustard
1/4 cup olive oil

In a small bowl, whisk together vinegar and sugar. Mix until sugar is dissolved. Add mustard and oil. Whisk until blended. Cover and refrigerate. Shake before serving. 1 cup.

Complete Menu

Cheesy Meat Loaf
- Saucy Vegetables, 21
- Bacon Cauliflower Salad, 176
- Sweet Dijon Salad Dressing, 287

Russian Dressing

2/3 cup sugar
1/4 cup red wine vinegar
1/3 cup ketchup
1 cup canola oil
1 teaspoon Worcestershire sauce
1/2 teaspoon celery salt
1/8 teaspoon celery seed
1 tablespoon chopped onion
1/8 teaspoon pepper
salt

Combine sugar and vinegar. Mix until sugar is dissolved. Place in blender. Add ketchup, oil, Worcestershire sauce, celery salt, celery seed, onion and pepper. Process until smooth. Add salt to taste. Cover and refrigerate. Shake before serving. 2 1/2 cups.

Complete Menu

Mayonnaise Chicken
- Spinach Bean Sprout Salad, 196
- Russian Dressing, 288
- Sour Cream Croissants, 371

Poppy Seed Dressing

1/2 cup apple cider vinegar
1/2 cup sugar
1 teaspoon poppy seeds
1 teaspoon onion salt
1/2 teaspoon ground mustard
1 teaspoon salt
1 cup canola oil

In a small bowl, combine vinegar and sugar. Whisk until smooth and sugar is dissolved. Add poppy seeds, onion salt, ground mustard and salt. Mix well. Add oil. Whisk until smooth and glossy. Cover and refrigerate. Shake before serving. 2 cups.

Complete Menu

Chicken a'la King
• Puff Bowls, 367
• Dried Cherry Salad, 185
• Poppy Seed Dressing, 289

 Best if prepared at least 24 hours before serving.

Celery Seed Dressing

1/4 cup sugar
1/3 cup corn syrup
1 teaspoon ground mustard
1 teaspoon salt
1/3 cup apple cider vinegar
1 cup canola oil
1 tablespoon onion
1 1/2 teaspoons celery seed
dash pepper

Combine sugar, corn syrup, ground mustard and salt. Stir in vinegar. Mix until sugar is dissolved. Whisk in oil. Press onion through garlic press. Stir onion, celery seed and pepper into dressing. Cover and refrigerate. Shake before serving. 2 cups.

Complete Menu

Cranberry Chicken
- Dried Cranberry Salad, 189
- Celery Seed Dressing, 290
- Honey Cranberry Muffins, 328

 Best if prepared at least 24 hours before serving.

Thousand Island Dressing

1 cup mayonnaise
1/4 cup ketchup
2 tablespoons apple cider vinegar
4 teaspoons sugar
4 teaspoons sweet pickle relish
2 teaspoons onion
1/4 teaspoon salt
dash of pepper

In a small bowl, whisk together mayonnaise, ketchup, vinegar, sugar and relish. Press onion through a garlic press. Add to bowl. Add salt and pepper. Mix well. Cover and refrigerate. Best served chilled. Stir before serving. 1 1/2 cups.

Complete Menu

Simply Lasagna
- Green Salad, 151
- Thousand Island Dressing, 291
- Buttery French Bread, 339

 Great as a spread for sandwiches. Especially good on burgers.

Simple Thousand Island Dressing

2 cups mayonnaise
1/2 cup ketchup
1/2 cup sweet pickle relish
2 tablespoons sugar

In a small bowl, combine mayonnaise and ketchup. Whisk until smooth and well mixed. Add pickle relish and sugar. Mix well. Wait about 5 minutes to allow the sugar to completely dissolve. Mix again. Best served chilled. Cover and refrigerate. Stir before serving. 3 cups.

Complete Menu

Swiss Ham and Noodles
- Swiss Spinach Salad, 194
- Simple Thousand Island Dressing, 292
- Cherry Freeze, 234

 A simpler version of the traditional Thousand Island dressing. Great on sandwiches and burgers.

Onion Dressing

3/4 cup apple cider vinegar
1 cup sugar
1/2 cup ketchup
1/8 teaspoon mustard
1/2 teaspoon salt
1/8 teaspoon pepper
2 teaspoons Worcestershire sauce
1/2 cup chopped onion
1 cup canola oil

Combine vinegar and sugar. Stir until sugar is dissolved. Place in blender. Add ketchup, mustard, salt, pepper, Worcestershire sauce, onion and oil. Process for about 30 seconds or until smooth. Cover and refrigerate. Shake before serving. 3 1/2 cups.

Complete Menu

French Onion Soup
• Strawberry Spinach Salad, 199
• Onion Dressing, 293
• Stuffed Crescent Rolls, 373

Try using a sweet onion, such as Walla Walla or Vidalia, for the 1/2 cup onion.

Ginger Dressing

1/4 cup minced onion
1/2 cup peanut oil
1/3 cup rice vinegar
2 tablespoon water
2 tablespoons minced ginger
1/2 teaspoon minced garlic
2 tablespoons minced celery
1 1/2 tablespoons soy sauce
1 tablespoon sugar
2 tablespoons ketchup
1 teaspoon lemon juice
1/2 teaspoon salt
1/4 teaspoon pepper

In a blender, combine onion, oil, vinegar and water. Add ginger, garlic, celery, soy sauce, sugar, ketchup, lemon juice, salt and pepper. Process for about 1 minute or until smooth. Cover and refrigerate. Shake before serving. 1 3/4 cups dressing.

Complete Menu

Meatball Spaghetti
- Fresh Pear Salad, 186
- Ginger Dressing, 294
- Cheese-Onion Bread Sticks, 349

For simple minced ginger, purchase a bottle of minced ginger. It is usually found in the produce section of the grocery store, near the fresh ginger.

Brown Sugar Dressing

1 cup packed brown sugar
2/3 cup white vinegar
2/3 cup ketchup
2 tablespoons Worcestershire sauce
1 cup canola oil
1/2 teaspoon salt
1/8 teaspoon pepper

In a medium bowl, combine brown sugar and vinegar. Stir until sugar is dissolved. Stir in ketchup, Worcestershire sauce and oil. Whisk until smooth and well blended. Add salt and pepper. Mix well. Cover and refrigerate. Shake before serving. 3 cups.

Complete Menu

Italian Shells
- Bacon Spinach Salad, 193
- Brown Sugar Dressing, 295
- Three Cheese Bread, 356

 A sweet dressing that doubles as a dip for vegetables or chicken.

Caesar Salad Dressing

1 cup mayonnaise
1/4 cup egg substitute
1/4 cup shredded fresh Parmesan cheese
2 tablespoons olive oil
2 tablespoons water
1 teaspoon lemon juice
2 teaspoons minced garlic
1 tablespoon sugar
1 tablespoon minced anchovy filets
1/2 teaspoon pepper
1/4 teaspoon salt
1/4 teaspoon dried parsley flakes

In a blender, combine mayonnaise and egg substitute. Add fresh Parmesan, oil, water, lemon juice, garlic, sugar, anchovies, pepper, salt and parsley. Process for about 1 minute or until smooth. Cover and refrigerate. Stir before serving. 2 cups.

Complete Menu

Italian Roast
- Corkscrew Broccoli, 137
- Caesar Salad, 155
- Caesar Salad Dressing, 296

Press garlic through a garlic press for instantly and uniformly minced garlic. For an even easier method, buy a small bottle of minced garlic, usually found in the produce department at the grocery store.

Simple Caesar Salad Dressing

1/3 cup mayonnaise
1/3 cup apple cider vinegar
1 teaspoon lemon juice
2 teaspoons sugar
1/4 cup shredded fresh Parmesan cheese
2 1/2 tablespoons Dijon mustard
1 teaspoon garlic powder
1/8 teaspoon pepper

Whisk together mayonnaise, vinegar, lemon juice and sugar. Allow to rest for about 5 minutes to allow sugar to dissolve. Stir in Parmesan cheese, mustard, garlic powder and pepper. Cover and refrigerate. Stir before serving. 1 cup.

Complete Menu

Cheesy Lasagna
- Elegant Salad, 154
- Simple Caesar Salad Dressing, 297
- Vegetable Cheese Texas Toast, 342

A great substitute for the real thing. Especially useful if you don't want to buy the anchovies that traditional Caesar Dressing calls for. Try substituting different mustards, such spicy brown or honey mustard.

Bleu Cheese Dressing

1 cup mayonnaise
1/4 cup buttermilk
2 tablespoons crumbled bleu cheese
1/8 teaspoon pepper
1/8 teaspoon onion powder
1/8 teaspoon garlic powder

Combine mayonnaise, butter-milk, cheese, pepper, onion powder and garlic powder in a small bowl. Mix well by hand, until mostly smooth. Chill at least 30 minutes before serving. Cover and refrigerate. Stir before serving. 1 1/2 cups.

Complete Menu

Lasagna
- Bleu Cheese Salad, 157
- Bleu Cheese Dressing, 298
- Bread Sticks, 348

For a cheesier dressing, whisk dressing until smooth. Add an additional 1 tablespoon (or more) of crumbled bleu cheese and mix briefly to leave small lumps.

Chinese Salad Dressing

1/2 cup mayonnaise
5 tablespoons rice vinegar
2 tablespoons sesame oil
2 tablespoons sugar
1 tablespoon soy sauce
1/4 teaspoon garlic powder

In a medium bowl, combine mayonnaise, vinegar, oil and sugar. Whisk until smooth and sugar is dissolved. Add soy sauce and garlic powder. Mix well. Best served chilled. Cover and refrigerate. Shake before serving. 1 cup.

Complete Menu

Tuna Chow Mein
- Oriental Salad, 175
- Chinese Salad Dressing, 299

Mandarin Dressing

1/4 cup chopped onion
1/2 cup peanut oil
1/3 cup rice vinegar
3 tablespoons Mandarin *orange juice* (see note below)
2 tablespoons chopped celery
2 tablespoons minced ginger
1/2 teaspoon minced garlic
1 1/2 tablespoons soy sauce
2 tablespoons ketchup
2 tablespoons sugar
1/2 teaspoon salt
1/8 teaspoon pepper

In a blender, combine onion, oil and vinegar. Add *orange juice*, celery, ginger, garlic, soy sauce, ketchup, sugar, salt and pepper. Process for about 45 seconds or until smooth. Cover and refrigerate. Shake before serving. 1 1/2 cups.

Complete Menu

Hawaiian Chicken
- Confetti Fried Rice, 112
- Mandarin Salad, 174
- Mandarin Dressing, 300

Use the *orange juice* from a can of Mandarin oranges. Save the orange segments for a salad such as Mandarin Salad. The *orange juice* is not actual orange juice but rather the light syrup that the oranges have been packed in. The flavor is much milder than orange juice. Using true orange juice will change the taste of the dressing. For more orange flavor, try adding a few orange segments.

Raspberry Dressing

1/2 cup raspberry jam
1/4 cup white wine vinegar
1/3 cup olive oil
1 teaspoon lemon pepper
1 1/2 teaspoon seasoned salt

In a small bowl, combine jam, vinegar and oil. Whisk until smooth. Stir in lemon pepper and seasoned salt. Mix until well blended. Cover and refrigerate. Shake before serving. 1 cup.

Complete Menu

Cheesy Chicken and Rice
- Baked Broccoli, 36
- Raspberry Avocado Salad, 214
- Raspberry Dressing, 301

For **Strawberry Dressing**, substitute strawberry jam for the raspberry jam.

Complete Menu

Continental Chicken
- Asparagus Linguine, 140
- Strawberry, Kiwi, Spinach Salad, 202
- Strawberry Dressing, 301

Cranberry Sauce

1 (12-ounce) bag fresh cranberries
1 ripe pear
1 tart apple (Granny Smith or Jonathan)
1 orange
1 cup sugar

Wash and sort cranberries. Remove any cranberries that are soft or do not bounce. Peel and chop the pear and apple. Peel the orange. Remove most of the skin and

Complete Menu

Turkey Dressing Pie
- Orange Candied Sweet Potatoes, 95
- Cranberry Sauce, 302

any seeds from each orange segment. Combine fruit and sugar in saucepan. Stir and bring to a boil. Reduce heat and simmer for 10 to 15 minutes or until thick. Cover and refrigerate. 12 servings.

To Freeze: Allow to cool and place in freezer container. Label and freeze.

To Serve: Thaw. Stir and serve.

 Cranberry Sauce may be used in any recipe that calls for canned cranberry sauce. Delicious!

Red Sauce

2 teaspoons minced garlic
1 tablespoon peanut oil
2 tablespoons soy sauce
2 tablespoons honey
2 tablespoons red wine vinegar
2 tablespoons tomato paste
2 teaspoons chili sauce
1 teaspoon cornstarch
1 tablespoon water

Stir-fry garlic in oil for about 1 minute. Stir in soy sauce, honey, vinegar, tomato paste and chili sauce. Combine water and cornstarch to make a paste. Stir into sauce mixture. Bring to a boil and cook for about 1 minute. Cover and refrigerate. 1/2 cup.

Complete Menu

Hawaiian Meatballs
- Rice Ring, 110
- Crispy Wonton, 382
- Red Sauce, 303

Press garlic through a garlic press for instantly and uniformly minced garlic. For an even easier method, buy a small bottle of minced garlic, usually found in the produce department at the grocery store.

Honey Butter

1 cup softened butter
1/4 cup honey

In small mixing bowl, beat butter until fluffy. Add honey and beat until completely mixed and smooth. Cover and refrigerate. 1 1/4 cups.

Complete Menu

Cabbage Patch Stew
- Corn Muffins, 330
- Honey Butter, 304

Marmalade Dipping Sauce

1/2 cup orange marmalade
2 tablespoons chili sauce
1 tablespoon apple cider vinegar
1/2 teaspoon ground mustard

In a small bowl, combine marmalade, chili sauce, vinegar and ground mustard. Mix well. Cover and refrigerate. 1/2 cup.

Complete Menu

Sweet and Sour Meatballs
- New Year Fried Rice, 113
- Coconut Shrimp, 387
- Marmalade Dipping Sauce, 305

Cocktail Sauce

3/4 cup ketchup
2 tablespoons tomato paste
1 tablespoon prepared horseradish
1/4 cup lemon juice
1 tablespoon sugar
dash cayenne pepper

In a small bowl, combine ketchup, tomato paste, horseradish and lemon juice. Stir well. Add cayenne pepper to taste. Cover and refrigerate. 1 cup.

Complete Menu

Mock Filet Mignon
- Garden Stuffed Baked Potatoes, 91
- Tomato Wedges, 101
- Batter Fried Shrimp, 388
- Cocktail Sauce, 306

Bread

What an amazing array of bread choices spring from different amounts and combinations of the same few ingredients! Bread makes a perfect accompaniment to almost any meal, from the simplest bowl of soup to an elegant multiple course dinner.

Mixing dough

Mixing biscuit and muffin dough is a simple process. Follow the recipe instructions for perfect results every time. Care should be taken to not overmix muffin batter, since overmixing can cause the muffins to be heavy and flat. Mix muffin batter briefly, just barely long enough to moisten most of the dry ingredients. Resist the desire to mix thoroughly.

There are several different methods of mixing and kneading yeast dough. Each yields beautiful bread, although some methods are significantly easier than others.

The traditional way of mixing bread dough is by hand with a wooden spoon. This method is effective but time consuming and labor intensive. Combine the dissolved yeast and about half of the dry ingredients and mix thoroughly. Continue adding flour, 1/2 cup at a time, until the dough becomes smooth and starts to pull away from the sides of the bowl. The dough should be a bit sticky.

Knead the dough on a floured board. If the dough is too wet, add one tablespoon of flour at a time, until the dough is smooth and elastic. This will take about 8 to 10 minutes.

One of the most common problems with homemade bread is that it turns out too dry. This is from adding too much flour. The amount of flour needed will depend on the flour. There are many factors that will affect how much liquid the flour will absorb. Factors that include, when and where the wheat was grown, the protein content and even the weather! There is no way to know for sure how much flour a recipe will require, so add the flour in small amounts. It is better to have a wetter, stickier dough than a dry, stiff dough.

Another common problem is heavy, dense bread. This is caused by insufficient kneading. If kneading bread by hand, it will take about 8 to 10 minutes to knead the bread properly. Set a timer if it will help you knead the dough for an adequate amount of time. *See the Kneading Test explained on page 309.*

Another option is to use a stand mixer. Use the flat paddle attachment to combine the wet ingredients and half of the dry ingredients. Switch to the dough hook for the remainder of the mixing. Add the remaining flour, 1/2 cup at a time, and mix thoroughly. Don't exceed speed 2 when kneading dough with the mixer. Run the mixer on low for about 5 minutes or until the dough is smooth and elastic. If the dough is too wet, add one tablespoon of flour at a time until the dough becomes smooth and elastic. It should pull into a ball and be slightly sticky. Turn the dough out onto a floured board and finish kneading with your hands until the dough passes the Kneading Test. *See the Kneading Test explained on page 309.*

A food processor can be used to mix bread dough if you use a plastic, smooth sided blade and not the chopping blade. Dissolve the yeast in the food processor bowl and then add half of the dry ingredients. Pulse the food processor a few times. Continue to add the remainder of the dry ingredients, 1/2 cup at a time, pulsing to combine after each addition. Then turn on the food processor and let it run for about 45 seconds until a ball forms on the side of the blade. The dough should still be a bit sticky. Turn the dough out onto a floured board and finish kneading with your hands until the dough passes the Kneading Test explained below.

Kneading Test

Stop kneading and pinch off a small piece of dough. Using both hands, slowly stretch the dough for an inch or two. The dough should stretch into a very thin "window" in the center of the stretched area.

• Stop kneading if the dough "window" stretches without breaking.

• Knead for about 1 minute more if the "window" tears.

• Continue kneading if the dough does not stretch easily and tears immediately.

After the dough has been kneaded, allow it to rise in a warm place. A recipe may give instructions for a specific length of rising time, but it is important to recognize that many factors will influence the actual time required for a yeast bread dough to rise adequately. The amount of kneading, the temperature of the room, the freshness of the yeast, even barometric pressure can all influence the amount of rising time. Recipes made from whole grains or that contain add-ins such as cheese, nuts and raisins can also take longer to rise. Be patient and be sure to allow the dough to rise properly.

Freezing Bread Dough

Almost any bread dough can be successfully frozen. If you are freezing a yeast bread dough, be sure to use the freshest yeast possible. Yeast is a living organism and has a limited shelf life. Be sure to check the date on your yeast to be sure you are using fresh yeast that will rise.

After the dough has risen for the first time, punch down the dough with your hand. If you are freezing a loaf of yeast bread, wrap the dough in plastic, place it in a freezer bag and immediately place it in the freezer. Do not allow yeast bread to rise the second time. Do not freeze raised bread dough. Once the bread thaws it will collapse and will not rise again unless the dough is kneaded again.

To freeze rolls, allow the dough to rise the first time and punch down. Wrap the dough and freeze immediately or form the dough into desired shapes. Place the shaped dough in a single layer on a cookie sheet. Cover with plastic and immediately place in the freezer. Do not allow rolls to start rising. After the shaped dough is frozen, transfer rolls to a freezer bag and return to the freezer.

When freezing a non-yeast dough such as biscuits, place the cut dough in a single layer on a cookie sheet. Cover with plastic and place the pan in the freezer until the dough is frozen. Then transfer the frozen biscuits to a freezer bag. It is so easy and convenient to bake any number of biscuits on the day you desire to serve them.

Do not freeze muffin batter. The muffins will be flat and dense. Freeze fresh baked muffins instead.

Thawing Bread Dough
For best results, dough should be thawed before baking. To thaw bread dough that will be shaped into rolls, remove the dough from the freezer but leave it wrapped while it thaws. When the dough is completely thawed, form the dough into the desired shapes. Cover loosely and allow to rise. Bake according to the recipe directions.

To thaw previously shaped rolls, place the desired number of rolls onto a greased baking sheet. Cover loosely and allow to thaw and rise in a warm place. Bake according to the recipe directions.

To thaw a loaf of bread, remove the dough from its freezer packaging and place in a greased bread pan. Spray a piece of plastic wrap and place the wrap, greased side down, over the bread in the pan. Allow the bread to sit at room temperature or warmer until thawed. It will begin to rise as soon as it begins to thaw. Allow to rise and then bake according to the recipe instructions.

An alternate choice is to allow the bread to thaw and rise in the refrigerator for about 8 hours or overnight. The bread will rise as it thaws. Place the frozen dough in the refrigerator at night and in the morning it should be ready to bake!

Storing Baked Breads
If the bread is already baked and it will be used within a day or two, wrap the bread airtight and store at room temperature. Do not store bread in the refrigerator. Refrigerated bread will become stale more rapidly. However, if the bread contains perishable ingredients, such as cheese, it should be stored in the refrigerator. If bread will not be used right away, freeze it as soon as possible.

Freezing Baked Breads
Freezing already baked bread allows you the convenience of warming one or any number of baked goods, without any preparation. All the mixing, kneading, rising and baking is already done! Just pull one or more from the freezer and in a few minutes it will be thawed and ready to eat. A few seconds in the microwave is all it takes to enjoy warm bread. Bread is best consumed on the day it was baked. However, a great deal of its freshness can be retained if it is frozen as

soon as it is baked. Wrap loaves in plastic and place in a freezer bag or wrap again in extra heavy foil. If you slice the bread before freezing, you can enjoy one piece at a time or the entire loaf. You can toast slices straight from the freezer. Wrap individual rolls, muffins and biscuits in plastic or place each in a plastic sandwich bag. Place multiples of wrapped baked goods together in a larger freezer bag.

Thawing Baked Bread
Baked breads will thaw rapidly after they are removed from the freezer. The length of time required to thaw the bread will depend on the size and shape of the bread.

If you desire warm bread or rolls, allow them to thaw and then wrap them in foil and heat for a few minutes in the oven. Rolls can be warmed in the microwave but care should be taken that they are not in the microwave for more than a few seconds. Overheating in the microwave will cause the bread to become tough and undesirable.

To thaw bread or rolls in the oven, wrap them tightly with foil. Allow them to thaw in the oven at 300° for about 20 to 35 minutes, depending on how large the quantity. Open the foil for the last 5 to 10 minutes to allow the crust to get slightly crisp. Give them a light coating of butter or frosting when appropriate and enjoy!

No matter which method you choose, enjoying bread with your meals is always a satisfying choice. Whether you bake and serve your bread on the same day, prepare and freeze the dough to be baked and served on another day, or freeze baked breads to be warmed and enjoyed with no fuss, the delicious comfort of bread is hard to top.

Bread Recipes

continued...

Cheese Biscuits

1 2/3 cups flour
2 teaspoons baking powder
1/4 teaspoon baking soda
1/2 teaspoon salt
1/4 cup shortening
1 1/2 cups shredded Cheddar cheese, divided
3/4 cup buttermilk

In a mixing bowl, combine flour, baking powder, baking soda and salt. Cut in shortening with fork or pastry cutter until crumbly. Add 1 cup of the cheese. Stir in buttermilk and stir just until moistened. Turn out dough onto a floured cloth. Knead until dough is soft and easy to handle. Roll dough into a 12 inch circle. Cut into 8 wedges. Sprinkle with remaining cheese. Starting at the wide end, roll up each wedge. Place biscuits on lightly greased baking sheet. Bake at 400° for 12 to 14 minutes or until golden brown. Serve warm. 8 biscuits.

Complete Menu

Salisbury Steak and Gravy
• Duchess Potatoes, 84
• Honey Mustard Peas, 29
• Cheese Biscuits, 315

To Freeze Baked Biscuits: While still warm, place each biscuit in sandwich bag. Press out air and seal. Allow to cool to room temperature. Place bagged biscuits in gallon freezer bag. Label and freeze.

To Serve: Thaw and serve. To serve warm, heat briefly in microwave, or wrap in foil and heat in oven.

To Freeze Unbaked Biscuits: Arrange unbaked biscuits close together in a single layer on a baking sheet. Place in freezer just until frozen. Transfer frozen biscuits to freezer bag. Label and freeze.

To Serve: Thaw. Bake at 400° for 12 to 14 minutes.

Cheddar Biscuits

2 1/2 cups biscuit/baking mix
1 cup shredded Cheddar cheese
3/4 cup milk
2 tablespoons melted butter
1/4 teaspoon garlic salt
4 tablespoons butter
1/2 teaspoon garlic salt
1/2 teaspoon dried parsley flakes

In a mixing bowl, combine biscuit/baking mix, cheese, milk, 2 tablespoons melted butter and 1/4 teaspoon garlic salt. Mix until well combined. Drop by heaping tablespoons on ungreased baking sheet. In a small bowl, combine remaining butter, garlic salt and the parsley flakes. Brush over the tops of unbaked biscuits. Bake at 400° for 14 to 16 minutes or until biscuits begin to brown. Serve warm. 12 biscuits.

Complete Menu

Chicken with Mushroom Gravy
- Italian Fettuccine, 139
- Crunchy Spinach Mushroom Salad, 192
- Honey Dressing, 270
- Cheddar Biscuits, 316

To Freeze Baked Biscuits: While still warm, place each biscuit in sandwich bag. Press out air and seal. Allow to cool to room temperature. Place bagged biscuits in gallon freezer bag. Label and freeze.

To Serve: Thaw and serve. To serve warm, heat briefly in microwave, or wrap in foil and heat in oven.

To Freeze Unbaked Biscuits: Arrange unbaked biscuits close together in a single layer on a baking sheet. Place in freezer just until frozen. Transfer frozen biscuits to freezer bag. Label and freeze.

To Serve: Thaw. Bake at 400° for 14 to 16 minutes.

Chili Cheddar Biscuits

1 1/3 cups flour
1 tablespoon baking powder
1 teaspoon chili powder
2 teaspoons dried parsley flakes
1/4 teaspoon salt
1/2 cup cold butter
1/2 cup milk
1 egg, beaten
1 1/2 cups shredded Cheddar cheese

In a large bowl, combine flour, baking powder, chili powder, parsley flakes and salt. Cut in butter with a fork or a pastry cutter until mixture forms pea-sized crumbs. Stir in milk and egg just until moistened. Stir in cheese. Turn onto floured surface. Roll 1/2-inch thick. Cut with round biscuit cutter. Place 1-inch apart on ungreased baking sheet. Bake at 450° for 10 minutes, or until golden brown. 12 biscuits.

Complete Menu

Nacho Meat Loaf
- Monterey Rice, 114
- Honey Glazed Stir-Fry, 18
- Chili Cheddar Biscuits, 317

To Freeze Baked Biscuits: While still warm, place each biscuit in sandwich bag. Press out air and seal. Allow to cool to room temperature. Place bagged biscuits in gallon freezer bag. Label and freeze.

To Serve: Thaw and serve. To serve warm, heat briefly in microwave, or wrap in foil and heat in oven.

To Freeze Unbaked Biscuits: Arrange unbaked biscuits close together in a single layer on a baking sheet. Place in freezer just until frozen. Transfer frozen biscuits to freezer bag. Label and freeze.

To Serve: Thaw. Bake at 450° for 10 minutes.

Sour Cream and Chive Biscuits

2 cups flour
1 tablespoon baking powder
1/4 teaspoon baking soda
1/2 teaspoon salt
1/3 cup shortening
1/4 cup milk
3/4 cup sour cream
1/4 cup minced chives

In a mixing bowl, combine flour, baking powder, baking soda and salt. Cut in shortening with a fork or a pastry cutter until mixture resembles coarse crumbs. Stir in milk, sour cream and chives. Turn out onto a floured surface and knead 5 or 6 times. Roll out to 3/4-inch thickness. Cut with round biscuit cutter. Place on ungreased baking sheet. Bake at 350° for 12 to 14 minutes or until golden brown. 12 biscuits.

Complete Menu

Corned Beef and Cabbage
- German Potato Salad, 218
- Sour Cream and Chive Biscuits, 318

To Freeze Baked Biscuits: While still warm, place each biscuit in sandwich bag. Press out air and seal. Allow to cool to room temperature. Place bagged biscuits in gallon freezer bag. Label and freeze.

To Serve: Thaw and serve. To serve warm, heat briefly in microwave, or wrap in foil and heat in oven.

To Freeze Unbaked Biscuits: Arrange unbaked biscuits close together in a single layer on a baking sheet. Place in freezer just until frozen. Transfer frozen biscuits to freezer bag. Label and freeze.

To Serve: Thaw. Bake at 350° for 12 to 14 minutes.

Bacon Biscuit Balls

2/3 cup milk
2 cups biscuit/baking mix
1/4 teaspoon pepper
2 tablespoons onion soup mix
1 egg, beaten
1 cup shredded Monterey Jack cheese

In a mixing bowl, combine milk, biscuit/baking mix, pepper and onion soup mix. Mix well. Shape into small balls. Arrange, sides touching, on ungreased baking sheet. Brush balls with beaten egg. Bake at 450° for 8 minutes. Sprinkle cheese on top of balls and bake an additional 2 minutes. About 24 biscuit balls.

Complete Menu

Jack Soup
• Bacon Biscuit Balls, 319

To Freeze: Do not separate biscuits. While still warm, wrap all together, tightly in extra heavy foil. Label and freeze.

To Serve: Thaw and serve. To serve warm, heat in oven for about 15 minutes. Open foil and heat for about 5 minutes more.

Sweet Potato Biscuits

2 3/4 cups flour
4 teaspoons baking powder
1 teaspoon salt
1/2 teaspoon cinnamon
2 cups cooked, mashed sweet potato
3/4 cup sugar
1/2 cup melted butter
1 teaspoon vanilla

In a large mixing bowl, combine flour, baking powder, salt and cinnamon. In separate bowl, combine sweet potato, sugar, butter and vanilla. Add to flour mixture and mix well. Turn onto floured cloth and knead 4 or 5 times. Roll dough 1/2-inch thick. Cut with a floured 2 1/2-inch biscuit cutter. Bake on lightly greased baking sheet at 450° for 12 minutes. 18 biscuits.

Complete Menu

Chicken and Dressing
- Baked Sweet Potatoes, 93
- Broccoli with Mustard Sauce, 32
- Sweet Potato Biscuits, 320

To Freeze Baked Biscuits: While still warm, place each biscuit in sandwich bag. Press out air and seal. Allow to cool to room temperature. Place bagged biscuits in gallon freezer bag. Label and freeze.

To Serve: Thaw and serve. To serve warm, heat briefly in microwave, or wrap in foil and heat in oven.

To Freeze Unbaked Biscuits: Arrange unbaked biscuits close together in a single layer on a baking sheet. Place in freezer just until frozen. Transfer frozen biscuits to freezer bag. Label and freeze.

To Serve: Thaw. Bake at 450° for 12 minutes.

Pimento Cheese Biscuits

3/4 cup corn meal
2 cups flour
1 1/2 tablespoons baking powder
1 1/2 teaspoons salt
1/3 cup cold butter
3 tablespoons chopped pimento
3/4 cups milk
1/2 cup melted butter
1 cup shredded Cheddar cheese

In a mixing bowl, combine corn meal, flour, baking powder and salt. Cut in cold butter until mixture is pea-sized crumbs. Mix in pimento. Add milk and stir just until moistened. Turn onto floured board. Knead gently a few times. Roll 3/4-inch thick. Cut with floured biscuit cutter. Cut each biscuit in half. Dip one side of each biscuit in melted butter, then in shredded cheese. In greased, square baking dish, stand each biscuit on cut edge, flat sides touching. There should be cheese between each biscuit. Sprinkle remaining cheese over all. Bake at 400° for 20 to 25 minutes. Allow to stand in pan for 2 to 3 minutes. Turn out onto serving plate. Turn right side up and brush with melted butter. Also beautiful baked in ring shaped pan. 12 servings.

Complete Menu

> Vegetable Beef Soup
> • Pimento Cheese Biscuits, 321

To Freeze: Do not separate biscuits. While still warm, wrap all together, tightly in extra heavy foil. Label and freeze.

To Serve: Thaw and serve. To serve warm, heat in oven for about 15 minutes. Open foil and heat for about 5 minutes more.

Apple Cider Biscuits

2 cups flour
1 tablespoon baking powder
2 teaspoons sugar
1/2 teaspoon salt
1/3 cup cold butter
3/4 cup apple cider
1/8 teaspoon cinnamon

In a large bowl, combine flour, baking powder, sugar and salt. Cut in butter with a fork or a pastry cutter until mixture resembles coarse crumbs. Stir in apple cider just until moistened. Turn onto a lightly floured surface and knead 8 to 10 times. Roll out to 1/2-inch thickness. Cut with a 2 1/2-inch biscuit cutter. Place on ungreased baking sheets. Sprinkle with cinnamon. Bake at 425° for 12 to 14 minutes. 12 biscuits.

Complete Menu

Country Barbequed Ribs
- Potato Skins, 89
- Apple Salad, 226
- Apple Cider Biscuits, 322

To Freeze Baked Biscuits: While still warm, place each biscuit in sandwich bag. Press out air and seal. Allow to cool to room temperature. Place bagged biscuits in gallon freezer bag. Label and freeze.

To Serve: Thaw and serve. To serve warm, heat briefly in microwave, or wrap in foil and heat in oven.

To Freeze Unbaked Biscuits: Arrange unbaked biscuits close together in a single layer on a baking sheet. Place in freezer just until frozen. Transfer frozen biscuits to freezer bag. Label and freeze.

To Serve: Thaw. Bake at 425° for 12 to 14 minutes.

Blueberry Muffins

2 cups flour
3/4 cup sugar
1 tablespoon baking powder
1/2 teaspoon salt
1 cup milk
1 tablespoon white vinegar
1 egg
1/4 cup canola oil
1 cup fresh or frozen blueberries

In a large mixing bowl, combine flour, sugar, baking powder and salt. In separate bowl, combine milk and vinegar. Beat in egg and oil. Pour into flour mixture. Stir just until moistened. Gently stir in blueberries. Fill paper lined muffin cups 2/3 full. Bake at 400° for 22 to 24 minutes. 12 muffins.

Complete Menu

Swiss Steak and Gravy
- Home-Style Potatoes, 64
- Blueberry Salad, 183
- Blueberry Muffins, 323

To Freeze: While still warm, place each muffin in a sandwich bag. Press out air and seal. Allow to cool to room temperature. Place bagged muffins in a gallon freezer bag. Label and freeze.

To Serve: Thaw and serve. Heat briefly, if desired.

Apple Carrot Muffins

2 cups flour
1 1/4 cups sugar
2 teaspoons cinnamon
1/2 teaspoon salt
2 teaspoons baking soda
2 cups shredded carrots
1/2 cup sweetened flaked coconut
1/2 cup raisins
1 cup canola oil
3 eggs
1 apple, peeled and shredded
2 teaspoons vanilla

In a large bowl, combine flour, sugar, cinnamon, salt and baking soda. Stir in carrots, coconut and raisins. In a small bowl, combine oil, eggs, apple and vanilla. Stir into dry ingredients just until moistened. Spoon into paper lined muffin cups. Bake at 350° for 15 minutes. 8 muffins.

Complete Menu

Swedish Meatballs
- Pasta Ring, 129
- Fruit and Lettuce Salad, 181
- Apple Carrot Muffins, 324

To Freeze: While still warm, place each muffin in a sandwich bag. Press out air and seal. Allow to cool to room temperature. Place bagged muffins in a gallon freezer bag. Label and freeze.

To Serve: Thaw and serve. Heat briefly, if desired.

Orange Cream Cheese Muffins

1 (3-ounce) package cream cheese
1/4 cup sugar
1 egg
1/2 cup orange juice
1 3/4 cups biscuit/baking mix
2 tablespoons orange marmalade

In a mixing bowl, beat together cream cheese and sugar. Add egg and orange juice. Mix well. Stir in biscuit/baking mix just until moistened. Spoon heaping tablespoon of batter into each of 12 paper lined muffin cups. Spoon 1/2 teaspoon orange marmalade into center of each muffin. Divide remaining batter over marmalade. Bake at 400° for 14 to 18 minutes until golden brown. Cool in pan 5 minutes. 12 muffins.

Complete Menu

Turkey and Stuffing Roll-Ups
- Maple Glazed Sweet Potatoes, 94
- Cranberry Pineapple Salad, 250
- Orange Cream Cheese Muffins, 325

To Freeze: While still warm, place each muffin in a sandwich bag. Press out air and seal. Allow to cool to room temperature. Place bagged muffins in a gallon freezer bag. Label and freeze.

To Serve: Thaw and serve. Heat briefly, if desired.

Ham and Cheese Muffins

2 cups flour
3 teaspoons baking powder
1/2 teaspoon baking soda
1 teaspoon salt
1 cup milk
1/2 cup mayonnaise
1/2 cup chopped ham
1/2 cup shredded Cheddar cheese

In a large bowl, combine flour, baking powder, baking soda and salt. In separate bowl, combine milk and mayonnaise. Stir in ham and cheese. Pour into dry ingredients. Stir sparingly, just until moistened. Fill paper lined muffin cups 2/3 full. Bake 425° for 16 minutes. 12 muffins.

Complete Menu

Old Fashioned Bean Soup
• Ham and Cheese Muffins, 326

To Freeze: While still warm, place each muffin in a sandwich bag. Press out air and seal. Allow to cool to room temperature. Place bagged muffins in a gallon freezer bag. Label and freeze.

To Serve: Thaw and serve. Heat briefly, if desired.

Buttermilk Oatmeal Muffins

1 cup quick cooking oatmeal
1 cup buttermilk
1 egg
1/2 cup packed brown sugar
1/4 cup canola oil
1 cup flour
1 teaspoon baking powder
1/2 teaspoon baking soda
1/2 teaspoon salt

Combine oatmeal and buttermilk in a mixing bowl. Allow to sit for 10 minutes. Stir in egg, brown sugar and oil. Combine flour, baking powder, baking soda and salt. Stir into oatmeal mixture just until moistened. Fill paper lined muffin cups 3/4 full. Bake at 400° for 16 to 18 minutes. 12 muffins.

Complete Menu

Pork Chops, Carrots and Gravy
- Cream Cheese Mashed Potatoes, 85
- Frog Eye Salad, 230
- Buttermilk Oatmeal Muffins, 327

To Freeze: While still warm, place each muffin in a sandwich bag. Press out air and seal. Allow to cool to room temperature. Place bagged muffins in a gallon freezer bag. Label and freeze.

To Serve: Thaw and serve. Heat briefly, if desired.

Honey Cranberry Muffins

2 cups bran flakes
1/2 cup sweetened dried cranberries
1 cup milk
1/4 cup honey
1 egg
3 tablespoons canola oil
1 1/4 cups flour
1 tablespoon baking powder
1/4 teaspoon salt

In a large mixing bowl, combine cereal, cranberries, milk and honey. Allow to stand for about 2 minutes. Add egg and oil. Mix well. Stir in flour, baking powder and salt, stirring just until moistened. Fill paper lined muffin cups 2/3 full. Bake at 400° for 18 to 20 minutes. Allow to cool in pan 10 minutes. 18 muffins.

Complete Menu

Cranberry Chicken
- Dried Cranberry Salad, 189
- Celery Seed Dressing, 290
- Honey Cranberry Muffins, 328

To Freeze: While still warm, place each muffin in a sandwich bag. Press out air and seal. Allow to cool to room temperature. Place bagged muffins in a gallon freezer bag. Label and freeze.

To Serve: Thaw and serve. Heat briefly, if desired.

Onion Cheese Muffins

1 1/2 cups biscuit/baking mix
3/4 cup shredded Cheddar cheese, divided
1 egg
1/2 cup milk
1/4 cup minced onion
1 tablespoon butter or margarine

In a mixing bowl, combine biscuit/baking mix and 1/2 cup cheese. In a small bowl, beat together egg and milk. In small skillet, melt butter. Add minced onion. Cook until onion is tender but not brown. Add onion to egg and milk mixture. Stir into baking mix and cheese mixture. Fill paper lined muffin cups 3/4 full. Top with remaining cheese. Bake at 400° for 18 to 20 minutes. Cool in pan for 10 minutes. Serve warm. 12 muffins.

Complete Menu

Oven Stew
• Onion Cheese Muffins, 329

To Freeze: While still warm, place each muffin in a sandwich bag. Press out air and seal. Allow to cool to room temperature. Place bagged muffins in a gallon freezer bag. Label and freeze.

To Serve: Thaw and serve. Heat briefly, if desired.

Corn Muffins

2 cups corn meal
2 cups flour
1 cup instant powdered milk
1/4 cup sugar
2 tablespoons baking powder
1/2 teaspoon baking soda
2 eggs, lightly beaten
2 2/3 cups water
1/2 cup melted butter
1 tablespoon apple cider vinegar

In a mixing bowl, combine corn meal, flour, powdered milk, sugar, baking powder and baking soda. Mix well. Add eggs, water, melted butter and vinegar. Stir just until moistened. Fill paper lined muffin cups 2/3 full. Bake 425° for 13 to 15 minutes. 24 muffins.

Complete Menu

Cabbage Patch Stew
• Corn Muffins, 330
• Honey Butter, 304

To Freeze: While still warm, place each muffin in a sandwich bag. Press out air and seal. Allow to cool to room temperature. Place bagged muffins in a gallon freezer bag. Label and freeze.

To Serve: Thaw and heat briefly. Serve with **Honey Butter** (page 304).

Southern Corn Muffins

1 cup corn meal
1 cup flour
1/4 cup sugar
1 tablespoon baking powder
1/2 teaspoon salt
1/4 teaspoon cayenne pepper
2 eggs
1 cup milk
1/2 cup canola oil
1 cup corn (fresh, frozen or canned)

In a mixing bowl, combine corn meal, flour, sugar, baking powder, salt and cayenne pepper. In separate bowl, combine eggs, milk, oil and corn. Pour into dry ingredients. Mix just until moistened. Spoon batter into paper lined muffin cups. Bake at 400° for 15 to 20 minutes. Cool 5 minutes in pan. 12 muffins.

Complete Menu

Honey Barbequed Ribs
- Potato Pancakes, 76
- Fresh Fruit Salad, 225
- Southern Corn Muffins, 331

To Freeze: While still warm, place each muffin in a sandwich bag. Press out air and seal. Allow to cool to room temperature. Place bagged muffins in a gallon freezer bag. Label and freeze.

To Serve: Thaw and serve. Heat briefly, if desired.

Calico Corn Muffins

1/4 cup butter
1/4 cup finely chopped red bell pepper
1/4 cup finely chopped green bell pepper
1/4 cup finely chopped yellow bell pepper
1 cup flour
1 cup corn meal
2 tablespoons sugar
1 tablespoon baking powder
3/4 teaspoon salt
1 cup milk
1/3 cup canola oil
2 eggs

Melt butter in small skillet. Cook peppers in hot butter for about 3 minutes, until tender. In a large bowl, combine flour, corn meal, sugar, baking powder and salt. In separate bowl, combine milk, oil and eggs. Add peppers and butter to milk. Pour all into flour mixture. Stir just until moistened. Spoon into paper lined muffin cups. Bake at 400° for 15 minutes. 12 muffins.

Complete Menu

Chili
• Calico Corn Muffins, 332

To Freeze: While still warm, place each muffin in a sandwich bag. Press out air and seal. Allow to cool to room temperature. Place bagged muffins in a gallon freezer bag. Label and freeze.

To Serve: Thaw and serve. Heat briefly, if desired.

Corn Bread

1 cup corn meal
1 cup flour
1/4 cup sugar
4 teaspoons baking powder
3/4 teaspoon salt
2 eggs
1 cup milk
1/4 cup shortening

In a mixing bowl, combine corn meal, flour, sugar, baking powder and salt. Add eggs, milk and shortening. Mix just until moistened. Pour into greased 9-inch square baking pan. Bake 425° for 20 to 25 minutes until golden brown. Or fill paper lined muffin cups 2/3 full. Bake 425° 15 to 20 minutes. 9 servings.

Complete Menu

Grandma's Beef Stew
• Corn Bread, 333

To Freeze: Remove corn bread from pan. While still warm, wrap loaf in extra heavy foil. For muffins, while still warm, place each muffin in a sandwich bag. Press out air and seal. Allow to cool to room temperature. Place bagged muffins in a gallon freezer bag. Label and freeze.

To Serve: Thaw and serve. Heat briefly, if desired.

Maple Corn Bread

1 1/4 cups flour
1/4 cup corn meal
1 1/2 teaspoons baking powder
1/2 teaspoon salt
1 egg
3/4 cup milk
1/2 cup maple syrup
3 tablespoons canola oil

In a bowl, combine flour, corn meal, baking powder and salt. In a separate bowl, beat egg, milk, syrup and oil. Stir into dry ingredients, just until moistened. Pour into a greased 9-inch square baking pan. Bake at 400° for 20 to 22 minutes. Cut into squares. Serve warm.
9 servings.

Complete Menu

Ham and Potato Scallop
• Maple Carrots, 39
• Maple Corn Bread, 334

To Freeze: Remove corn bread from pan. While still warm, wrap entire loaf in extra heavy foil. Or place individual pieces in sandwich bags and place all together in a freezer bag. Label and freeze.

To Serve: Thaw and serve. Heat briefly, if desired.

Corn Meal Bread

1 cup corn meal
1 cup flour
1 tablespoon baking powder
4 tablespoons sugar
1 teaspoon salt
1 (6-ounce) box instant vanilla pudding
1/3 cup softened butter
1 cup milk

In a mixing bowl, combine corn meal, flour, baking powder, sugar, salt and pudding mix. Mix well. Stir in softened butter until crumbly. Stir in milk just until moistened. Pour into a greased 9-inch square baking pan. Bake at 400° for 25 minutes. 9 servings.

Complete Menu

Slow Cooked Chili
• Zucchini Rounds, 99
• Corn Meal Bread, 335

To Freeze: Remove corn bread from pan. While still warm, wrap entire loaf in extra heavy foil. Or place individual pieces in sandwich bags and place all together in a freezer bag. Label and freeze.

To Serve: Thaw and serve. Heat briefly, if desired.

Sour Cream Corn Bread

1 cup corn meal
1 cup flour
2 tablespoons sugar
2 teaspoons baking powder
1/2 teaspoon salt
1 egg, slightly beaten
1 cup sour cream
1/3 cup milk
2 tablespoons melted butter
1 teaspoon minced dried onion

In a mixing bowl, combine corn meal, flour, sugar, baking powder and salt. Add egg, sour cream, milk, melted butter and dried onion. Mix just until moistened. Pour into greased 9-inch baking pan. Bake 400° for 20 to 25 minutes until golden brown. Or fill paper lined muffin cups 2/3 full and bake 400° for 15 to 20 minutes. 9 servings.

Complete Menu

Slow Cooked Stew
• Sour Cream Corn Bread, 336

To Freeze: Remove corn bread from pan. While still warm, wrap loaf in extra heavy foil. For muffins, while still warm, place each muffin in a sandwich bag. Press out air and seal. Allow to cool to room temperature. Place bagged muffins in a gallon freezer bag. Label and freeze.

To Serve: Thaw and serve. Heat briefly, if desired.

Corn Pudding

1 (7-ounce) box corn bread mix
1/3 cup melted butter
1 (15-ounce) can corn, drained
1 (15-ounce) can creamed corn
1 cup sour cream
1 (4-ounce) can diced green chiles

In a mixing bowl, combine corn bread mix and butter. Stir in corn and creamed corn. Add sour cream and diced green chiles. Mix well. Turn into greased baking dish. Bake at 350° for 1 hour. Spoon into center of individual servings of stew or chili. 8 servings.

Complete Menu

Southwest Stew
• Corn Pudding, 337

To Freeze: Mix as above and spoon into 8 paper lined cups of a muffin tin. Bake at 350° for 50 minutes. Allow to cool. Remove from pan and place in freezer bag. Label and freeze.

To Serve: Thaw. Heat briefly in microwave, just until hot. Unwrap and place in center of individual servings of stew or chili.

Corn Pudding is not really *pudding*, but rather a very moist corn bread.

French Loaves

2 tablespoons yeast
1/2 cup warm water
1 tablespoon salt
3 tablespoons sugar
5 tablespoons canola oil
2 cups water
6 cups flour, divided
1 egg white, beaten

Dissolve yeast in warm water. Allow to stand for 10 minutes. In a large bowl, combine salt, sugar, oil and water. Stir in 3 cups flour. Mix well. Stir in dissolved yeast. Stir in remaining 3 cups flour. Mix well and leave spoon in batter. Allow batter to rest for 10 minutes. Stir vigorously and allow to rest 10 minutes. Repeat vigorous stirring and resting 3 more times. Turn dough out onto floured board. Knead lightly. Divide dough in half. Roll each half into a 9 x 12-inch rectangle. Starting with long edge, roll dough loosely into a jelly roll shaped loaf. Seal edges. Place loaves, seam side down, on greased baking sheet. Make 3 diagonal slashes on top of each loaf. Brush with beaten egg white. Allow to rise for about 30 minutes. Bake at 400° for 35 minutes, or until golden brown. 2 loaves.

To Freeze Bread Dough: Wrap unraised, shaped loaves tightly in plastic. Place in a freezer bag. Label and freeze.

To Serve: Thaw, then rise and bake as directed.

To Freeze Baked Bread: Allow loaves to cool. Wrap each loaf tightly in extra heavy foil. Label and freeze.

To Serve: Thaw. Slice and serve. Heat briefly, if desired.

Complete Menu

Almost Ravioli
- Italian Salad, 167
- Simple Italian Dressing, 285
- French Loaves, 338

Buttery French Bread

1/2 cup softened butter
1/2 teaspoon dried parsley flakes
1/4 teaspoon celery seed
1/4 teaspoon paprika
1 loaf French bread

Combine butter, parsley, celery seed and paprika. Cut bread into thick slices. Butter both sides of each slice. Arrange slices back into loaf and spread more butter over the top of the loaf. Wrap in foil and bake at 375° for 15 minutes. Unwrap foil and bake 5 additional minutes. 8 servings.

Complete Menu

Simply Lasagna
- Green Salad, 151
- Thousand Island Dressing, 291
- Buttery French Bread, 339

To Freeze: Prepare bread as directed and wrap in extra heavy foil. Do not bake. Label and freeze.

To Serve: Thaw. Bake foil wrapped loaf at 375° for 15 minutes. Unwrap foil and bake 5 minutes.

Ranch Garlic Bread

1 cup softened butter
2 tablespoons Ranch dressing mix (from 1-ounce envelope)
2 teaspoons garlic powder
1 loaf French bread

In a small bowl, combine butter, dressing mix and garlic powder. Mix well. Cut bread in half lengthwise. Spread butter mixture over cut sides of the bread. Place on a baking sheet. Broil 4 inches from heat for 3 to 4 minutes or until golden brown. 8 servings.

Complete Menu

Bird's Nest Pie
- Italian Broccoli, 30
- Ranch Garlic Bread, 340

To Freeze: Prepare bread as directed. Put halves of bread back together to form a loaf. Wrap in extra heavy foil. Do not bake. Label and freeze.

To Serve: Thaw. Unwrap bread. Split bread halves. Place on baking sheet, cut sides up. Broil 4 inches from heat for 3 to 4 minutes until toasted.

Toasted Garlic French Bread

1 loaf French Bread
1/2 cup melted butter
1/4 cup shredded Parmesan cheese
2 teaspoons minced garlic
1/2 teaspoon oregano

Slice bread lengthwise. Place with cut sides up on large baking sheet. In a small bowl, combine butter, cheese, garlic and oregano. Brush onto cut sides of bread. Broil 4 inches from heat for 2 to 3 minutes or until lightly toasted. Cut crosswise into serving pieces. 8 servings.

Complete Menu

Spaghetti and Meatballs
- Parmesan Pimento Salad, 164
- Parmesan Dressing, 276
- Toasted Garlic French Bread, 341

To Freeze: Prepare bread as directed. Do not broil. Put halves of bread back together to form a loaf. Wrap loaf in extra heavy foil. Label and freeze.

To Serve: Thaw. Unwrap bread. Split bread halves. Place on baking sheet, cut sides up. Broil 4 inches from heat for 2 to 3 minutes until toasted.

Vegetable Cheese Texas Toast

1/2 cup shredded carrots
3 green onions, sliced
1/4 cup mayonnaise
1/2 teaspoon Italian seasoning
2 cups shredded Mozzarella cheese
8 slices Texas toast

In a mixing bowl, combine shredded carrots, onions and mayonnaise. Mix well. Stir in Italian seasoning and shredded cheese. Place bread slices in single layer on an ungreased baking sheet. Broil 2 minutes or until lightly browned. Turn bread slices over and divide cheese mixture among the 8 slices. Spread to cover. Bake at 350° until cheese is melted. 8 servings.

Complete Menu

Cheesy Lasagna
- Elegant Salad, 154
- Simple Caesar Salad Dressing, 297
- Vegetable Cheese Texas Toast, 342

To Freeze: While still warm, place each baked slice in a sandwich bag. Press out air and seal. Allow to cool to room temperature. Place bagged slices in a gallon freezer bag. Label and freeze.

To Serve: Thaw. Heat in oven or toaster oven.

Texas toast is a square loaf of thick sliced bread, usually found between regular sliced bread and specialty breads.

Cheesy Texas Toast

8 slices Texas Toast
4 tablespoons softened butter
1/2 teaspoon garlic salt
2 cups shredded Mozzarella cheese
2 tablespoons minced green onion

Spread butter on one side of each bread slice. Sprinkle with garlic salt. Sprinkle generously with Mozzarella cheese. Arrange on an ungreased baking sheet. Bake at 400° for about 5 minutes, until cheese is bubbly and barely begins to brown on edges. Sprinkle with green onions. 8 servings.

Complete Menu

Italian Meat Sauce
• Garlic Pasta, 135
• Lime Avocado Salad, 187
• Cheesy Texas Toast, 343

To Freeze: While still warm, place each baked slice in a sandwich bag. Press out air and seal. Allow to cool to room temperature. Place bagged slices in a gallon freezer bag. Label and freeze.

To Serve: Thaw. Heat in oven or toaster oven.

Texas toast is a square loaf of thick sliced bread, usually found between regular sliced bread and specialty breads.

Garlic Cheese Bread

1/2 cup butter
1 cup shredded Cheddar cheese
1/4 cup shredded fresh Parmesan cheese
1/2 teaspoon garlic salt
1/4 teaspoon Worcestershire sauce
12 slices Texas toast

Soften (do not melt) butter and mix with cheeses, garlic salt and Worcestershire sauce. Spread on one side of each of the slices of Texas toast. Arrange on baking sheet. Bake at 400° for 10 to 12 minutes or until cheese begins to brown and bubble. 12 servings.

Complete Menu

Pizza in a Dish
- Frozen Sour Cream Fruit Salad, 237
- Garlic Cheese Bread, 344

To Freeze Unbaked Slices: Cover each slice of Texas toast with spread. Freeze in single layer. When frozen, place each slice in sandwich bag. Place bagged slices gallon freezer bag.

To Serve: Thaw. Unwrap and bake as directed.

To Freeze Baked Slices: While still warm, place each baked slice in a sandwich bag. Press out air and seal. Allow to cool to room temperature. Place bagged slices in a gallon freezer bag. Label and freeze.

To Serve: Thaw. Heat in oven or toaster oven.

Vegetable Bread

2 cups milk
1 tablespoon yeast
1/4 cup warm water
2 tablespoons sugar
2 teaspoons salt
2 tablespoons softened butter
2 eggs, beaten
6 cups flour
1/4 cup finely shredded red cabbage
1/2 cup shredded carrots
1/4 cup minced onion
2 tablespoons minced celery
2 tablespoons minced green pepper
2 tablespoons chopped cucumber
1/2 teaspoon minced garlic

Scald milk by heating just to a boil. Remove from heat. In a small bowl, dissolve yeast in warm water. In a mixing bowl, combine scalded milk, sugar, salt and butter. Allow to cool. Stir in beaten eggs. Stir in yeast and flour. Beat until well combined. Stir in cabbage, carrots, onion, celery, green pepper, cucumber and garlic. Place dough in a greased bowl. Turn once to grease surface. Cover and let rise until double. Punch down, cover and allow to rise again until double. Punch down. Shape into 2 smooth loaves. Cover and allow to rest 10 minutes. Place into greased loaf pans. Cover and allow to rise until double. Bake at 375° for 35 minutes or until dough leaves the sides of the pan. Brush tops with butter. 2 loaves.

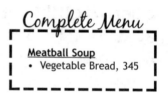

Complete Menu

Meatball Soup
• Vegetable Bread, 345

To Freeze: Prepare bread as directed and wrap in extra heavy foil. Label and freeze.

To Serve: Thaw. Slice and serve. Heat briefly, if desired.

Western Zucchini

3 cups sliced zucchini
1/4 cup chopped onion
4 eggs, beaten
1/2 cup canola oil
1 cup biscuit/baking mix
1 teaspoon salt
1/8 teaspoon pepper
1 cup shredded Cheddar cheese

Arrange zucchini and onion in a greased baking dish. In a bowl, combine eggs, oil, baking mix, salt and pepper. Mix well. Stir in shredded cheese. Pour over zucchini. Mix lightly. Bake uncovered at 350° for 25 minutes or until brown and bubbly. 8 servings.

Complete Menu

Skillet BBQ Chicken
- Crisp New Potatoes, 69
- Speedy Fruit Salad, 224
- Western Zucchini, 346

To Freeze: Cut in squares. Place each square in individual sandwich bags. Place single servings inside a large freezer bag. Or, freeze squares in a single layer. When frozen, transfer to a large freezer bag. Label and freeze.

To Serve: Thaw. Heat briefly, if desired.

---

 2 1/2 cups shredded zucchini may be substituted for the sliced zucchini.

Italian Twists

1 loaf frozen bread dough, thawed
1 cup canned Parmesan cheese
1 1/2 teaspoons Italian seasoning
1/2 cup melted butter
garlic salt

Cut dough into 8 sections. Cut each section into 4 pieces. (32 equal pieces). Mix Parmesan cheese and Italian seasoning in a shallow dish. Roll each piece of dough into a 4-inch rope. Dip into melted butter and then roll in cheese and seasoning mixture. Twist each rope 3 times and place on greased baking sheet. Sprinkle lightly with garlic salt. Bake at 450° for 7 or 8 minutes. 32 twists.

Complete Menu

Spaghetti Sauce
- Tangy Linguini, 138
- Italian Broccoli Salad, 211
- Italian Dressing, 284
- Italian Twists, 347

To Freeze: While still warm, place one or two twists in a sandwich bag. Press out air and seal. Allow to cool to room temperature. Place bagged twists in a gallon freezer bag. Label and freeze.

To Serve: Thaw and serve. Heat briefly, if desired.

Bread Sticks

1 1/4 cups flour
1 teaspoon salt
1 tablespoon sugar
1 1/2 teaspoons baking powder
1/2 cup milk
2 tablespoons melted butter

In a mixing bowl, combine flour, salt, sugar and baking powder. Stir in milk and beat 30 strokes. Add 1 tablespoon milk if mixture is too dry. Turn onto a floured cloth. Knead 10 times. Roll out into a rectangle and cut in half. Cut each half into 1-inch strips. Dip each strip in melted butter, twist and place on greased baking sheet. Bake at 375° for 15 to 20 minutes or until golden brown. 12 bread sticks.

To Freeze: While still warm, place each bread stick in a sandwich bag. Press out air and seal. Allow to cool to room temperature. Place bagged bread sticks in a gallon freezer bag. Label and freeze.

To Serve: Thaw and serve. Heat briefly, if desired.

Complete Menu

Lasagna
- Bleu Cheese Salad, 157
- Bleu Cheese Dressing, 298
- Bread Sticks, 348

Cheese-Onion Bread Sticks

1 tablespoon yeast
1/3 cup warm water
1 cup flour
1 tablespoon dried parsley flakes
1 tablespoon shortening
1 teaspoon sugar
3/4 teaspoon salt
1/8 teaspoon garlic powder
1 egg
1 tablespoon minced dried onion
1/4 cup shredded fresh Parmesan cheese
1 tablespoon butter, melted

In a mixing bowl, dissolve yeast in warm water. Add flour, parsley flakes, shortening, sugar, salt, garlic powder and egg. Beat with electric mixer on medium speed 30 seconds. Scrape bowl, beat on medium speed 2 more minutes. Stir in onion and cheese. With floured hands, pat dough evenly in greased 9 x 13-inch baking pan. Cut dough into 3 x 1-inch pieces. Let rise in warm place until almost double, about 20 minutes. Brush with melted butter. Bake at 450° for 12 to 15 minutes, until edges are brown. 3 dozen bread sticks.

Complete Menu

Meatball Spaghetti
- Fresh Pear Salad, 186
- Ginger Dressing, 294
- Cheese-Onion Bread Sticks, 349

To Freeze: Remove from pan and wrap warm bread sticks in extra heavy foil. Allow to cool. Label and freeze.

To Serve: Thaw. Place foil wrapped bread in 350° oven for 15 minutes or until warm. Open foil and bake 5 minutes. Serve warm.

Onion Cake

3 cups chopped onion
1/2 cup butter
1 1/2 teaspoons salt
1 1/2 teaspoons paprika
3/4 teaspoon pepper
4 cups flour
1/2 cup cornstarch
1 tablespoon sugar
1 tablespoon packed brown sugar
1 tablespoon baking powder
1 1/4 cups cold butter
1/4 cup melted butter
3/4 cup milk
5 eggs
3/4 cup sour cream

In large skillet, cook onions in butter over low heat for about 10 minutes. Stir in salt, paprika and pepper. Cook until golden, stirring constantly. Remove from heat and set aside. In a mixing bowl, combine flour, cornstarch, sugar, brown sugar and baking powder. Cut in cold butter until mixture forms pea-sized crumbs. In a separate bowl, whisk together the melted butter, milk, eggs and sour cream. Pour into dry ingredients and mix just until moistened. Spread in a greased 10-inch springform pan. Spoon onion mixture over batter. Place pan on a baking sheet. Bake at 350° for 35 minutes or until a toothpick inserted near the center comes out clean. Serve warm. 10 servings.

Complete Menu

Beef Noodle Onion Bake
- Celery Bacon Green Beans, 56
- Onion Cake, 350

To Freeze: Remove from pan and wrap warm bread in extra heavy foil. Allow to cool. Label and freeze.

To Serve: Thaw. Place foil wrapped bread in 350° oven for 15 minutes or until warm. Open foil and bake 5 minutes. Serve warm.

Onion Poppy Seed Bread

2 tablespoons butter
1 cup chopped onion
1 1/2 cups biscuit/baking mix
1 egg, lightly beaten
1/2 cup milk
1/2 cup shredded sharp Cheddar cheese
1 tablespoon poppy seed
1/2 cup shredded sharp Cheddar cheese
2 tablespoons melted butter

Melt butter in a small skillet. Add chopped onion. Cook and stir until onion is soft and golden. In a mixing bowl, combine biscuit/baking mix, beaten egg and milk just until moistened. Stir in onion and 1/2 cup shredded cheese. Spread dough in greased 8-inch round baking pan. Sprinkle poppy seed and 1/2 cup shredded cheese over top of dough. Drizzle melted butter over all. Bake at 400° for 20 to 25 minutes. Serve warm. 8 servings.

Complete Menu

Green Chile Chicken Soup
• Onion Poppy Seed Bread, 351

To Freeze: Remove from pan and wrap warm bread in extra heavy foil. Allow to cool. Label and freeze.

To Serve: Thaw. Place foil wrapped bread in 350° oven for 15 minutes or until warm. Serve warm.

Cheese Squares

1/2 cup flour
1 teaspoon baking powder
1 cup cottage cheese
5 eggs, beaten
1 (4-ounce) can diced green chiles
1 1/2 cups shredded Cheddar cheese
1 1/2 cups shredded Monterey Jack cheese
1/2 cup melted butter

In a large bowl, combine flour and baking powder. Stir in cottage cheese and beaten eggs. Mix well. Stir in green chiles, cheeses and melted butter. Pour into a greased 9 x 13-inch baking dish. Bake at 400° for 10 minutes. Reduce heat to 350°. Continue to bake for 30 to 35 minutes. Cut into squares. 12 servings.

Complete Menu

Chicken Tortellini Soup
• Cheese Squares, 352

To Freeze: Place each warm square in a sandwich bag. Press out air and seal. Place bagged squares in freezer bag. Label and freeze.

To Serve: Thaw and serve. Heat briefly, if desired.

Hawaiian Sweet Bread

1 tablespoon yeast
1/4 cup warm water
4 tablespoons softened butter
1/4 cup sugar
1/2 cup milk
3 eggs
1/4 teaspoon salt
2 drops yellow food coloring
3 3/4 cups flour

Dissolve yeast in warm water. Allow to stand for 10 minutes. In a mixing bowl, beat butter and sugar until well combined. Add milk, eggs, salt and food coloring. Mix well. Stir in yeast mixture. Gradually add flour. Mix well. Turn onto floured board. Knead 10 minutes, adding more flour, a little at a time, if necessary. Place in large greased bowl. Cover. Allow to rise until double. Turn onto floured board and knead 2 minutes. Divide in half. Shape into loaves and place on greased baking sheet. Cover and allow to rise until double. Bake at 350° for 30 minutes, until golden brown. 2 loaves.

Complete Menu

Corkscrew Chicken
- Broccoli Tomato Salad, 210
- Green Goddess Dressing, 277
- Hawaiian Sweet Bread, 353

To Freeze Bread Dough: Wrap unraised, shaped loaves tightly in plastic. Place in a freezer bag. Label and freeze.

To Serve: Thaw, then rise and bake as directed.

To Freeze Baked Bread: Wrap each loaf in extra heavy foil. Label and freeze.

To Serve: Thaw. Slice and serve. Heat briefly, if desired.

Sweet Braided Bread

3 to 3 1/2 cups flour, divided
1/2 cup sugar, divided
1 tablespoon yeast
3/4 teaspoon salt
1/2 cup milk
1/4 cup water
1/4 cup butter
1 egg
1 egg, separated
1 tablespoon water

In a large bowl, combine 1 cup flour, 1/4 cup sugar, yeast and salt. In saucepan, heat milk, water and butter until very warm. Gradually add to the flour. Beat for about 2 minutes with electric mixer. Add the egg, egg yolk and 1/4 cup sugar. Beat for 2 minutes with electric mixer. Stir in enough flour to make a soft dough. Knead dough on a lightly floured surface until smooth and elastic, about 10 minutes. Cover and allow to rest for about 10 minutes. Divide dough into 3 pieces. Roll each into a 20-inch rope. Braid the 3 ropes together. Pinch ends and tuck under. Place on a greased baking sheet. Cover with sprayed plastic wrap. Allow to rise in a warm place until doubled. In a small bowl, whisk together egg white and water. Brush over bread braid. Bake at 375° for 25 minutes. Remove from baking sheet. Allow to cool on wire rack. 1 loaf.

Complete Menu

New England Baked Beans
- Paradise Pasta Salad, 254
- Sweet Braided Bread, 354

To Freeze: Wrap loaf in extra heavy foil. Label and freeze.

To Serve: Thaw. Slice and serve. Heat briefly, if desired.

Bread Bowls

1 1/4 cups very warm water
1 tablespoon yeast
1 1/2 teaspoons salt
1 1/2 teaspoons sugar
1 tablespoon canola oil
3 to 4 cups flour
1 egg, beaten
1 tablespoon milk

In a large bowl, combine warm water and yeast. Stir until yeast is dissolved. Add salt, sugar, oil and 1 1/2 cups flour. Beat until smooth. Add enough flour to make a stiff dough. Turn out onto a floured board. Knead for 10 minutes, until smooth and elastic. Place dough in a greased bowl. Turn dough to grease the top. Cover. Allow to rise in a warm place for about 1 hour or until doubled. Grease outsides of 6 custard cups or oven proof bowls. Punch dough down. Divide into 6 pieces. Cover and allow to rest for 10 minutes. Spread each piece into a 6-inch circle. Place dough over outsides of bowls. Work dough over bowl until it fits. Set bowls, dough side up, on greased baking sheet. Cover loosely with plastic wrap. Allow to rise in a warm place for about 30 minutes or until doubled. Combine egg and milk. Gently brush over dough. Bake at 400° for 15 minutes or until golden brown. Carefully remove bowl. Set bowls, open sides up, on baking pan. Return to oven and bake 5 minutes. Fill with thick soup, stew, chili or chowder. 6 bread bowls.

Complete Menu

Corn Chowder
• Bread Bowls, 355

To Freeze: Wrap each bread bowl carefully in plastic. Nest 2 or 3 bowls together and place in gallon freezer bag. Label and freeze.

To Serve: Thaw and serve.

Three Cheese Bread

2 tablespoons yeast
1 cup very warm water
1 cup soft butter
6 eggs, beaten
4 1/2 cups flour
1 teaspoon salt
2 teaspoons sugar
1 cup cubed Swiss cheese
1 cup cubed sharp Cheddar cheese
1/2 cup shredded fresh Parmesan cheese

In a small bowl, dissolve yeast in warm water. In a large mixing bowl, beat butter until fluffy. Beat in eggs. Stir in dissolved yeast and water. In a separate bowl, combine flour, salt and sugar. Gradually add to egg and butter mixture. Continue to beat until smooth. Stir cheese cubes and shredded cheese into mixture. Turn dough out into a large greased bowl. Cover and allow to rise until doubled. Stir gently with a spoon. Cover bowl and allow to rise until doubled again. Gently stir dough down. Drop by spoonfuls into a greased 10-inch tube pan. Allow to rise again until doubled. Bake at 400° for 35 to 40 minutes. Remove from oven. Cool 10 minutes. Lift bread out of tube and cool 20 minutes. Serve while warm. 12 servings.

Complete Menu

Italian Shells
- Bacon Spinach Salad, 193
- Brown Sugar Dressing, 295
- Three Cheese Bread, 356

To Freeze: Wrap carefully in extra heavy foil. Label and freeze.

To Serve: Thaw. Unwrap. Heat tube pan (the same pan it was baked in) in oven. Place bread in warm pan. Cover loosely with foil. Heat for about 15 minutes in 350° oven.

Potato Bread

1 tablespoon yeast
2 cups warm potato water
3 tablespoons sugar
1 tablespoon salt
5 1/2 to 6 cups flour
2 tablespoons melted butter

Dissolve yeast in warm potato water. Allow to rest for about 5 minutes. Stir in sugar, salt and 3 cups flour. Beat well. Stir in melted butter. Gradually add enough remaining flour to make a soft dough. Turn out on a floured board and knead for about 10 minutes until smooth and elastic. Place in a greased bowl. Turn dough to grease the top. Cover and allow to rise in a warm place for about 2 hours or until doubled. Knead dough down in bowl. Divide dough in half. Shape into balls and place in well greased round baking pans. Cover and allow to rise for about 1 hour or until almost doubled. Dust loaves lightly with flour. Bake at 400° for 35 to 40 minutes. Makes 2 loaves.

Complete Menu

Meatballs in Gravy
- Garlic Mashed Potatoes, 81
- Simple Spinach Salad, 191
- Buttermilk Dressing, 265
- Potato Bread, 357

To Freeze Bread Dough: After dough rises the first time, knead dough, divide in half and wrap tightly in plastic. Place wrapped dough in a freezer bag. Label and freeze.

To Serve: Thaw. Shape into balls and place in well greased round baking pans. Cover and allow to rise, dust with flour and bake at 400° for 35 to 40 minutes.

To Freeze Baked Bread: Wrap each loaf in extra heavy foil. For individual servings, pull bread apart, place each piece in a sandwich bag and place all together in a freezer bag. Label and freeze.

To Serve: Thaw. Pull apart and serve. Heat briefly, if desired.

Scones

2 cups warm buttermilk
1 tablespoon yeast
2 tablespoons sugar
1 egg
1 tablespoon canola oil
4 to 5 cups flour
1 1/2 teaspoons baking powder
1/4 teaspoon baking soda
1 teaspoon salt
oil for deep-frying

In a large mixing bowl, combine warm buttermilk, yeast and sugar. Let stand for about 5 minutes. Stir to dissolve. Add egg and oil. Mix well. Stir in 2 cups flour, baking powder, baking soda and salt. Continue to add flour until soft dough pulls away from sides of bowl. Cover and let rise until doubled in size (about an hour). Turn onto a floured cloth. Roll to 1/4-inch thickness. Cut into 3 or 4-inch circles. Deep-fry in hot oil (375°) until golden brown. Serve with **Honey Butter** (page 358). 8 servings.

Complete Menu

Crab, Shrimp, or Lobster Newberg
• Shrimp Salad, 213
• Scones, 358

To Freeze Scone Dough: After dough rises the first time, knead dough and wrap tightly in plastic. Place wrapped dough in a freezer bag. Label and freeze.

To Serve: Thaw. Roll to 1/4-inch thickness. Cut in circles and deep-fry in hot oil.

To Freeze Scones: While still warm, place scones in a gallon freezer bag. Allow to cool to room temperature. Label and freeze.

To Serve: Thaw and serve. Heat briefly, if desired.

Easy Yeast Rolls

1 tablespoon yeast
3/4 cup warm water
2 1/2 to 2 3/4 cups biscuit/baking mix
2 tablespoons melted butter

Dissolve yeast in warm water. Allow to stand for 10 minutes. Add enough biscuit/baking mix to make a fairly stiff dough. Knead on lightly floured board until smooth. Form into rolls

Complete Menu

Country Chicken and Vegetables
- Five Fruit Salad, 221
- Honey Lime Dressing, 272
- Easy Yeast Rolls, 359

and place on greased baking sheet. Cover with waxed paper and let rise in warm place for 1 hour or until double. Brush with melted butter and bake at 400° for 10 to 12 minutes or until golden brown. Remove from oven and brush with melted butter. Makes 12 to 16 rolls.

To Freeze Dough: Do not allow dough to rise. Wrap dough tightly in plastic. Place in a freezer bag. Or, shape dough into rolls and place in a single layer, close together but not touching on a baking sheet. Cover and allow to freeze. Transfer frozen dough to a freezer bag. Label and freeze.

To Serve: Thaw. Allow to rise. Bake at 400° for 10 to 12 minutes. Brush with melted butter.

To Freeze Baked Rolls: While still warm, place each roll in a sandwich bag. Press out air and seal. Allow to cool to room temperature. Place bagged rolls in a gallon freezer bag. Label and freeze.

To Serve: Thaw and serve. Heat briefly, if desired.

Dinner Rolls

2 tablespoons yeast
1 cup very warm water
1/2 cup melted butter
1/2 cup sugar
3 eggs, beaten
1 teaspoon salt
4 to 4 1/2 cups flour

In a large bowl, dissolve yeast in warm water. Allow to stand for about 5 minutes. Stir in melted butter, sugar, eggs and salt. Stir in half the flour. Mix well. Continue to add flour until dough is too stiff to stir. Cover with plastic wrap and refrigerate for at least 2 hours. Turn dough out onto a floured surface. Roll into smooth balls. Place balls in a greased 9 x 13-inch baking dish. Cover and allow to rise in a warm place for about an hour, or until double in size. Uncover and bake at 375° for 15 to 20 minutes. Brush warm rolls with melted butter. 24 rolls.

Complete Menu

Manhattan Clam Chowder
- Apple Pasta Salad, 256
- Dinner Rolls, 360

To Freeze Dough: Do not allow dough to rise. Wrap dough tightly in plastic. Place in a freezer bag. Or shape dough into rolls and place in a single layer, close together but not touching on a baking sheet. Cover and allow to freeze. Transfer frozen dough to a freezer bag. Label and freeze.

To Serve: Thaw. Allow to rise. Bake at 375° for 15 to 20 minutes. Brush with melted butter.

To Freeze Baked Rolls: Wrap each loaf tightly in extra heavy foil. Label and freeze.

To Serve: Thaw. Pull apart and serve. Heat briefly, if desired.

One Hour Rolls

2 tablespoons yeast
1 cup very warm water
1/4 cup sugar
1/3 cup canola oil
1 teaspoon salt
1 egg, beaten
3 1/2 to 4 cups flour
1/4 cup melted butter

In a large mixing bowl, combine yeast, warm water and sugar. Let stand for 5 minutes. Stir to dissolve. Add oil and salt. Mix well. Stir in egg and 2 cups flour. Continue to add flour until soft dough forms and pulls away from sides of bowl. Turn onto a floured cloth. Knead until smooth and elastic. Shape into 2 balls. Roll out into circles. With pizza cutter, cut each circle into 12 wedges. Brush with melted butter. Roll up, starting at wide end. Place on greased baking sheet. Allow to rise until double in size. Bake at 375° for 12 minutes. 24 rolls.

Complete Menu

New England Clam Chowder
• One Hour Rolls, 361

To Freeze Dough: Do not allow dough to rise. Wrap dough tightly in plastic. Place in a freezer bag. Or shape dough into rolls and place in a single layer, close together but not touching on a baking sheet. Cover and allow to freeze. Transfer frozen dough to a freezer bag. Label and freeze.

To Serve: Thaw. Allow to rise. Bake at 375° for 12 minutes.

To Freeze Baked Rolls: While still warm, place each roll in a sandwich bag. Press out air and seal. Allow to cool to room temperature. Place bagged rolls in a gallon freezer bag. Label and freeze.

To Serve: Thaw and serve. Heat briefly, if desired.

 For Orange Rolls, brush wedges with orange marmalade instead of butter. Allow to rise and bake as directed.

Cloverleaf Rolls

4 to 4 1/2 cups flour, divided
1/4 cup sugar
2 tablespoons yeast
1 1/2 teaspoons salt
3/4 cup milk
1/2 cup water
1/3 cup cold butter
1 egg
1/3 cup melted butter

In a large bowl, combine 1 1/2 cups flour, sugar, yeast and salt. In a saucepan, heat milk, water and butter until very warm. Gradually add to the flour mixture. Beat for 2 minutes with electric mixer. Add egg and 1 cup flour. Beat for 2 minutes with electric mixer. Stir in remaining flour to make a stiff batter. Cover with greased plastic wrap. Refrigerate for 2 hours. Turn dough onto a floured board. Divide into 18 pieces. Divide each into 3 pieces and roll into balls. Place 3 balls into each cup of greased muffin tin. Cover. Allow to rise in a warm place until double. Bake at 375° for 12 to 15 minutes or until golden. Brush tops with melted butter. Remove from pan and cool on wire rack. 18 rolls.

Complete Menu

Slow Cooked Goulash
- Noodles Romanoff, 132
- Wilted Salad, 165
- Cloverleaf Rolls, 362

To Freeze Dough: Do not allow dough to rise. Wrap dough tightly in plastic. Place in a freezer bag. Or shape dough into cloverleaf rolls and place in a single layer, close together but not touching on a baking sheet. Cover and allow to freeze. Transfer frozen dough to a freezer bag. Label and freeze.

To Serve: Thaw. Allow to rise. Bake at 375° for 12 to 15 minutes. Brush with melted butter.

To Freeze Baked Rolls: While still warm, place each roll in a sandwich bag. Press out air and seal. Allow to cool to room temperature. Place bagged rolls in a gallon freezer bag. Label and freeze.

To Serve: Thaw and serve. Heat briefly, if desired.

Potato Rolls

1 cup milk
1/2 cup mashed potatoes
3 tablespoons butter
1/2 cup sugar
1 teaspoon salt
1 tablespoon yeast
1 egg
4 cups flour

Heat milk in saucepan just to boiling. Remove from heat. In a large bowl, combine mashed potatoes, butter, sugar and salt. Pour milk over all and stir until butter melts and sugar is dissolved. Stir in yeast. Add egg and mix well. Gradually add flour and stir until dough no longer clings to sides of bowl. Knead into a smooth ball. Grease lightly and cover. Allow to rise until double. Punch down and shape into desired rolls. Place rolls on greased baking sheet or in a greased muffin tin. Allow to rise until double. Bake at 350° for 25 to 30 minutes. 18 rolls.

Complete Menu

Meatballs in Sour Cream Sauce
- Baked Rice, 123
- Snow Pea Stir-Fry, 27
- Potato Rolls, 363

To Freeze Dough: After dough rises the first time, punch down and wrap dough tightly in plastic. Place in a freezer bag. Or shape dough into rolls and place in a single layer, close together but not touching on a baking sheet. Cover and allow to freeze. Transfer frozen dough to a freezer bag. Label and freeze.

To Serve: Thaw. Allow to rise. Bake at 400° for 10 to 12 minutes. Brush with melted butter.

To Freeze: While still warm, place each roll in a sandwich bag. Press out air and seal. Allow to cool to room temperature. Place bagged rolls in a gallon freezer bag. Label and freeze.

To Serve: Thaw and serve. Heat briefly, if desired.

Sweet Potato Rolls

1 cup mashed sweet potatoes
1/4 cup melted butter
1 tablespoon yeast
1/2 cup warm water
1/2 cup milk
2 eggs, beaten
3 tablespoons sugar
1 teaspoon salt
3 1/2 to 4 cups flour

In a mixing bowl, combine mashed sweet potatoes and melted butter with electric mixer. In a small bowl, dissolve yeast in warm water. Stir into potatoes. Heat milk just to boiling and stir into potatoes. Add the eggs, sugar, salt and 2 cups of the flour. Cover bowl and allow to rise in a warm place until the dough is doubled. Add the remaining flour and knead until very smooth. Form dough into 1 1/2-inch rolls and place close together on a buttered baking sheet. Let rise until double. Bake at 375° for 20 to 30 minutes or until golden brown. 18 rolls.

Complete Menu

Polynesian Pork Roast
- Shrimp Rice, 121
- Carrot Pineapple Salad, 248
- Sweet Potato Rolls, 364

To Freeze Dough: After dough rises the first time, add flour and knead. Wrap dough tightly in plastic. Place in a freezer bag. Label and freeze.

To Serve: Thaw. Shape into 1 1/2-inch rolls and place close together on buttered baking sheet. Allow to rise. Bake at 375° for 20 to 30 minutes.

To Freeze: Wrap each loaf tightly in extra heavy foil. For individual servings, pull bread apart, place each piece in a sandwich bag and place all together in a freezer bag. Label and freeze.

To Serve: Thaw. Pull apart and serve. Heat briefly, if desired.

Cheese Rolls

1 package *brown and serve* rolls
2 cups shredded Cheddar cheese
2 tablespoon soft butter
1/2 teaspoon ground mustard
1/2 teaspoon salt
1/8 teaspoon pepper

Split rolls most of the way through, top to bottom. In a mixing bowl, combine shredded cheese, soft butter, ground mustard, salt and pepper. Mix well. Spoon cheese mixture, full to overflowing, into each split roll. Bake at 350° for 15 minutes or until rolls are browned and cheese is bubbly. 12 rolls.

Complete Menu

Tomato Beef Stew
• Cheese Rolls, 365

To Freeze: Split and stuff rolls. Wrap tightly in extra heavy foil. Label and freeze.

To Serve: Thaw. Open foil and bake at 350° for 15 to 20 minutes.

Broiled Garlic Rolls

1 cup softened butter
1 cup salad dressing
1 cup shredded Monterey Jack cheese
1 cup shredded Cheddar cheese
1 cup shredded Mozzarella cheese
garlic salt
12 fresh Hard Rolls

Whip butter. Mix in salad dressing. Stir in cheeses. Cut each roll in half. Spread cheese mixture onto cut side of each half. Sprinkle each with garlic salt. Broil 2 to 4 minutes until cheese is melted. 24 pieces.

Complete Menu

Beef and Cheese Rolls
• Tortellini Primavera, 133
• Broiled Garlic Rolls, 366

To Freeze: Place unbaked rolls close together on baking sheet. Cover with plastic and freeze. When frozen transfer to a freezer bag. Label and freeze.

To Serve: Broil for about 4 minutes until bread is thawed, warm and cheese is melted.

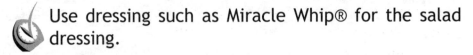 Use dressing such as Miracle Whip® for the salad dressing.

Hard Rolls can usually be found at the bakery of the grocery store. Hard Rolls are not actually *hard*, it's just a name!

Puff Bowls

2 eggs
1/2 cup flour
1/2 cup milk
1/4 teaspoon salt
2 tablespoons butter, melted

In small mixer bowl, beat eggs until frothy. Gradually beat in flour until smooth. Add milk, salt and melted butter. Mix well. Pour into well greased 9-inch pie plate. Bake at 425° for 15 minutes. Do not open oven. Reduce oven temperature to 350°. Do not open oven. Continue baking for 15 minutes. Batter will puff up off bottom of pan forming an inverted bowl. Serve filled with stew, chili, chowder, etc. For individual puff bowls, pour 1/8 cup batter into each well greased cup of a 12-cup muffin tin. Bake 11 minutes. Reduce oven temperature to 350° and continue baking for 12 minutes. For bite-sized servings, pour 1 1/2 teaspoons batter into each well greased cup of a 24-cup miniature muffin tin. Bake 6 minutes. Reduce oven temperature to 350° and continue baking 5 minutes. Try these filled with sweetened sliced strawberries and top with whipped cream! 12 servings.

Complete Menu

Chicken a'la King
- Puff Bowls, 367
- Dried Cherry Salad, 185
- Poppy Seed Dressing, 289

To Freeze: Place baked, unfilled puff bowls in a freezer bag. Label and freeze.

To Serve: Thaw. Fill and serve.

Pepperoni Puffs

1 (4-ounce) package sliced pepperoni
1 1/2 cups shredded Mozzarella cheese
2 (7.5-ounce) cans refrigerated biscuit dough
oil for deep-frying

Coarsely chop pepperoni. Shred Mozzarella cheese. Separate biscuits. Press each biscuit flat and place 1 tablespoon of cheese and 1 tablespoon of chopped pepperoni

Complete Menu

Italian Chili
• Pepperoni Puffs, 368

on center. Carefully fold biscuit dough around filling. Press edges closed, pinching to make sure well sealed. Heat oil in deep-fryer to 350° degrees or heat one inch of oil in a heavy skillet. Place filled biscuits in hot oil. Deep-fry 1 to 2 minutes or until puffy and golden brown. Turn over and fry until golden brown. Watch carefully, they brown quickly. Drain the puffs on paper towels. 20 puffs.

To Freeze: While still warm, place puffs in a gallon freezer bag. Allow to cool to room temperature. Label and freeze.

To Serve: Thaw and serve. Heat briefly, if desired.

 Pepperoni Puffs are delicious served with warm spaghetti sauce.

Corn Fritters

2/3 cup flour
1/4 teaspoon salt
1/2 teaspoon baking powder
1/2 teaspoon paprika
2 eggs, separated
1 1/2 cups frozen corn, thawed
oil for deep-frying

In a mixing bowl, combine flour, salt, baking powder and paprika. In a separate bowl, combine egg yolks and corn. Add to flour mixture and mix well. Beat egg whites until soft peaks form. Fold into flour mixture. In deep-fryer or electric skillet, heat oil to 375°. Drop heaping table-spoons of batter into hot oil. Deep-fry for 3 to 4 min-utes or until golden brown. Drain on paper towels. 8 servings.

Complete Menu

Minestrone
• Corn Fritters, 369

To Freeze: Drain corn fritters and allow to cool. Wrap each fritter in plastic or place in sandwich bag. Allow to cool completely. Place wrapped fritters in gallon freezer bag. Label and freeze.

To Serve: Heat frozen or thawed fritters briefly in microwave. For crisper fritters, heat in toaster oven.

Mushroom Puffs

6 mushrooms, chopped
1 (3-ounce) package cream cheese, softened
1 tablespoon minced green onion
dash pepper
1 (8-ounce) can refrigerated crescent roll dough

In a small bowl, combine mushrooms, cream cheese, onion and pepper. Separate crescent roll dough into 4 rectangles. Press together perforations. Divide mushroom filling among the 4 rectangles. Spread to the edges of each. Starting with the long side, roll up each rectangle. Cut each roll into 5 slices. Place on ungreased baking sheet. Bake at 425° for 10 minutes. Rolls should be puffed and golden. 20 puffs.

> *Complete Menu*
>
> **Chicken Stuffed Manicotti**
> • Red, White and Green Salad, 152
> • Creamy Italian Dressing, 286
> • Mushroom Puffs, 370

To Freeze: Arrange baked puffs in a single layer on a baking sheet. Cover and place in freezer just until frozen. Transfer frozen puffs to a freezer bag. Label and freeze.

To Serve: Thaw. Heat briefly in microwave. For crisper puffs, heat briefly under broiler or in toaster oven.

Sour Cream Croissants

1 (8-ounce) can refrigerated crescent roll dough
2 tablespoons sour cream
1 tablespoon minced green onion
1/4 teaspoon celery salt
1/8 teaspoon pepper

Unroll crescent roll dough and separate into triangles. In a small bowl, combine sour cream, green onion, celery salt and pepper. Spread over each triangle. Starting with the short side, roll up each triangle. Place on an ungreased baking sheet with pointed side down. Curve ends to form a crescent shape. Bake at 375° for 12 minutes or until golden brown. 8 servings.

Complete Menu

Mayonnaise Chicken
• Spinach Bean Sprout Salad, 196
• Russian Dressing, 288
• Sour Cream Croissants, 371

To Freeze: While still warm, place croissants in a gallon freezer bag. Allow to cool to room temperature. Label and freeze.

To Serve: Thaw and serve. Heat briefly in microwave, under broiler or in toaster oven, if desired.

Cheddar and Chile Pinwheels

3/4 cup shredded Cheddar cheese
1 (4-ounce) can diced green chiles
2 tablespoons salsa
1 (8-ounce) package cream cheese, softened
1/4 teaspoon chili powder
1/4 teaspoon garlic salt
1 (8-ounce) can refrigerated crescent roll dough

In a mixing bowl, combine Cheddar cheese, green chiles, salsa, cream cheese, chili powder and garlic salt. Unroll crescent roll dough and separate into 4 rectangles. Press together perforations. Divide the filling among the 4 rectangles. Spread filling edge to edge. Starting with the short side, roll up. Wrap in plastic and chill for about an hour. Cut each roll into 6 slices. Place on an ungreased baking sheet. Bake at 350° for 10 minutes or until golden brown. Makes 24 pinwheels.

Complete Menu

Chili Soup
• Cheddar and Chile Pinwheels, 372

To Freeze: Arrange baked pinwheels in a single layer on a baking sheet. Cover and place in freezer just until frozen. Transfer frozen pinwheels to a freezer bag. Label and freeze.

To Serve: Thaw. Heat briefly in microwave. For crisper pinwheels, heat briefly under broiler or in toaster oven.

Stuffed Crescent Rolls

1 cup softened cream cheese
2 cups cooked, shredded chicken
1 cup sliced mushrooms
1 tablespoon minced green onion
2 (8-ounce) cans refrigerated crescent roll dough
2 tablespoons melted butter
1/2 cup dry bread crumbs

Combine cream cheese, chicken, mushrooms and green onion. Separate crescent roll dough into triangles. Spoon 1 tablespoon filling onto center of each. Fold dough in half to form smaller triangle. Press edges together to seal. Dip into melted butter then in bread crumbs. Place on baking sheet. Bake at 375° for 12 minutes or until golden brown. 16 rolls.

Complete Menu

French Onion Soup
- Strawberry Spinach Salad, 199
- Onion Dressing, 293
- Stuffed Crescent Rolls, 373

To Freeze: While still warm, place one or two rolls in a sandwich bag. Press out air and seal. Allow to cool to room temperature. Place bagged rolls in a gallon freezer bag. Label and freeze.

To Serve: Thaw. Heat briefly in microwave. For crisper rolls, heat briefly under broiler or in toaster oven.

Serve with soup or serve with gravy made from 1 can cream of chicken soup mixed with 1/2 cup sour cream.

Substitute 2 cups chopped ham for the chicken to make delicious **Ham Stuffed Crescent Rolls.**

Onion Poppy Seed Rolls

1/4 cup butter
1 1/2 cups sliced onion
1/4 cup sugar
1 tablespoon poppy seed
1 (8-ounce) can refrigerated crescent roll dough

Melt butter in a large skillet. Cook onion in butter over medium heat until onion is soft. Add sugar and poppy seed. Cook until the sugar melts. Remove from heat and allow to cool to room temperature. Unroll and separate crescent rolls. Divide onion mixture among the 8 triangles. Starting with the short side of each triangle, roll onions in dough and place rolls on baking sheet. Sprinkle lightly with poppy seeds. Bake at 400° for 10 minutes, until golden brown. 8 rolls.

Complete Menu

Beefy Macaroni
- Green and Gold Salad, 162
- Onion Poppy Seed Rolls, 374

To Freeze: While still warm, place each roll in a sandwich bag. Press out air and seal. Allow to cool to room temperature. Place bagged rolls in a gallon freezer bag. Label and freeze.

To Serve: Thaw. Heat briefly in microwave. For crisper rolls, heat briefly under broiler or in toaster oven.

Everything Else

"Everything Else" in this case means all of the recipes that didn't really fit in any of the other categories. They are, however, just as yummy, and certainly some meals would not be complete without them.

Many of the recipes in this chapter may be prepared in advance and, in some cases, can even be frozen. When deciding whether to freeze a recipe or not, consider your desire or need for convenience in serving. Performing much of the preparation in advance, leaving only the brief cooking or heating for later, can make the difference between enjoying the recipe with a meal or going without.

If you decide to freeze ahead, be sure to package the items properly for the freezer. Freezer burn happens rapidly and can occur wherever air is present. Even trapped air can allow freezer burn. Individually wrap items that are especially susceptible to drying out.

Many foods can be frozen before or after they have been cooked. To freeze them before cooking, prepare and place in a single layer in the freezer. Be sure to cover them since they will dry out rapidly. They should be completely frozen in about 2 or 3 hours. After they are frozen, place them in a freezer bag or container.

Foods that have been baked or deep-fried should be cooled first, then quickly frozen in a single layer. This usually takes only 2 or 3 hours. They should be placed in a freezer bag or container as soon as they are frozen.

Most items may be thawed first or cooked from frozen, although, if they are cooked from frozen, they may require a longer cooking time. If deep-frying a frozen food, you may need to add an extra minute or two to the cooking time.

Baked and deep-fried foods have a crispy exterior that will be compromised when frozen. This crispiness can be partially regained by placing the item under the broiler or in a toaster oven for a minute or two. For speedy serving of a frozen deep-fried food such as a wonton or eggroll, microwave it briefly to thaw and heat, then place under the broiler or toaster oven for about a minute to make the outside crisp.

The recipes in this section, whether made today or frozen for tomorrow, will add the extra pizzazz that will make a good meal fabulous.

Everything Else Recipes

Steak Taco Quesadillas

1 cup water
2 teaspoons sugar
2 teaspoons mesquite-flavored liquid smoke
1 teaspoon salt
1/4 teaspoon pepper
1 (8-ounce) sirloin steak
2 tablespoons olive oil
1 small red bell pepper, sliced
1 small green bell pepper, sliced
1 small yellow onion, sliced
4 large flour tortillas
3 cups shredded Monterey Jack cheese
1/4 cup taco sauce

Combine water, sugar, liquid smoke, salt and pepper in a bowl. Add steak and coat completely. Cover and refrigerate for one hour. After meat has marinated, grill for 4 or 5 minutes per side OR broil for 3 or 4 minutes per side. Cut into thin strips. Heat oil in a large skillet. Add peppers and onion. Cook until peppers and onion start to brown. Remove from skillet. Leave skillet on burner. One at a time, place a tortilla in the skillet. Over half of the tortilla, arrange 1/2 cup cheese, 1/4 of the vegetables, and 1/4 of the sliced steak. Spoon 1 tablespoon taco sauce over the meat and top with 1/4 cup of cheese. Fold tortilla in half over filling and press down. Cook for about 2 minutes until the tortilla is a golden brown. Turn and cook for about another 2 minutes until all the cheese has melted. Slide onto a plate and cut into wedges. 4 quesadillas.

Complete Menu

Taco Soup
• Steak Taco Quesadillas, 378

Substitute 1 boneless skinless chicken breast half for the steak for delicious **Chicken Taco Quesadillas**.

Jalapeño Quesadillas

1/4 cup mayonnaise
2 teaspoons minced canned jalapeño peppers
2 teaspoons jalapeño pepper juice (from the can)
1 teaspoon sugar
1/2 teaspoon cumin
1/8 teaspoon garlic salt
1/2 teaspoon paprika
dash cayenne pepper
4 chicken tenders
2 tablespoons olive oil
4 large flour tortillas
1 cup shredded Cheddar cheese
1 cup shredded Monterey Jack cheese

In small bowl, whisk together mayonnaise, jalapeño peppers, jalapeño pepper juice, sugar, cumin, garlic salt, paprika and cayenne pepper. Brush chicken tenders with oil. Grill or broil chicken for 3 or 4 minutes per side. Cut into thin slices. Heat large skillet over medium heat. One at a time, place tortillas in hot skillet. Over half of the tortilla, arrange 1/4 cup Cheddar cheese, 1/4 cup Monterey Jack cheese and 1/4 of the chicken. Spread about 1 tablespoon of the jalapeño sauce over the other half of the tortilla. Fold the tortilla in half and press down. Cook for about 2 minutes until the tortilla is golden brown. Turn and cook for about another 2 minutes until all the cheese has melted. Slide onto a plate and cut into wedges. 4 quesadillas.

Complete Menu

Mexican Beef Stew
• Jalapeño Quesadillas, 379

For **Steak Jalapeño Quesadillas**, substitute 1 (8-ounce) sirloin steak for the chicken tenders.

Pot Stickers

1/2 pound ground pork
1 teaspoon minced ginger
2 green onions, minced
2 teaspoons minced water chestnuts
1 teaspoon soy sauce
1 teaspoon sugar
1/4 teaspoon garlic salt
1/4 teaspoon crushed red pepper flakes
1/2 (16-ounce) package round wonton wraps
1 egg, beaten
oil for deep-frying

In a medium bowl, combine meat, vegetables and seasonings. Mix well. Place about 1 tablespoon filling on each wrapper. Brush beaten egg half way around the edge of the wrapper. Fold the wrapper over the filling. Gather the wrapper while sealing so that it is crinkled around the edge on one side. Heat about 2 inches of oil over medium heat or to 375°. Deep-fry a few at a time in hot oil for 3 to 5 minutes or until golden brown. 24 Pot Stickers.

Complete Menu

Teriyaki Chicken
- Oriental Noodles, 144
- Pot Stickers, 380

To Freeze: Arrange cooked or uncooked filled pot stickers in a single layer on a baking sheet. Cover and place in freezer. When pot stickers are frozen, transfer to freezer bag. Label and freeze.

To Serve: Cooked: Heat briefly in microwave. For crisper pot stickers, heat briefly in toaster oven.

Uncooked: Thaw. Deep-fry a few pot stickers at a time for about 3 to 5 minutes until golden brown.

 Prepared minced ginger can be found in small jars in the produce section of the grocery store. It is easy and convenient, and will keep for a long time in the refrigerator.

Chinese Dumplings

4 cups flour
3/4 cup boiling water
1/2 cup cold water
2 cups ground pork
2 cups peeled, chopped shrimp
1/2 cup minced green onion
1 tablespoon minced ginger
1 tablespoon soy sauce
1 1/2 teaspoons salt
1/8 teaspoon pepper
1 cup shredded cabbage
5 1/2 tablespoons peanut oil
2 tablespoons rice vinegar
2 tablespoons soy sauce
dash cayenne pepper

In a mixing bowl, combine flour and boiling water. Beat until smooth. Allow to rest for 3 minutes. Stir in the cold water and knead until smooth. Roll the dough into a long cylinder and slice into 1 1/2-inch pieces. Roll each one first

Complete Menu

Teriyaki Beef
• Oriental Rice Pilaf, 117
• Chinese Dumplings, 381

into a ball and then roll flat into small, thin pancakes. In a separate bowl, combine pork, shrimp, green onion, ginger, soy sauce, salt and pepper. Mix in the cabbage and peanut oil. Spoon 1 tablespoon of filling onto each thin pancake. Fold in half. Pinch edges together to close firmly. Heat a large wok or skillet and add 3 tablespoons peanut oil. Turn heat to high and deep-fry for 2 to 3 minutes to brown the underside of dumplings. Do not turn dumplings. Add 1/2 cup water to the wok or pan and cover. Steam the dumplings over high heat until almost all the water has evaporated. Remove cover and add 1 1/2 tablespoons oil. Reduce heat and cook until all the liquid has absorbed. Combine vinegar, soy sauce and cayenne pepper for dipping. May be frozen before or after cooking. (see **Pot Stickers**, page 380). 40 dumplings.

Crispy Wonton

3 tablespoons soy sauce
1 tablespoon rice vinegar
2 cups ground pork
1 teaspoon packed brown sugar
1 teaspoon minced garlic
1 teaspoon minced ginger
2 cups frozen spinach, thawed
1/2 (16-ounce) package square wonton wraps
oil for deep-frying
Red Sauce (page 303)

In a mixing bowl, combine soy sauce, vinegar and pork. Mix well. Add sugar, garlic and ginger. Squeeze spinach to remove most of the liquid. Add to mixture and mix well. Spoon 1 tablespoon of filling onto center of each wonton square. Dampen edges with water. Fold in half to form triangles and press edges together firmly. Heat oil to 350° or until one wonton edge dipped in the oil sizzles immediately. Deep-fry the wonton, a few at a time, for about 5 minutes or until golden brown. Drain on paper towels. Serve with **Red Sauce** for dipping. 30 wonton.

Complete Menu

Hawaiian Meatballs
- Rice Ring, 110
- Crispy Wonton, 382
- Red Sauce, 303

To Freeze: Arrange cooked or uncooked filled wonton in a single layer on a baking sheet. Cover and place in freezer. When the wonton are frozen, transfer to freezer bag. Label and freeze.

To Serve: Cooked: Heat briefly in microwave. For crisper wonton, heat briefly in toaster oven. **Uncooked:** Thaw. Deep-fry a few wonton at a time for about 5 minutes until golden brown.

Cream Cheese Wonton

1/2 (16-ounce) package square wonton wraps
1 (8-ounce) package cream cheese
oil for deep-frying

Separate wonton wraps. Spread about 2 teaspoons cream cheese on center of each wrap. Dampen edges with water. Fold in half to form triangles. Press edges together firmly. Heat oil to 350° or until one wonton edge dipped in the oil sizzles immediately. Deep-fry the wonton, a few at a time, for about 3 minutes or until golden brown. Drain on paper towels. 30 wonton.

Complete Menu

Maple Almond Beef
- Fried Noodles, 145
- Cream Cheese Wonton, 383

Egg Rolls

3 tablespoons canola oil
4 cups shredded cabbage
1 cup chopped onion
1 cup shredded carrots
1 cup shredded zucchini
1 cup cooked, shredded chicken
1/2 cup teriyaki sauce
1/4 teaspoon pepper
1 (16-ounce) package large egg roll wrappers
oil for deep-frying

Heat oil in a large skillet. Add cabbage, onion, carrots and zucchini. Cook and stir until limp. Stir in chicken, teriyaki sauce and pepper. Remove from heat. Spoon about 1/4 cup onto each egg roll wrapper. Fold the bottom corner up over the filling. Fold the side corners over the filling. Brush water on all top edges. Roll the wrapper up, keeping it tight, until it rolls over the top corner. It should stick. Repeat with the remaining wraps. Heat oil in large skillet or deep-fryer to 350° degrees. Deep-fry for about 5 minutes or until the outside is golden brown. Drain on paper towels. 16 egg rolls.

Complete Menu

Sweet and Sour Chicken
• Oven Steamed Rice, 109
• Egg Rolls, 384

To Freeze: Arrange cooked or uncooked egg rolls in a single layer on a baking sheet. Cover and place in freezer. When egg rolls are frozen, transfer to freezer bag. Label and freeze.

To Serve: Cooked: Heat briefly in microwave. For crisper egg rolls, heat briefly in toaster oven.
Uncooked: Thaw. Deep-fry a few egg rolls at a time for about 5 to 7 minutes until golden brown.

Cheese Wraps

1 (16-ounce) package large egg roll wrappers
2 cups shredded Cheddar cheese
2 cups shredded Monterey Jack cheese
1 (4-ounce) can diced Jalapeño peppers
1 bunch green onions, finely chopped
oil for deep-frying

Arrange 2 tablespoons of Cheddar cheese, 2 tablespoons of Jack cheese, 1 teaspoon of Jalapeño pepper and 1 teaspoon of green onion lengthwise on the center of each eggroll wrapper. Fold the bottom corner up over the filling. Fold the side corners over the filling. Brush water on all top edges. Roll the wrapper up, keeping it tight, until it rolls over the top corner. It should stick. Repeat with the remaining wraps. Heat oil in large skillet or deep-fryer to 350° degrees. Deep-fry wraps for 2 1/2 to 3 minutes or until the outside is golden brown. Drain the wraps on paper towels. 16 wraps.

Complete Menu

Ravioli Soup
• Cheese Wraps, 385

To Freeze: Arrange cooked or uncooked wraps in a single layer on a baking sheet. Cover and place in freezer. When wraps are frozen, transfer to freezer bag. Label and freeze.

To Serve: Cooked: Heat briefly in microwave. For crisper wraps, heat briefly in toaster oven.
Uncooked: Thaw. Deep-fry a few wraps at a time for about 3 minutes until golden brown.

Lettuce Wraps

1 pound lean ground beef
1/2 pound ground pork
1/2 cup hoisin sauce
1/2 cup Asian peanut sauce
1 cup diced cucumber
1/2 cup shredded carrots
1 teaspoon salt
1/4 teaspoon pepper
12 large lettuce leaves

Brown ground beef and ground pork in a large skillet over medium heat, stirring often to form very small pieces. Stir in hoisin sauce and peanut sauce. Heat through. Stir in cucumber, carrots, salt and pepper. Cook and stir for about 2 minutes. Spoon beef mixture into lettuce leaves and wrap up to serve. 12 wraps.

Complete Menu

Cantonese Meatballs
- Carrot Rice, 119
- Sweet and Sour Vegetables, 17
- Lettuce Wraps, 386

To Freeze: Do not spoon filling into lettuce. Place filling in freezer bag. For individual servings, spoon filling into greased cups of a muffin tin. Place in freezer. When frozen, pop out and place in freezer bag.

To Serve: Heat filling in microwave. Spoon into lettuce leave. Wrap up and serve.

To cut lettuce for lettuce wraps, start with whole, firm head of Iceberg lettuce. Cut off bottom of head of lettuce. Loosen individual leaves from bottom of head.

Coconut Shrimp

24 large uncooked shrimp
1/2 cup cornstarch
1 teaspoon salt
1/4 teaspoon cayenne pepper
3 egg whites
2 1/2 cups sweetened flaked coconut
Marmalade Dipping Sauce (page 305)

Peel and devein shrimp, leaving tails on. Make a slit about 1/2 way through along the inner curve of each shrimp. Press open and gently flatten. In shallow dish, combine cornstarch, salt and cayenne pepper. In a mixing bowl, beat egg whites until stiff peaks form. Place the coconut in another shallow dish. Coat shrimp first in cornstarch mixture, then in egg whites, then coat with coconut. Heat oil to 375° in electric skillet or deep-fryer. Fry shrimp 1 to 1 1/2 minutes on each side or until golden brown. Drain on paper towels. Serve with **Marmalade Dipping Sauce.** 24 pieces.

Complete Menu

Sweet and Sour Meatballs
• New Year Fried Rice, 113
• Coconut Shrimp, 387
• Marmalade Sauce, 305

To Freeze: Arrange prepared but uncooked shrimp in single layer on a baking sheet. Cover and freeze. Transfer to freezer bag. Label and freeze.

To Serve: Thaw. Fry shrimp about 2 minutes on each side until golden.

 Cooked shrimp may be frozen but be very careful to not overcook shrimp when reheating.

Batter Fried Shrimp

24 large uncooked shrimp
1 cup evaporated milk
2 cups complete pancake mix
oil for deep-frying
Cocktail Sauce (page 306)

Peel and devein shrimp, leaving
tails on. Make a slit about 1/2
way through along the inner
curve of each shrimp. Press open
and gently flatten. Place evaporated milk in a small bowl. Place
pancake mix in a shallow dish.

Complete Menu

Mock Filet Mignon
- Garden Stuffed Baked Potatoes, 91
- Tomato Wedges, 101
- Batter Fried Shrimp, 388
- Cocktail Sauce, 305

Dip shrimp first in milk, then in pancake mix. Lay out in a single layer on a baking sheet. After all have been coated, dip
each shrimp in the pancake mix a second time. Allow to rest
on the baking sheet for about 20 minutes. Heat oil to 375° in
electric skillet or deep-fryer. Deep-fry shrimp 1 to 1 1/2 minutes on each side or until golden brown. Drain on paper towels. Serve with **Cocktail Sauce**. 24 pieces.

To Freeze: Arrange prepared but uncooked shrimp in
single layer on a baking sheet. Cover and freeze.
Transfer frozen shrimp to freezer bag. Label and freeze.

To Serve: Deep-fry shrimp for about 2 minutes on each
side or until golden brown.

Cooked shrimp may be frozen but be very careful
to not overcook shrimp when reheating.

Nachos

36 plain tortilla chips
2 1/2 cups shredded Cheddar cheese
1 (2.25-ounce) can sliced black olives, drained
1/2 pound bacon, cooked and crumbled
1/4 cup sliced green onion
1/2 cup sour cream

Arrange tortilla chips in a single layer on an oven proof serving platter. Arrange cheese evenly over chips. Sprinkle with olives, bacon and green onion. Place in 350° oven until cheese melts. Remove from oven and top with dollops of sour cream. Serve with salsa. 6 servings.

Complete Menu

Chili Beef and Rice
- Piñata Salad, 171
- Chile Dressing, 283
- Nachos, 389

For Nacho variations, substitute one or more of the following for the bacon:
- 1 cup cooked, shredded chicken
- 1 cup cooked, shredded beef
- 1 cup cooked, shredded pork
- 1 cup taco seasoned ground beef

Chicken and Rice Burritos

2 cups cooked, shredded chicken
1 (1.25-ounce) envelope taco seasoning
3/4 cup water
2 tablespoons canola oil
1 cup uncooked rice
2 1/2 cups water
1 (8-ounce) can tomato sauce
1 teaspoon lemon pepper
1 bunch green onions, sliced
1 tomato, diced
8 flour tortillas

In a large skillet, combine chicken, taco seasoning and 3/4 cup water. Simmer for about 10 minutes. Remove chicken. In same skillet, heat oil. Stir in uncooked rice. Cook and stir until rice is golden brown. Stir in remaining 2 1/2 cups water, tomato sauce and lemon pepper. Bring to a boil. Reduce heat. Cover and simmer for 20 minutes. Stir in chicken, green onion and tomato. Wrap tortillas in foil. Warm in oven. Spoon 1/2 cup chicken and rice onto each tortilla. Roll up and serve. 8 burritos.

Complete Menu

Beefy Spanish Rice
- Chicken and Rice Burritos, 390
- Refried Beans, 59

To Freeze: Prepare chicken and rice filling but do not add the green onion or tomato. Allow filling to cool and place in freezer bag. Label and freeze.

To Serve: Thaw and heat chicken and rice filling. Fluff with a fork. Stir in green onion and tomato. Spoon onto warm tortillas, roll up and serve.

Recipe Index